Township Violence
and the End of Apartheid

Related James Currey titles on South & Southern Africa

South Africa. The Present as History:
From Mrs Ples to Mandela & Marikana
John S. Saul & Patrick Bond

Liberation Movements in Power: Party & State in Southern Africa
Roger Southall

The New Black Middle Class in South Africa
Roger Southall

Mandela's Kinsmen: Nationalist Elites & Apartheid's First Bantustan
Timothy Gibbs

Women, Migration & the Cashew Economy in Southern Mozambique
Jeanne Marie Penvenne

Remaking Mutirikwi:
Landscape, Water & Belonging in Southern Zimbabwe
Joost Fontein

Writing Revolt: An Engagement with African Nationalism, 1957–67
Terence Ranger

Colonialism & Violence in Zimbabwe: A History of Suffering
Heike I. Schmidt

The Road to Soweto: Resistance & the Uprising of 16 June 1976
Julian Brown

Markets on the Margins: Mineworkers, Job Creation
& Enterprise Development
Kate Philip

The War Within: New Perspectives on the Civil War in Mozambique,
1976–1992
Eric Morier-Genoud, Michel Cahen & Domingos M. do Rosário (eds)

*Limpopo's Legacy: Student Politics & Democracy in South Africa**
Anne K. Heffernan

*forthcoming**

Township Violence
and the End of Apartheid

War on the Reef

GARY KYNOCH

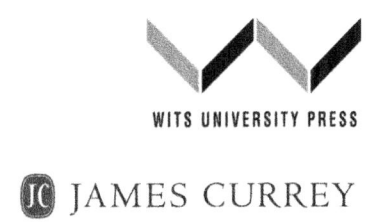

WITS UNIVERSITY PRESS

JAMES CURREY

James Currey
is an imprint of Boydell & Brewer Ltd
PO Box 9
Woodbridge, Suffolk IP12 3DF (GB)
www.jamescurrey.com

and of

Boydell & Brewer Inc.
668 Mt Hope Avenue
Rochester, NY 14620-2731 (US)
www.boydellandbrewer.com

Published in paperback in Southern Africa in 2018
(South Africa, Namibia, Lesotho, Zimbabwe & Swaziland)
by Wits University Press
1 Jan Smuts Avenue
Braamfontein
Johannesburg 2017
South Africa

© Gary Kynoch 2018
First published 2018

All rights reserved. No part of this book may be reproduced in any form, or by electronic or mechanical means, including information storage and retrieval systems, without permission in writing from the publishers, except by a reviewer who may quote brief passages in a review.

The right of Gary Kynoch to be identified as the author of this work has been asserted in accordance with sections 77 and 78 of the Copyright, Designs and Patents Act 1988

British Library Cataloguing in Publication Data
A catalogue record for this book is available on request from the British Library

ISBN 978-1-84701-212-8 (James Currey cloth edition)
ISBN 978-1-77614-322-1 (Wits University Press)

The publisher has no responsibility for the continued existence or accuracy of URLs for external or third-party internet websites referred to in this book, and does not guarantee that any content on such websites is, or will remain, accurate or appropriate.

This book is printed on acid-free paper

Typeset in 10/12 Melior
by Avocet Typeset, Somerton, Somerset, TA11 6RT

Printed and bound in Great Britain by
TJ International Ltd, Padstow, Cornwall

Contents

List of Maps and Photographs	vii
Acknowledgements	ix
List of Acronyms	xi
Introduction	1
Part 1 War on the Reef	**15**
1 Beginnings	17
2 Rule of the Gun THE ANC AND IFP AT WAR	36
3 Rule of the Gun VIOLENCE ON MULTIPLE FRONTS	62
4 State Security Forces and Township Conflict	85
Part 2 Katlehong and Thokoza	**121**
5 A Tale of Two Townships	123
6 Combatant Stories	143
7 Living in a War Zone	174
Conclusion	193
Bibliography	203
Index	219

Maps and Photographs

Maps
1 South Africa   xiii
2 The Reef townships   xiv
3 The townships of Katlehong and Thokoza   122

Photographs
1 Zulu hostel residents advance down Khumalo Street toward Phola Park at the start of the war in 1990   34
2 Thokoza SDU members in action, 1990s   53
3 Police load bodies into a trailer following a night of fighting in Thokoza, 1993   98
4 MK leave a message for police in Phola Park, 1990s   100
5 Thokoza SDU member during an assault on Mshayazafe Hostel, 1994   142
6 Thokoza residents walk to work through burning barricades on Khumalo Street, 1990   175
7 Ruined, yet still inhabited building in Mshayazafe Hostel, 2008   195
8 Grounds of Madala Hostel, 2008   196

Acknowledgements

I am indebted to all the people who shared their stories of extremely trying times. Without them, this book would not have been possible. Most remain anonymous, but of those I can name I would like to express my gratitude to Hein Kilian, Greg Marinovich, Robert McBride, Duma Nkosi, Sally Sealey and David Storey. SDU and ISD veterans made a vital contribution to this book. Even if you don't agree with my conclusions, I hope I have accurately represented your views and experiences.

Zodwa Radebe did most of the interviews for this study. We spent a lot of time together in Thokoza and Katlehong, and Zodwa hunted down many interviews on her own. The connections that she made with former SDUs were invaluable. Zodwa, a massive thank you for your dedication to this project and for the great company. My first forays into Thokoza and Katlehong were with June Ngcobo when neither of us knew where we were going. With patience and charm, June paved the way for the first set of hostel interviews. Thokoza residents Dimpho and Teboho Siphoro conducted several interviews in their home town.

Thanks are due to Greg Marinovich and Joao Silva for the use of their photos and to Kate Kirkwood who produced the maps. Anemari Jansen generously provided a photo and shared her manuscript on ISD Unit 6. Michele Pickover and Carol Archibald at Historical Papers in the University of the Witwatersrand's William Cullen Library were extraordinarily helpful in locating valuable material, and always fun to talk with. Rian Malan alerted me to Daniel Reed's book, which was a fantastic resource. I am grateful to two anonymous reviewers for their careful reading, incisive criticisms, and useful suggestions, and to Phil Zachernuk for his thoughts on improving the introduction. I would be remiss if I failed to acknowledge my favourite girls, Buffy and Lilly. Fazeela Jiwa is a hero.

The Social Sciences and Humanities Research Council of Canada funded the research for this study. Some of the material in this book was previously published in two *African Affairs* articles: 'Reassessing Transition Violence: Voices from South Africa's Township Wars, 1990–94', 112, 447 (2013) and 'Crime, Conflict and Politics in Transition Era South Africa', 104, 416 (2005).

Acknowledgements

Finally, this book is dedicated to the most important people in my life, Theresa Ulicki and Nathaniel Konstantyn Kynoch-Ulicki, masters of the label game. Theresa for sharing with me our South African journey and all that life has to offer; and to Nate, dedicated conversationalist, empathetic listener, and the best fishing and football buddy one could ever wish for.

List of Acronyms

ANC	African National Congress
ANCYL	African National Congress Youth League
APLA	Azanian People's Liberation Army
AZAPO	Azanian People's Organisation
BEYCO	Bekkersdal Youth Congress
CASE	Community Agency for Social Enquiry
COSAS	Congress of South African Students
COSATU	Congress of South African Trade Unions
FAWU	Food and Allied Workers Union
FOSATU	Federation of South African Trade Unions
G & D	Germiston and District Taxi Association
HRC	Human Rights Commission
IBIIR	Independent Board of Inquiry into Informal Repression
IFP	Inkatha Freedom Party
ISCOR	Iron and Steel Corporation
ISD	Internal Stability Division (sometimes referred to as (ISU) Internal Stability Unit)
KATO	Katlehong Taxi Association
KZN	KwaZulu-Natal
LHR	Lawyers for Human Rights
LPC	Local Peace Committee
LRC	Legal Reference Centre
MDM	mass democratic movement
MK	Umkhonto weSizwe
NGO	non-governmental organisation
NP	National Party
NPA	National Peace Accord
NPKF	National Peacekeeping Force
NUMSA	National Union of Metalworkers of South Africa
PAC	Pan Africanist Congress
PASO	Pan Africanist Student Organisation
PTSD	Post-traumatic Stress Disorder
PWV	Pretoria-Witwatersrand-Vaal region
SABC	South African Broadcasting Corporation
SACP	South African Communist Party

List of Acronyms

SADF	South African Defence Force
SAP	South African Police
SDU	Self Defence Unit
SIPP	Special Integrated Presidential Project for urban planning
SPU	Self Protection Unit
TEC	Transitional Executive Council
TRC	Truth and Reconciliation Commission
TTA	Thokoza Taxi Association
UDF	United Democratic Front
UWUSA	United Workers' Union of South Africa

Map 1 South Africa

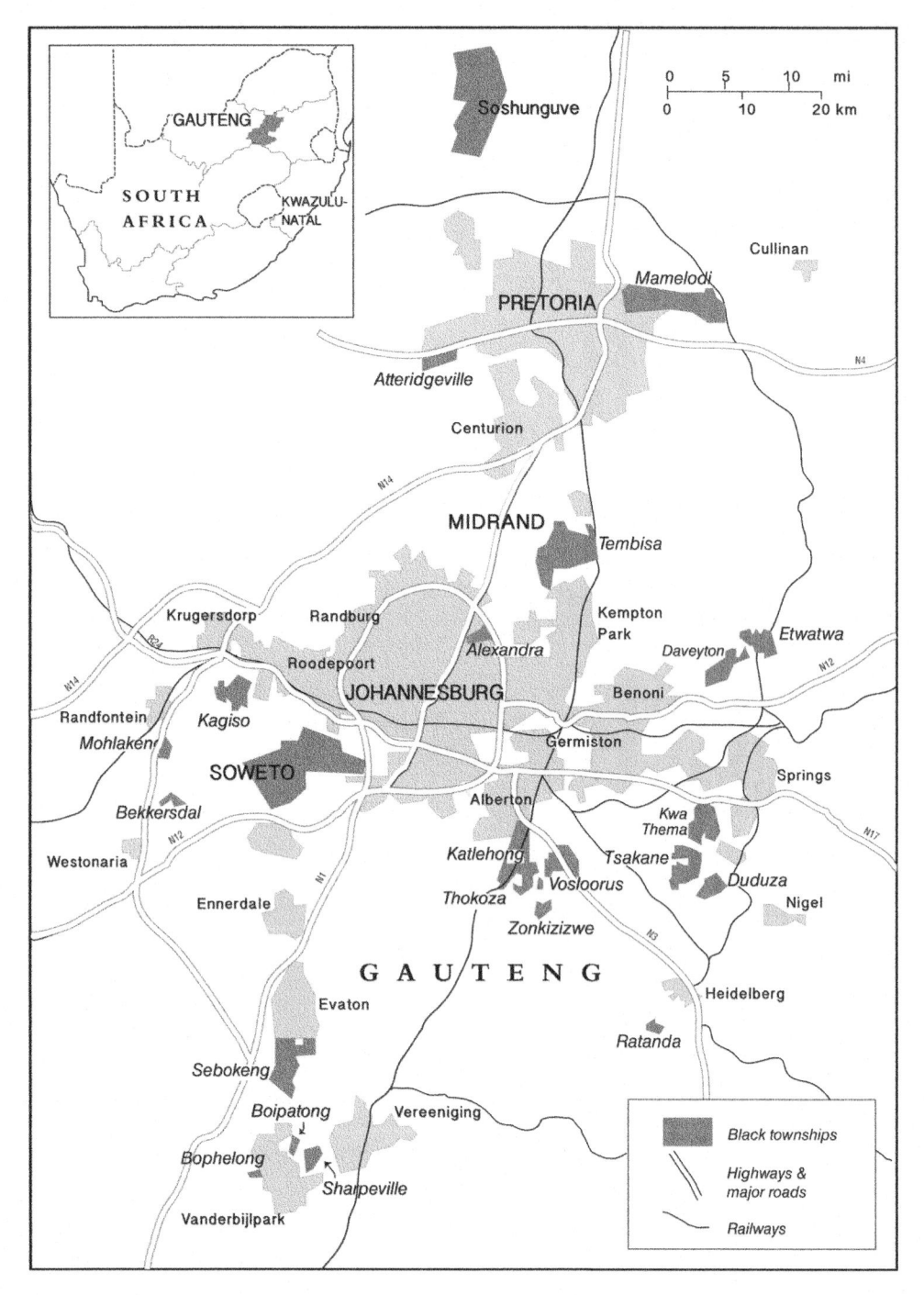

Map 2 The Reef townships

Introduction

In 1993 South African state president, F.W. de Klerk, and African National Congress (ANC) leader, Nelson Mandela, were awarded the Nobel Peace Prize 'for their work for the peaceful termination of the apartheid regime'.[1] Both men deserved credit for entering negotiations leading to the April 1994 elections that formally ended racial rule. However, apartheid did not enjoy a 'peaceful termination'. The four years of the transition era preceding the elections were the bloodiest of the entire apartheid period with an estimated 14,000 deaths attributed to politically related violence.[2] The primary divide in these conflicts pitted ANC supporters against those of the Inkatha Freedom Party (IFP), with state security forces also figuring prominently. This work is the first book-length study devoted to the fighting that plagued black residential areas in South Africa's industrial core surrounding Johannesburg, an area known as the Rand (shorthand for Witwatersrand) or the Reef (because of the gold-bearing reefs that sustained the local mining industry for decades).

Over the course of the transition period and in its immediate aftermath, an enduring narrative emerged which attributed the bulk of the violence to a joint state security force and IFP onslaught against ANC supporters. I argue that this standard account is mired in the conventional binaries that defined South African struggle history. The governing National Party (NP) and its black proxies assume the 'oppressor' role, while those associated with the ANC and the liberation struggle are accorded the mantle of 'resisters'. The oppressor–resister dyad simplified the myriad contestations of the apartheid period and, given the seismic political shifts of the transition era, is especially problematic when applied to the conflicts of the early 1990s. In February 1990, de Klerk announced the unbanning of opposition parties including the ANC, the Pan Africanist Congress (PAC) and

---

[1] 'The Nobel Peace Prize 1993', *Nobelprize.org* (Nobel Media AB 2014), https://www.nobelprize.org/nobel_prizes/peace/laureates/1993/.

[2] *Truth and Reconciliation Commission of South Africa Final Report* (Truth and Reconciliation Commission, Cape Town, 1999), vol. 2, ch. 7, p. 584. These figures, however, constitute guesswork as there were no specific classification criteria for politically related homicides.

the South African Communist Party (SACP), released Nelson Mandela from prison, and committed his government to negotiations with its foremost adversary. Some form of democratic elections in which black South Africans would play a pivotal role were clearly on the horizon, and political competition intensified as the three major parties – NP, ANC and IFP – manoeuvred for advantage throughout the transition period. These changing political dynamics were crucial in shaping the conflicts that raged through many black townships – urban areas set aside for African settlement. The NP, IFP and ANC all had blood on their hands during this turbulent period and no party appropriated the moral high ground in relation to transition violence. The history of exclusionary, exploitive and racist rule embodied in almost five decades of NP governance created the conditions that were foundational to the violence, but within the transition period itself all parties vied for power, all used violence to promote their interests and all bear responsibility for the suffering that accompanied the end of apartheid.

The actions, perspectives and memories of combatants and non-combatants highlight a more nuanced reality than prevailing interpretations which unfailingly cast the IFP as aggressors and the police and military as uniformly hostile to the ANC. Identifying the multiplicities of violence and the diversity of security force involvement is essential to grasping how these conflicts affected township communities. Many townships were drawn into the fighting, but Katlehong and Thokoza, adjoining neighbourhoods twenty or so kilometres southeast of Johannesburg, experienced the most intensive and protracted violence. Residents of these two townships, along with police officers who served there, provided the oral testimony upon which much of this work is based.[3]

[3] Interviews in Thokoza and Katlehong were conducted primarily through door-to-door canvassing. Research assistants accompanied by me or working alone knocked on doors, explained the nature of the project and asked residents if they would agree to an interview. If respondents were comfortable in English, I conducted the interview; if they preferred isiZulu, isiXhosa or Sesotho, the interview was conducted by a research assistant. Research assistants also interviewed acquaintances and neighbours who lived in Thokoza and Katlehong. The only qualifications for respondents was they had to have been resident in the township during the early 1990s and at least in their teens during this period. Obtaining interviews in the IFP-dominated hostels was a different process. The hostels are governed by community leaders, known as *indunas*. In some hostels, the *indunas* agreed immediately after the initial consultation, and we were free to wander the hostel complexes asking for volunteers. In one complex, a general meeting was called in which we were introduced to the residents who were encouraged to ask questions about our project and, if interested, to volunteer for interviews. All hostel interviews were conducted in isiZulu by research assistants. About sixty township and sixty hostel interviews were completed. Five former ANC-aligned Self Defence Unit (SDU) members were uncovered during township canvassing with an additional seventeen interviews obtained through liaising with a Thokoza-based ex-combatants' association. I conducted several in English, and the remainder were conducted by a research assistant in isiZulu, isiXhosa or Sesotho. I interviewed eight former police officers from the

Introduction

Party politics

By the 1980s it had become obvious to all but the most hard-line NP members that the grand vision of apartheid, in which disenfranchised black South Africans were contained in ethnic homelands and only tolerated in 'white' South Africa so long as white businesses or householders employed them, was unworkable. South Africa's commitment to apartheid had made it an international pariah, and internal opposition was unrelenting. In a final campaign to preserve white rule, the government ruthlessly suppressed dissent while also attempting to appease domestic and international critics by amending different aspects of legalised discrimination. State repression had effectively curbed militant action by the end of the 1980s, but piecemeal reforms had failed to satisfy opponents of the regime, bolster the economy or win international approval. While the liberation movement led by the ANC had no hope of overthrowing the state by force of arms, the long-term future of white rule looked increasingly untenable. The pragmatic F.W. de Klerk's ascendancy to the state presidency in September 1989 opened a new chapter in South African politics. His bold initiative to unban exiled opposition parties in February 1990 marked the beginning of a new political era and set the stage for the Rand conflicts.

Fighting between IFP and ANC supporters on the Rand began a few months after Mandela's release. Inkatha was a Zulu cultural movement with roots going back to the 1920s. Mangosuthu Buthelezi revived Inkatha in the mid-1970s with the intent of structuring a mass organisation based in the KwaZulu homeland. Buthelezi had been on good terms with the ANC and had even briefly been a member of the ANC Youth League. He was an ambiguous figure in liberation circles prior to the 1980s as he spoke out against apartheid and refused independence for KwaZulu, but his power derived from his senior position within a homeland structure created by the apartheid government. Differences over the ANC's prosecution of an armed struggle against the apartheid regime and its call for economic sanctions led to a formal split between the two organisations in 1979. Buthelezi and Inkatha claimed that armed resistance would only result in black casualties and that economic sanctions would weaken the already precarious position of black workers. Noting that his stance on these issues echoed those of the government that paid his salary as a homeland leader, many in the ANC dismissed

^(contd) Internal Stability Division (ISD – sometimes erroneously referred to as ISU) along with a handful of township police, local ANC and IFP officials, non-governmental organisation (NGO) personnel, journalists and peace monitors. Additional testimony was gleaned from Truth and Reconciliation Commission transcripts, SDU and police interview material gathered by the University of Witwatersrand Missing Voices Project and interviews housed in the O'Malley archives.

Buthelezi as a National Party puppet. When supporters of the United Democratic Front (UDF), a collection of civic, worker, student and church groups broadly sympathetic to and in some cases unofficially aligned with the ANC, began organising stayaways and boycotts in the predominantly Zulu province of Natal and adjacent KwaZulu in the early 1980s, Inkatha mobilised resistance to these campaigns. From the mid-1980s much of contemporary KwaZulu-Natal (KZN) province was locked in a Zulu civil conflict between UDF/ANC and IFP supporters. With the remaking of the political landscape in 1990, Inkatha launched as a political party – the IFP – in July. The already bitter Inkatha–ANC dispute acquired a new significance with the onset of negotiations. Primarily black parties, which had previously been denied meaningful political authority, were now poised to compete for influence as black voters were sure to be enfranchised in any political settlement. Inkatha had been founded as a Zulu movement and appeals to Zulu nationalism, imbedded in a deep attachment to the monarchy and invocations to a proud martial history, were central to Inkatha identity. The IFP proved incapable of making significant inroads beyond its ethnic base and recruitment efforts outside of KZN were limited to Zulu labour migrants on the Rand, where the ANC was also building branches and campaigning. Years of deadly feuding in KZN fuelled inflammatory rhetoric as both parties denounced the other. A July 1990 IFP rally in Sebokeng township, south of Johannesburg, served as a catalyst for the fighting that did not end until the April 1994 elections. Unlike in KZN, the Rand violence acquired an ethnic dimension with Zulu migrants associated with the IFP confronting ANC-supporting, multi-ethnic communities with a strong isiXhosa-speaking contingent. These conflicts have been referred to as 'hostel wars' because many IFP supporters were housed in municipal hostel complexes built for migrant labourers. As the conflicts progressed, predominantly Zulu hostels functioned as IFP fortresses surrounded by ANC-dominated townships.

The government reluctantly accepted the need to negotiate with the ANC but remained intent on weakening its old enemy prior to any elections. White South Africa had been conditioned to fear the ANC and for years many police and military units had sought to root out and destroy ANC 'terrorists'. With the ANC returned from exile and preparing for elections, many security force personnel needed little encouragement to continue old patterns of policing. There is much debate about the extent to which President de Klerk and his inner circle knew about, sanctioned or directed covert security force operations to assist the IFP in its conflict against the ANC, but it is indisputable that such actions took place. The NP initially co-operated with the IFP to undermine the ANC but changed tack midway through the transition period when it realised that reaching a political settlement acceptable to the majority required a working partnership with the ANC. The apartheid state was dysfunctional in some regards, but right to the end it was remarkably effective in safeguarding white privilege and security. Even while it was losing ground in the negotiations, the state retained its ability to insulate whites from violence. Black South Africans were not so lucky. Starting in mid 1990, the ANC–IFP conflict turned many Rand townships into warzones and the militarisation of these areas had profound consequences.

Historiography

Despite contributions that point to the targeting of migrant Zulus associated with the IFP, the excesses of some ANC-affiliated militants and instances of ethnic partisanship within the police force, the fundamental concept of the ANC under siege by an IFP-security force alliance has retained its influence.[4] The ANC condemned the 1990s violence as a state-initiated campaign to destabilise the liberation movement. It argued that Inkatha had joined forces with a duplicitous government that publicly pursued negotiations while secretly instigating violence against ANC supporters. A sinister collection of police and military, referred to as the 'third force', are key actors in this narrative. The third force covertly served government interests by attacking ANC supporters, assisting IFP fighters and provoking conflict between ANC and IFP groups. In the words of a contemporary analyst, 'The present crisis represents a new phase in the long war waged by the state against the liberation movement in general and the

---

[4] Heribert Adam and Kogila Moodley's work is notable for its inclusion of internecine ANC violence as well as clashes between ANC–AZAPO supporters. Lauren Segal's interviews during the conflict describe incidents of Xhosa police backing Xhosa township combatants and Zulu police assisting their 'brothers' in the hostels. Philip Bonner and Vusi Ndima acknowledge the aggression of ANC-affiliated fighters and are sensitive to the plight of migrant Zulus caught up in the conflict. Bonner and Noor Nieftagodien recognise that the SDUs often took the fight to the IFP and their analysis of the TRC's findings on East Rand hostilities highlights the centrality of criminal activity. See Heribert Adam and Kogila Moodley, 'Political Violence, "Tribalism", and Inkatha', *Journal of Modern African Studies* 30, 3 (1992), pp. 485–510; Lauren Segal, 'The Human Face of Violence: Hostel Dwellers Speak', *Journal of Southern African Studies* 18, 1 (1992), pp. 190–231; Philip Bonner and Vusi Ndima, 'The Roots of Violence and Martial Zuluness on the East Rand' in Benedict Carton, John Laband and Jabulani Sithole (eds), *Zulu Identities: Being Zulu past and present* (Columbia University Press, New York, 2009), pp. 363–82; Philip Bonner and Noor Nieftagodien, *Kathorus: A History* (Maskew Miller Longman, Cape Town, 2001); Philip Bonner and Noor Nieftagodien, 'The Truth and Reconciliation Commission and the Pursuit of "Social Truth": The Case of Kathorus' in Deborah Posel and Graeme Simpson (eds), *Commissioning the Past: Understanding South Africa's Truth and Reconciliation Commission* (Wits University Press, Johannesburg, 2002), pp. 173–203.

ANC in particular.'[5] Stephen Ellis argued that third force networks 'were not responsible for all the political violence that occurred in this period, but there is reason to believe that they were by some way its most important sponsors'.[6] David Everatt insisted that 'the analysis of monitoring data leads to the conclusion that the violence was manipulated by elements from the security forces of the apartheid state to guarantee their position under a new democratic dispensation'.[7] Monitoring and press reports of massacres also led Rupert Taylor and Mark Shaw to claim that Inkatha was the principal aggressor and 'the security forces transported, escorted and joined Inkatha offences or remained inactive during Inkatha attacks'.[8] Two recent works illustrate the persistence of such convictions. A study of the East Rand region, now known as Ekurhuleni, classifies the violence as freedom fighters' continued resistance against the oppressive state:

> The violence than [sic] engulfed the township in the early 1990s had a profound effect on the negotiations that were taking place only a few kilometres away in Kempton Park. The violence was intended to derail the negotiations process and, when that objective failed, to influence the outcome of the negotiations in their favour. The attempt to endanger the birth of democracy was thwarted by hundreds of activists, many of whom were barely in their teens and who organized themselves into [ANC-aligned] Self Defence Units (SDUs) to defend their communities and the promise of freedom.[9]

In their examination of Reef violence, Sekibakiba Lekgoathi and Sifiso Ndlovu conclude that, 'In all strife-torn areas, the police and soldiers publicly colluded with Inkatha ... On the other hand, the attitude of the security forces towards township residents and those in squatter settlements was quite hostile and combative.'[10]

A convergence of factors explains this narrative's ascendance. The ANC, led by international icon Mandela, exemplified the struggle to end racist rule. The NP, by contrast, was the founding party of apart-

---

[5] Morris Szeftel, 'Manoeuvres of war in South Africa', *Review of African Political Economy* 19, 51 (1991), p. 64.
[6] Stephen Ellis, 'The Historical Significance of South Africa's Third Force', *Journal of Southern African Studies* 24, 2 (1998), p. 264.
[7] David Everatt, 'Analysing political violence on the Reef, 1990–1994' in Ran Greenstein (ed.), *The Role of Political Violence in South Africa's Democratisation* (Community Agency for Social Enquiry, Johannesburg, 2003), p. 95.
[8] Rupert Taylor and Mark Shaw, 'The Dying Days of Apartheid' in D. Howarth and A. Norval (eds), *South Africa in Transition: New Theoretical Perspectives* (MacMillan Press Ltd., London, 1998), p. 22.
[9] Philip Bonner and Noor Nieftagodien with Sello Mathabatha, *Ekurhuleni: The Making of an Urban Region* (Wits University Press, Johannesburg, 2012), p. 183.
[10] Sekibakiba Peter Lekgoathi and Sifiso Mxolisi Ndlovu, 'Political Violence in the PWV region, 1990–94' in *The Road to Democracy in South Africa*, vol. 6, part 2, South African Democracy Education Trust (Unisa Press, Pretoria, 2013), p. 963.

heid and its security forces were associated with decades of racist brutality. Inkatha did not have the same struggle credentials as the ANC. Its power was centred in an apartheid-constructed homeland and the movement and its leader, Buthelezi, were seen in many circles as NP clients. Moreover, Inkatha supporters, sometimes with the assistance of state security forces, had been battling ANC-aligned groups in KZN since the mid 1980s. Given these circumstances, the ANC held the moral high ground over its foes. ANC officials and the ANC Department of Information and Publicity took every opportunity to impress upon an increasingly sympathetic domestic and international English language media that the IFP and the security forces were conducting an offensive against ANC supporters.

This message was reinforced by various violence monitoring organisations that identified with the liberation struggle. From the beginning of politicised violence on the Rand in 1990, the IFP complained that monitoring groups and much of the English press were biased. As a result, IFP supporters and officials often refused to interact with these outfits and, as the violence intensified, it became difficult for reporters to work in Inkatha areas.[11] Political ideals, ease of access and language affinities ensured that the majority operated in ANC-dominated territory and interacted primarily with ANC officials and supporters.[12] The government's campaign – abetted by much of the Afrikaans press – to establish the ANC as the source of township violence did not achieve much traction beyond a limited domestic white audience. As Hermann Giliomee notes, the state was 'unable to counter the ANC's ability to influence large sections of the English press to accept its version of the conflicts in the townships'.[13] For most South African and international observers, the apartheid regime, with its history of deception and media manipulation, was almost entirely discredited as a reliable source of information. Moreover, the NP's long history of persecuting nationalist opposition rendered plausible virtually any report of

[11] Writing about the fighting in Thokoza, photo-journalists Greg Marinovich and Joao Silva report that IFP militants were openly hostile towards journalists: 'As the first year of the war wore on, venturing into the hostels became a scary gamble... Later still, entering the hostels at all was out of the question.' Greg Marinovich and Joao Silva, *The Bang Bang Club: Snapshots from a hidden war* (Arrow Books, London, 2001), p. 111.

[12] Far more ANC-aligned township residents could speak English than the typically less-educated migrant labourers who made up the bulk of the IFP. This state of affairs was not confined to the Rand. For KZN violence, see Phillipe Denis, Radikobo Ntsimane and Thomas Cannel, *Indians versus Russians: An oral history of political violence in Nxamalala (1987–1993)* (Cluster Publications, Pietermaritzburg, 2010). They observed that, 'Because they were perceived to be sympathetic to the ANC, the violence monitors sometimes were incapable of obtaining information on the "other side"', p. 13.

[13] Hermann Giliomee, *The Last Afrikaner Leaders: A Supreme Test of Power* (Tafelberg Publishers Limited, Cape Town, 2012), p. 317.

government-sponsored violence. For many journalists and violence monitors, IFP accounts of the violence were similarly suspect, not least because of the IFP's ties to the state and elements within the security forces.

The more influential English coverage tended to reflect the ANC's version of events. M.L. Thotse and J.E.H. Grobler's examination of media and violence-monitoring organisations' portrayals of transition violence notes that much of the Afrikaans media and, of course, the state-run South African Broadcasting Corporation, essentially parroted the government's side of the story. In the same vein, they argue that five prominent and ostensibly impartial South African monitoring groups – Community Agency for Social Enquiry (CASE), Human Rights Commission (HRC), Independent Board of Inquiry into Informal Repression (IBIIR), Lawyers for Human Rights (LHR) and the Legal Reference Centre (LRC) – did much the same for the ANC. They observe that 'HRC representatives did not even attempt to conceal their loyalty to the ANC.'[14] The authors pay particular attention to the backgrounds of monitoring personnel and judge that these organisations were predisposed to favour the ANC's version of events. Indeed, they conclude that, 'at least some, if not all of the organisations, had actively tried to convince the international public opinion of the existence of a "third force" to mount international pressure on the government and to weaken the latter's negotiation position.'[15]

The regional director for the National Peace Accord (NPA) responsible for the Rand was also sceptical of violence monitors' impartiality, particularly the HRC:

> You can read HRC reports and there are two types of reports – there are Inkatha attacks and there are unknown men. It's very clear that unknown men were ANC but they don't say it, they never dared; and they were hated, absolutely hated, by all other parties: the police hated them, the army hated them, Inkatha hated them.[16]

CASE compiled a database of political violence on the Rand between 1990 and 1994 in which, whenever possible, it recorded the affiliation of aggressors. In these reports, 'a massive 80 per cent of incidents were ascribed to Inkatha, 13 per cent to the SAP [South African Police] or SADF [South African Defence Force], and 5 per cent to ANC supporters'.[17] The IBIIR produced volumes of material on Rand violence,

---

[14] M.L Thotse and J.E.H. Grobler, 'Standpoints on "Black-on-Black" vs "Third Force" Violence during South Africa's Transitional Negotiations', *Historia* 48, 2 (2003), p. 151.
[15] Thotse and Grobler, 'Standpoints', p. 152.
[16] Interview, David Storey, former Wits-Vaal regional director, National Peace Accord, Johannesburg, 26 May, 2006.
[17] Everatt, 'Analysing political violence', p. 126.

including a series of monthly reports, and regularly briefed international human rights groups, journalists, government-appointed inquiries such as the Goldstone Commission and other interested parties. The IBIIR was formed in 1989 to investigate attacks on anti-apartheid activists, and its political leanings were well established. IBIIR senior investigator Sally Sealey collaborated closely with Duma Nkosi, the ANC's chairperson in Thokoza, and was seen by all parties to the conflict as an ally of the ANC.[18] Sealey claimed that the IBIIR attempted to gain the co-operation of IFP supporters but admitted, 'I don't suppose I can blame the IFP for not trusting us. Under the circumstances it would have been very difficult for them to trust us.'[19] Almost without exception, the IBIIR identified the IFP and state security forces as aggressors in the violence. It sometimes chided the ANC for not exerting sufficient control over SDUs that preyed on their host communities, but IBIIR reports on the ANC–IFP conflict consistently depict township residents associated with the ANC as victims. The material disseminated by violence-monitoring agencies was critical in shaping the narrative as media and other sources, including academic works, often relied on 'data' generated by violence monitors to inform their accounts of the violence.

Coverage of the 1992 Boipatong massacre provides a well-documented example of uncritical reporting related to police complicity in communal violence. As James Simpson points out, 'it was successfully broadcast as an event that epitomised unending state-sponsored violence. This decisive interpretation remains widespread in scholarship and popular memory.'[20] After IFP supporters in KwaMadala Hostel slaughtered dozens of non-combatant township residents during a night-time raid on Boipatong township, the ANC immediately accused the police of assisting the attackers. Simpson describes how the ANC intervened to control the flow of information. On the morning after the massacre, 'ANC officials went around the township instructing residents not to talk to police or outsiders. Statements were made to violence monitoring groups with ANC-supporters among their membership such as the Human Rights Commission and Peace Action. Journalists were guided around the township and introduced to witnesses.'[21] In its initial public statement that day, the ANC claimed that armoured police vehicles ferried the attackers from the hostel and

---

[18] Interview, Duma Nkosi, Ekurhuleni, 27 June, 2008. Sealey stated in a TRC hearing that she had been 'threatened and intimidated' by both IFP supporters and SAP officers during the violence. See TRC Amnesty Hearing, Sally Sealy submission, 23 November, 1998, Palm Ridge, http://www.justice.gov.za/trc/amntrans/1998/9811231210_pr_981123th.htm.

[19] Interview, Sally Sealey, London, July 2006.

[20] James Simpson, 'Boipatong: The Politics of a Massacre and the South African Transition', *Journal of Southern African Studies* 38, 3 (2012), p. 623.

[21] Simpson, 'Boipatong', p. 630.

that police participated in the massacre. An official commission of inquiry and judicial proceedings subsequently refuted these findings and, although the police were criticised for inaction and incompetence in investigating the massacre, they were cleared of having participated in the attack.[22] Nevertheless, 'ANC accusations quickly developed into popular conviction in Boipatong, South Africa and around the world.'[23] In fact, several years after the massacre, the Truth and Reconciliation Commission (TRC), established to investigate human rights abuses committed between 1960 and 1994, concluded that 'KwaMadala Hostel residents, together with the police, planned and carried out an attack on the community of Boipatong ... The Commission finds that the police colluded with the attackers and ... that white men with blackened faces participated in the attack'.[24] The ANC's efforts to discredit the government and smear the security forces often bore fruit, even when the evidence for security force transgressions was questionable.

In the years following the ANC's 1994 election victory, the established narrative was reinforced by the IFP boycott of the TRC. The TRC was supported by the ANC-led government and the IFP castigated it as an exercise run by and for ANC interests. Philip Bonner and Noor Nieftagodien have noted how the TRC's interpretations of the violence were affected by the absence of IFP testimony. They specifically mention ANC supporters' destruction of Lindela Hostel in Katlehong as a crucial event in the escalation of local violence that was completely missed by the TRC:

> The only means of remedying this deficiency would have been the extensive interviewing of participants in or bystanders to these events. But seeing that the victims of the Lindela hostel slaughter were migrant Zulus, whose political party, the IFP, refused to co-operate with the Commission, a major source of information was automatically cut off.[25]

Only a handful of IFP militants on the Rand, most of whom were in prison, applied to the TRC for amnesty, so the perspectives and experiences of IFP supporters are almost entirely lacking in the TRC archive. Partially by default, the ANC's interpretation of the township conflicts continues to enjoy the widest currency.

The ANC version also gathered strength because many of its assertions were true. As the transition period unfolded it became clear that Inkatha and the NP had a mutual interest in destabilising the ANC, and covert units within the security forces provided Inkatha mili-

---

[22] See the report from the British consultant appointed by the Goldstone Commission to investigate police conduct at Boipatong: P.A.J. Waddington, 'Policing South Africa: The View from Boipatong', *Policing and Society* 4, (1994), pp. 83–95.
[23] Simpson, 'Boipatong', p. 634.
[24] TRC Report, vol. 3., ch. 6, 'Regional Profile, Transvaal, 1990–94'.
[25] Bonner and Nieftagodien, 'Pursuit of "Social Truth"', p. 188.

tants with weapons and training and protected leading IFP officials from prosecution. Some of these operations were exposed during the transition period and additional examples of state security force–IFP collusion came to light through the offices of the TRC. These events represent a partial truth, however, as the fixation with IFP and security force aggression deflected attention from violence that did not conform to this model.[26]

Reassessing transition violence and structure of the book

Studies of violence elsewhere offer valuable insights for the South African conflicts. In his analysis of loyalism during the Mau Mau rebellion, Daniel Branch argues that instead of pre-existing political or socio-economic positions, 'loyalism was much more a reaction to the conduct and direction of the conflict'. He cites vengeance, press-ganging and a desire to be on the winning side as crucial determinants.[27] Because the dominant account is concerned with laying blame for the violence, it overstates the role of party agendas in shaping conflict. ANC–IFP hostilities instigated and justified the formation of armed groups that at times engaged 'the enemy', but also used force to secure dominance over rivals, the compliance of local populations and material advantages. National-level political antagonisms triggered, defined and sustained hostilities as parties incited and armed their followers, but neither the ANC nor the IFP could contain or manage township violence that was largely determined by parochial dynamics. People fought to protect their homes, to safeguard loved ones, to avenge the suffering they had endured and to achieve local advantage; some were conscripted into fighting units. Lauren Segal's interviews with hostel residents conducted during the conflict led her to conclude that, 'actors in the violence are motivated by a host of factors, which at times

[26] A much less influential counter-narrative does exist. Its foremost proponent, Anthea Jeffrey, identifies the ANC as the primary force behind the politicised violence of apartheid's last decade. She classifies IFP violence as a response to the ANC's revolutionary onslaught, waged to get power at all costs. Jeffrey's zeal to denounce the ANC and rehabilitate the IFP is evident throughout and the selective use of sources further undermines the credibility of this impassioned story. Stuart Kaufman also draws attention to ANC militarism, declaring that the ANC won control of the country by 'defeating their black opponents in combat while blaming de Klerk for the violence'. Kaufman's assertion ignores the level of support the ANC enjoyed across the country and the fact that the ANC had the least to gain by resorting to violence. If none of the major parties had sponsored violence, the ANC was best placed to win the elections. Moreover, many militants associated with the ANC did not answer to the party. See Anthea Jeffrey, *People's War: New light on the struggle for South Africa* (Jonathan Ball Publishers, Johannesburg, 2009); Stuart Kaufman, *Nationalist Passions* (Cornell University Press, Ithaca, 2015), p. 208.
[27] Daniel Branch, *Defeating Mau Mau, Creating Kenya: Counterinsurgency, Civil War and Decolonisation* (Cambridge University Press, New York, 2009), p. 223.

intersect with, and at other times radically diverge from, popular explanations or expressed party political lines.'[28] Political loyalties mattered, but the involvement of township and hostel residents in the violence often depended on who held power in their area, which group presented the foremost threat and the potential benefits provided by party affiliation.

Stathis Kalyvas' characterisation of civil wars as 'welters of complex struggles rather than simple binary conflicts neatly arrayed along a single-issue dimension'[29] provides a useful framework for situating Rand violence. Kalyvas notes that although civil wars are typically defined by a 'master' cleavage – religious, ethnic, political, etc. – tangential 'local' cleavages frequently drive the violence on the ground. Rather than privileging a top-down or bottom-up perspective, he outlines an alternative model based on 'alliance' in which civil wars function as 'concatenations of multiple and often disparate local cleavages more or less loosely arrayed around the master cleavage'.[30]

Exploring these alliances and intersections through the perceptions and memories of residents from war-torn areas, along with security force members, politicians and violence monitors, offers new possibilities for understanding South Africa's transition violence. IFP testimony adds an element that, with few exceptions, is notable by its absence[31] and oral testimony from township residents collected at least ten years after the end of the conflict arguably allows for a more measured response than information provided to violence-monitoring agencies and media during the war. Violence that does not fit neatly into the limiting prism of state repression/IFP aggression must be explored more fully. This need not involve downplaying the magnitude of state or IFP responsibility, only a recognition that various forms of violence emerged in the transition period that do not necessarily align with the conventional binaries.

It is notoriously difficult to distinguish 'criminal' from 'political' violence, however; as townships became locked into the ANC–IFP rivalry, business and personal interests, along with acquisitive criminality, became bound up with politics in an explosive cocktail of localised violence. Scholars have focused attention on the wartime activities of criminal gangs and predatory militias in different settings. Alex de Waal identifies the commercialisation of violence in African conflicts, in which many combatants engage in extortion, robbery and looting.[32] In the Liberian civil war of the 1990s, many youth joined

[28] Segal, 'Human Face of Violence', p. 192.
[29] Stathis Kalyvas, *The Logic of Violence in Civil War* (Cambridge University Press, New York, 2006), p. 371.
[30] Kalyvas, *Logic of Violence*, p. 384.
[31] Segal's 'Human Face of Violence' is the foremost exception. Bonner and Ndima's 'Roots of Violence' also incorporates the voices of East Rand hostel dwellers.
[32] Alex de Waal, *Demilitarizing the Mind: African Agendas for Peace and Security* (Africa World Press, Philadelphia, 2003).

the fighting in the hope of enriching themselves. In anticipation of looting opportunities, one rebel advance on Monrovia was referred to as 'Operation Pay Yourself'.[33] Similar behaviours were in evidence during politicised fighting in South Africa. Hostel dwellers looted homes during raids into the townships and comrades responded in kind when attacking Inkatha areas. For some militants, hijacking delivery trucks and stealing cars proved to be a profitable sideline. Peter Andreas's study of the 1992–95 Bosnian war recommends integrating the criminalised dimensions of war into analyses, not least because of the 'profound effects that the criminalized aspects of conflict can have on postwar social order'.[34] His observation that 'criminality and private predation does not simply trump politics in wartime but rather interacts with it in complex ways'[35] has particular relevance for an understanding of transition-era violence in South Africa. State security forces, IFP and ANC structures all made use of and/or allied with criminal gangs to further their goals.

A more expansive approach to the Rand violence requires a critical examination of ANC militants' aggression, clashes between ANC-aligned groups, conflicts between the ANC and rival nationalist organisations, the PAC and the Azanian People's Organisation (AZAPO), the roles of different security force personnel and the intersection of criminal and political violence. Forces associated with both Inkatha and the ANC committed atrocities in an environment that sanctioned violence against all people categorised as the enemy, regardless of combatant status. There was no shortage of victims on either side of the political divide and, by the latter stages of the Rand conflict, IFP members were under siege and on the defensive. ANC structures occasionally battled with PAC and AZAPO groups and the ANC frequently had to contend with episodes of internecine violence. The ANC was a broad church, allied with civic, labour and student movements and with different component parts such as its armed wing Umkhonto weSizwe (MK), the Youth League and the Women's League. It had connections to the hundreds of SDUs whose formation it had encouraged. Newly unbanned and returned from exile, the ANC did not have the institutional means to monitor and control diverse constituencies with competing interests. As the ANC built its networks and enlarged its capacity during the transition period, struggles for authority between local structures sometimes erupted into bloody conflict. This aspect of transition violence has been largely overlooked.

---

[33] Stephen Ellis, *The Mask of Anarchy: The Destruction of Liberia and the Religious Dimensions of an African Civil War* (New York University Press, New York, 1999).

[34] Peter Andreas, 'The Clandestine Political Economy of War and Peace in Bosnia', *International Studies Quarterly*, 28 (2004), p. 49.

[35] Andreas, 'War and Peace in Bosnia', p. 32.

Introduction

A detailed study of security force involvement complicates standard assertions regarding state security forces' relationships with the ANC and IFP, as well as the extent of third force influence. Some covert operators provided military assistance to the IFP and many security force members abhorred the ANC. However, police and military groups functioned independently of one another, and security force personnel did not share a standard political orientation. Some favoured the IFP, a much smaller number backed the ANC, while others had no stake in the violence and performed their jobs, competently or otherwise, without discernible bias. Moreover, various groups within the townships, of all political persuasions, were active players in the violence with their own interests, and state security personnel lacked the capability to engineer and manage wide-ranging conflicts. Without discounting the destructiveness of third force interventions, a more consequential development was the utter collapse of the rule of law in war-torn areas. Black South Africans had long distrusted the South African police but as their communities were consumed by armed conflicts that the police could not contain, and in which they were often implicated, the state abdicated any vestiges of remaining authority and the rule of the gun prevailed. What this book attempts therefore is to present a re-reading of modern South African history during the transition years and how this was enacted in the key African townships of the Witwatersrand.

The book is structured in two parts: the first takes a broad view of the fighting across the Rand in several different townships. It locates the beginning of the ANC-IFP conflict on the Reef from July 1990, highlights the activities of a multiplicity of combatant groups, and analyses state security forces' contributions to politicised hostilities. Chapter 1 identifies the forces that triggered and shaped the war on the Reef and examines the initial outbreaks of violence. The formation, composition, and agendas of ANC and IFP-affiliated armed groups provides the focus for Chapter 2, while Chapter 3 demonstrates that politicised violence was not confined to the ANC-IFP rivalry. Chapter 4 investigates the different roles played by various police and military units. Part 2 is concerned exclusively with Katlehong and Thokoza. Chapter 5 traces the course of the conflict in the two townships from 1990–94. Chapters 6 and 7, respectively, explore the experiences of combatants and non-combatants during this period. The Conclusion summarises the main findings and considers the connections between transition-era militarisation and post-apartheid political violence.

Part 1
War on the Reef

1 Beginnings

Years of fighting in KZN ensured that ANC–IFP relations were steeped in hostility when political campaigning on the Rand began following Mandela's release from prison in February 1990. This division operated along pre-existing fault lines as many Zulu migrant labourers – the IFP's natural constituency on the Reef – had been alienated by the militancy of liberation politics in the workplace and the townships. To preserve and expand their authority, both the ANC and the IFP sanctioned violence and armed their supporters. Some state security forces actively assisted the IFP, far fewer supported the ANC, and the rest proved incapable of stopping the violence. Urban Africans had experienced the burden of oppressive policing long before the 1980s insurrections, but the role of the police in suppressing these protests brought them into direct confrontation with youthful ANC supporters. This history rendered it next to impossible for the police to be accepted (or, often, to act) as impartial arbiters in the 1990s ANC–IFP violence. Initial skirmishes sparked cycles of revenge that drew in ever greater numbers of people. The massive civil conflicts that ensued provided fertile terrain for armed groups of all descriptions to advance their agendas, sometimes in line with the main political contenders and sometimes independent of party interests.

Township histories

The war on the Reef began in 1990, but Johannesburg's black townships had experienced different forms of state, criminal and vigilante violence for decades. These segregated urban spaces were adjacent to, but physically apart from, white cities and towns.They contained a mixture of government housing projects, backyard shacks, squatter camps and municipal hostels built for migrant workers. Successive white governments prioritised racial control over crime prevention in black communities, and state violence was most glaringly apparent in the ubiquitous pass and liquor raids that traumatised generations of township residents. To make matters worse, the widespread poverty and marginalisation inevitably produced a criminal element whose violence greatly contributed to the insecurity of township life. In the absence of state protection, many township communities organised initiatives that utilised violence to deter crime and punish suspects.

The direct precursor of transition-era violence occurred during the latter half of the 1980s. In response to the state's 1983 reforms, which allowed increased participation by the Coloured and Indian minorities but still excluded the African majority from parliamentary politics, the ANC called on its supporters within South Africa to make the country ungovernable. This call further invigorated a process that had already begun in some areas as activists had taken to the streets to protest local hardships but also in solidarity against apartheid rule. As protests on the Rand escalated, the ANC's Radio Freedom declared, 'We must destroy the enemy organs of government. We must render them ineffective and inoperative.'[1] From the mid-1980s many townships experienced different forms of anti-government collective action with boycotts, stayaways and other mass protests being accompanied by attacks on local black councillors, police officers and suspected collaborators/informers, along with occasional bombings by guerrillas of the ANC's armed wing, MK. The government responded with ferocious repressive measures, declaring states of emergency first in 1985 for certain areas of South Africa and then again in 1986 for the entire country. In 1987 the state of emergency was extended for a further two years. Policing focused on suppressing dissent and thousands of SADF troops were deployed in volatile townships.

Anti-apartheid activists mobilised under the banner of the UDF and the organisations affiliated to it often directed protest campaigns while township activists presided over 'liberated zones'. Although celebrated by some township residents, the rise of youthful militants known as 'comrades' or 'young lions' was also a source of division and conflict. Comrades demanded adherence to boycotts and stayaways, which were sometimes called without consultation, enforced through violence and could be a source of hardship. Young activists assumed positions of influence and often inverted traditional generational hierarchies by dictating to their elders. Some township residents, especially workers with tenuous employment security and business people who had much to lose by defying the state, confronted the comrades, occasionally with the support of the security forces. The police relied heavily on networks of informers to neutralise political opposition and the hatred these *izimpimpi* (singular *impimpi*) engendered led to the notorious 'necklace', in which suspects had a rubber tire placed around their necks, were doused with petrol and burnt alive. In some cases, this treatment was extended to 'sell-outs' suspected of collaborating with the apartheid regime and those who fraternised with such unde-

[1] J. Seekings, *The UDF: A History of the United Democratic Front in South Africa 1983–1991* (David Philip Publishers, Cape Town, 2000), p. 125.

sirables. Whispering campaigns could easily lead to public executions, and scapegoating and mistakes were inevitable. Distrust, paranoia and heightened insecurity were a by-product of these campaigns to eradicate enemies of the struggle.

In many townships militants routinely clashed with security forces and, more than ever before, the police were seen as an oppressive entity. Township policing had long suffered from a lack of legitimacy and the position of black police became increasingly untenable throughout the 1980s conflicts. Officers and their families were targeted and forced to flee their homes. Images of young militants, throwing stone and petrol bombs and engaging with well-armed security force personnel, were standard fare in international news broadcasts and the South African government was heavily censured. Sensitive to the appearance of white police abusing black youth, the government imported hastily trained and poorly qualified black auxiliaries from rural areas, derisively referred to as 'kitskonstabels' (instant constables), to police the townships. These shotgun-toting outsiders soon became notorious for their indiscipline and propensity for violence. Their introduction further soured the relationship between the SAP and township communities.

As civil policing receded further into the background, violent crime continued unchecked. In addition, several townships experienced deadly clashes between 'Charterists' – those who subscribed to the ANC's Freedom Charter commitment to non-racialism – and the followers of other anti-apartheid groups such as the PAC and AZAPO. Charterists favoured white participation in the struggle against apartheid and the UDF co-operated with and included multi-racial and white organisations. AZAPO and the PAC were not expressly anti-white but followed the principles of the Black Consciousness Movement, which preached that blacks alone should liberate South Africa for the black majority. Disagreements over protest tactics initiated conflicts and, while ideological differences existed, much of the fighting had to do with local influence. The worst of the UDF–AZAPO violence took place in Port Elizabeth and Johannesburg townships in 1985 and 1986. Jeremy Seekings writes that these clashes were largely attributable to Charterist political intolerance: 'Many Charterist activists assumed that ... the UDF and ANC embraced the whole of the "people's camp", and anyone else must therefore be part of the "ruling camp."'[2] The conflicts cost dozens of lives, with attacks and counter-attacks, kidnappings, assassinations and house burnings. According to Seekings, 'AZAPO's Port Elizabeth leadership not unreasonably claimed that "the UDF is out to eliminate AZAPO entirely"'.[3] Leaders on both sides generally spoke out against the violence, but disdain for rivals on the ground was so intense that these interventions often had little

[2] Seekings, *The UDF*, p. 146.
[3] Seekings, *The UDF*, p. 146.

impact. Gail Gerhart and Clive Glaser's description of 1980s violence also applies to the transition-era conflicts: 'Once violence was touched off, it tended to spiral out of control as members of rival organisations and their allied youth and student groups tried to dominate particular patches of urban turf and wreak vengeance on the other side.'[4] In 1986 this conflict spread to Soweto. An AZAPO activist testified that, 'Here in Johannesburg, it was a general thing that the UDF and AZAPO were in a state of war.'[5] The rivalry was particularly intense in Soweto until the Charterist/UDF movement emerged dominant by the late 1980s. When transition violence erupted in 1990, Rand townships housed a core of battle-hardened activists who had been conditioned to using violence in a variety of local struggles.

Hostel–township divide

The defining feature of the Rand conflicts was the prominence of municipal hostels, large dormitory-like complexes built for unskilled, black, male migrants, primarily employed in the lowest-status urban occupations such as factory and foundry work. These structures were managed by municipalities and/or industrial firms and most were decades old by the 1990s.[6] Hostels accommodated migrant workers from many areas of South Africa, but rural Zulus from KZN and isiXhosa speakers from the Transkei and Ciskei homelands tended to dominate hostel populations. With the end of influx controls in 1986, which had restricted the movement of black people to the urban areas, municipal administration of the hostels began to collapse. By the time violence took hold in 1990, these hostels were effectively self-governing with resident leaders and committees supervising hostel life. They were overcrowded and overwhelmingly male but, in the absence of municipal oversight, increasing numbers of female occupants moved into the hostels. Historically, these migrants had a complex relationship with the surrounding, more urbanised township communities. There were points of interaction and friendship through work, churches, soccer teams and social activities, and some hostel occupants had romantic partners and relatives in the townships. Despite these connections,

---

[4] Gail Gerhart and Clive Glaser, *From Protest to Challenge: A Documentary History of African Politics in South Africa, 1882–1990, Volume 6: Challenge and Victory, 1980–1990* (Indiana University Press, Bloomington, 2010), p. 82

[5] TRC Amnesty Hearing, Motlana Mphoreng, AM2740/96, 8 June 1998, Johannesburg, http://sabctrc.saha.org.za/hearing.php?id=52691

[6] The Khumalo Street hostels in Thokoza, for example, were built in the 1960s and 1970s. See Colin Marx and Margot Rubin, *Divisible Spaces: Land Biographies in Diepkloof, Thokoza and Doornfontein, Gauteng*, Report prepared for Urban LandMark, May 2008, http://www.urbanlandmark.org.za/downloads/Land_Biographies_Full_Report_LowRes.pdf

hostel-based migrants lived apart from township residents, typically had a more rural orientation including attachments to traditional authorities, were less educated and kept their families in their home areas. Politically inspired protest campaigns produced friction between township activists and hostel residents. Migrants complained that, although they were rarely consulted beforehand, township activists demanded compliance with stayaways and boycotts and abused those who did not go along with such protests. These sporadic tensions came to a head during the 1980s.

One of the outgrowths of NP reforms to moderate aspects of apartheid during the 1970s and 1980s was the greater freedom of organisation granted to black trade unions. This development had significant repercussions for the 1990s violence. Migrant mine and factory workers initially embraced trade unionism for the potential workplace benefits that membership offered, and unions distanced themselves from nationalist politics to avoid government repression. However, as anti-apartheid activism gathered steam in the mid 1980s the character of union politics underwent a fundamental shift. The established Federation of South African Trade Unions (FOSATU) came together with other unions to form the new conglomerate Congress of South African Trade Unions (COSATU) in 1985. COSATU, unlike its predecessors, was overtly political and linked to the nationalist struggle. This attachment was formalised in 1988 when COSATU joined the UDF. As mass democratic movement (MDM) unionism prevailed by the mid 1980s, urban, well-educated and often youthful men assumed the majority of leadership positions, and poorly educated migrants who were less proficient in English were sidelined in the union movement.[7] Ari Sitas argues that changes in the industrial workforce further contributed to the marginalisation of migrant workers. In the metal industry, for example, downsizing meant the loss of unskilled positions that were disproportionately filled by migrants. Consequently, 'unions tended to be dominated by the more established sectors, which had more skilled workforces and were in growth areas like electrical engineering, petrochemicals, electronics and so on. By 1986/7 COSATU's leadership on the Reef was to be drawn from urban semi-skilled workers.'[8] Unions reduced their mobilisation efforts in hostels and with union activism becoming inseparable from anti-apartheid politics, droves of migrant Zulus deserted the MDM unions in the late 1980s. A National Union of Metalworkers of South Africa (NUMSA – a COSATU affiliate) organiser observed the alienation of migrants through the 1980s:

[7] The MDM was a broad resistance front comprised of the UDF, COSATU and other activist groups opposed to minority rule.
[8] Ari Sitas, 'The New Tribalism: Hostels and Violence', *Journal of Southern African Studies* 22, 2 (1996), p. 242.

Once unions became easier to join, and more fashionable and successful, the urban workers started to join and took the leadership positions. And migrant workers were pushed out of the leadership positions because they spoke no English and how could you elect a shop steward who couldn't speak English to the boss? ... We stopped going to the hostels and stopped having meetings there ... Then Inkatha got into the hostels ... That was a major strategic error.[9]

As a result, 'the link between union organisation and hostel life in the early nineties was shown to be virtually non-existent'.[10]

Zulu labourers, who often depended on Inkatha patronage at home and who, more than many other migrant groups, took urban work to sustain a rural livelihood, wanted their unions to concentrate on bettering their terms of employment rather than serving as platforms for militant politics. This was especially true in the economic downturn of the late 1980s when Zulu migrants feared dismissal. Chipkin explains, 'Faced with the ever-present possibility of replacement, migrant workers were disinclined to take orders from township youths who did not fully appreciate the threat of unemployment. Many migrant workers saw incitements to "reckless" action as risking their families' often already tenuous subsistence.'[11] Many migrants blamed militant union politics for factory closures, as COSATU promoted disinvestment in line with the ANC's call for foreign companies to take a stand against apartheid by divesting their holdings in South Africa. 'And as the IFP and Inkatha endlessly reiterated, disinvestment cost jobs.'[12] Prioritising employment over support for liberation politics put these men directly at odds with nationalist activists. As Jason Hickel notes, for Zulu migrants 'the obligation to build the homestead was more important than political transformation. ... ANC cadres from the townships regarded this position as indefensible – they saw migrants as a weak link in the chain of solidarity.'[13] Zulu migrants - attached to a monarchy, and to rural hierarchies and modes of living, were out of step with the democratic, 'modern' vision of a new order espoused by MDM nationalism. The ANC, by contrast, was urban, educated, modern and led on the ground by youth.[14] To enlist these disaffected workers and counter the power of MDM unions, Inkatha launched the United Workers' Union of South Africa (UWUSA) in 1986 and it

---

[9] Bonner and Nieftagodien, *Kathorus*, p. 115.
[10] Segal, 'Human Face of Violence', p. 204.
[11] Ivor Chipkin, 'Nationalism as Such: Violence during South Africa's Political Transition', *Public Culture* 16, 2 (2004), p. 331.
[12] Bonner and Nieftagodien, *Kathorus*, p. 116.
[13] Jason Hickel, *Democracy as Death: The Moral Order of Anti-Liberal Politics in South Africa* (University of California Press, Oakland, 2015), p. 42.
[14] Hickel also argues that male Zulu migrants objected to ANC/COSATU social ordering that accorded greater authority to youth and women and that stigmatised as primitive migrants' beliefs in ancestors as arbiters of people's fortunes.

quickly made gains among Zulu migrants on the Rand.[15] Moreover, Inkatha took advantage of the vacuum of authority to increase its institutional presence in the hostels. 'Inkatha established and controlled hostel committees, businesses that catered for the hostel trade and, increasingly, taxi routes. By 1990 Inkatha had made serious inroads into hostel affairs thus counter-mobilising against the civics' initiatives and mass action.'[16] As the transition era approached many migrant Zulus found themselves outside the world of the political activists who led the township civics, the unions and the anti-apartheid struggle in general.[17] A Katlehong hostel resident lamented that, in 1990,

> The school children said we hostel dwellers were delaying progress because we were not co-operative when they were giving orders. We would go to work when they said it was a stayaway. It was that confusion, because we never knew about these stayaways until we go to work and they tell us that we went to work while it was a stayaway and then they will attack us.[18]

The ANC's call to transform single-sex migrant hostels into family housing and accommodation for returned exiles further exacerbated this divide. With the end of influx controls in 1986 many migrants from different ethnic groups began moving with their families into townships, but hostels remained particularly important for Zulu men because many parts of KZN still had a viable subsistence economy.[19] A substantial nucleus of Zulu migrants left their families at home and the hostels provided an affordable urban base that made a rural livelihood possible. No doubt, other migrants were also disillusioned with MDM politics, but Zulu workers were particularly dependent on the hostels. Moreover, no other migrant group had a powerful political organisation favoured by the apartheid state to defend its interests.

Party politics

The ANC was determined to build its support on the Rand into political capital for the coming elections and Inkatha was desperate to expand from its KZN base to become a national political player. Its best opportunity to do so was in South Africa's industrial core, which accommo-

---

[15] Sitas, 'New Tribalism', p. 243.
[16] Sitas, 'New Tribalism', p. 244.
[17] See Hickel, *Democracy as Death* and Ivor Chipkin, *Do South Africans Exist? Nationalism, Democracy and the Identity of 'the People'* (Wits University Press, Johannesburg, 2007) for a broader discussion of Zulu migrants' estrangement from MDM politics.
[18] Interview, Z45, male resident, Mazibuko Hostel, July 2006.
[19] Chipkin, *Do South Africans Exist?*, p. 126; Anthony Minnaar, 'Hostels and Violent Conflict on the Reef' in Minnaar (ed.), *Communities in Isolation: Perspectives on Hostels in South Africa* (Human Sciences Research Council, Pretoria, 1993), p. 25.

dated tens of thousands of migrant Zulu workers and job seekers. ANC officials condemned Buthelezi and Inkatha as ignorant sell-outs – IFP, they said, stood for 'Inkatha Fears Progress'. Inkatha leaders stoked fears of the ANC's reputed anti-Zulu stance, including its antagonism towards migrant Zulus. Party allegiances often converged with ethnic identities on the Rand, as migrant Zulus were associated with the IFP and the ANC was seen by IFP supporters as a Xhosa-dominated organisation. Many respondents listed party rivalries as a key element triggering the violence. 'These fights occurred right after Mandela was released. The Zulus were jealous that the ANC was going to overpower their political party.'[20] ANC supporters often cited what they believed to be the backwardness of migrant Zulus to explain their opposition to the ANC. 'When Mandela was released from prison, Inkatha leadership told its supporters that he was coming to take over and that he was a communist who did not believe in traditional beliefs, and you know that Inkatha is a Zulu party, and Zulus are traditionalists.'[21] Hostel dwellers also believed that Nelson Mandela's release from prison heightened political tensions but attributed this to ANC supporters' arrogance. 'The problem started when Mandela was going to be released and the Xhosas said, "Mandela is going to be the president, and Buthelezi will make tea for him and King Zwelithini [Zulu monarch] will be the security guard and open the gate for Mandela", that led to disagreements.'[22] Many township residents invested in the liberation struggle dismissed IFP militants as pawns of the apartheid regime. 'Township people were fighting to defend themselves and Zulus were fighting for money. They were bought by the apartheid government to kill township people.'[23]

Although resembling a civil war in many respects, politicised violence in South Africa differed from most civil wars in that neither of the two primary non-state antagonists was attempting to capture the state through military action. Rather, the ANC and the IFP directed violence against each other, with the NP intervening to pursue its objectives. Each approached the Rand conflict differently, but all three invested in militarisation to maximise their political prospects. Both the ANC and the IFP pinned their hopes on building support among the black majority that would determine South Africa's political future. In a terrible irony, the prospect of democracy – for which many had fought and died – introduced a new conflict dynamic as contested black areas became battlegrounds for political influence. To this end, the ANC and IFP employed violence to secure a political following and to impede the other's ability to do the same.

[20] Interview, D2, female resident, Thokoza, 3 June 2006.
[21] Interview, T8, male resident, Thokoza, 22 May 2006.
[22] Interview, Z11, male resident, Buyafuthi Hostel, 4 July 2006.
[23] Interview, T5, male resident, Thokoza, 20 March 2006.

After decades of armed struggle having a negligible impact, the ANC accepted that the military option had no immediate prospect of ending white rule. Instead, a negotiated settlement that enfranchised the majority population offered the quickest and surest route to power. To facilitate negotiations the ANC suspended its armed struggle in August 1990. The police and ANC-aligned activists had a long history of animosity and the negotiations process did little to dampen these hostilities. Consequently, clashes continued throughout the transition period but at the level of local skirmishes as opposed to an armed campaign against the state. As the pre-eminent liberation movement, with a broad base of support among black South Africans, the ANC was well positioned to contest national elections and, when large scale politicised conflict erupted on the Rand in mid-1990, the leadership took a measured approach. It was not in the ANC's best interests to intensify hostilities by instructing MK to take a leading role in the fighting or to encourage violent uprisings. Any such move would have prompted a massive security force response and threatened the negotiations that represented the ANC's best opportunity to replace the NP as the next government. On the other hand, with elections approaching, the ANC could not afford to abandon its supporters and soon-to-be voters to IFP and security force violence. Nor was it prepared to surrender political terrain to the IFP without a fight. Consequently, the ANC adopted a middle ground between party militants who advocated a more confrontational approach towards government and the IFP, and moderates invested in the negotiation process.[24] It engaged in a limited war to shore up township support as part of the campaign to achieve a political victory. This included promoting community-based militias as a means of local protection and offering limited assistance to these structures, stressing that SDUs were community rather than ANC initiatives. Returned MK veterans living in the townships were urged to lend their expertise to SDUs, and a handful of ANC/MK officials facilitated training and provided a regulated supply of weapons to selected SDUs. This delicate balancing act served the ANC well. Despite complaints from some residents that the ANC was not doing enough to protect them, SDUs actively combatted IFP militants while the negotiations stayed on track.

The Rand hostels, packed with Zulu migrants, provided an ideal venue for IFP recruitment campaigns. Many of these migrants had already abandoned ANC-affiliated unions and were alienated from liberation politics. As hostel dwellers, they were not fully integrated into surrounding township populations, which tended to be sympathetic to the ANC. The IFP set itself up as the champion of these isolated communities and emphasised ANC hostility to Zulu traditions, culture

---

[24] For a discussion of tensions between ANC militants and moderates, see Kaufman, *Nationalist Passions*, ch. 6, 'The End of Apartheid in South Africa'.

and migrant networks. Campaigning in the hostels often led to violence as those who refused to support the IFP in majority-Zulu hostels were forced out, sometimes with significant casualties. In the KZN conflict the IFP had forged close ties with different state military and police units. Some two hundred Inkatha members had received military training in Namibia from the SADF in the 1980s and some of these men were deeply involved in the KZN fighting. Although it is possible that a few of these Caprivi trainees, as they were known, may have been deployed or independently made their way to the Rand, the IFP did not have a military capacity on the Reef when the conflict began. In the absence of existing armed structures, IFP officials invoked Zulu martial traditions, including the carrying of 'traditional' weapons, and relied on IFP-connected headmen known as *indunas* to organise hostel dwellers into fighting regiments. As the violence escalated, the IFP formed hostel-based militias called Self Protection Units (SPUs). IFP leaders on the Rand successfully liaised with state security force operatives to procure arms for these militants, who largely avoided conflict with the police. At the beginning of the transition period the NP viewed the ANC as an adversary, whereas the IFP was considered a potential bulwark against the ANC. Accordingly, the IFP did not worry that anti-ANC violence would damage its relationship with the government and there was little incentive for the IFP to exercise restraint in its conflict with the ANC. In fact, the IFP sought to leverage its capacity for violence into political relevance on the national stage. Violence raised the profile of the IFP and served to warn the other major parties that any political settlement had to take the IFP into account. The IFP's position was undermined in mid-1992 when the NP abandoned their alliance. By this time, however, the IFP was entrenched in conflict with the ANC and the violence on the Rand continued until the eve of elections.

Because the government was not under attack, state security forces presided over a conflict between non-state parties, albeit in ways aimed at securing the NP's political future. Initially, the government sought to profit from ANC–IFP fighting, which it characterised as 'black-on-black' violence. It argued that the ANC's commitment to violence made it unfit to assume a major role in government. As time went on, however, the unrelenting conflict worked against the NP. It was discredited by the barrage of allegations concerning security force involvement in politicised fighting. At the least, the government appeared incapable of stemming the violence. By mid-1992 as the ANC threatened to abandon negotiations unless the government took decisive steps to curtail the conflicts, de Klerk and his inner circle calculated that a lasting political settlement could only be reached by working with its old enemy. The government began to rein in security forces that were engaged in anti-ANC covert operations, but policing practices on the ground did not always reflect this political turn.

Taxi wars

In the East Rand townships of Katlehong and Thokoza, communal violence began as a dispute between competing taxi associations. When the government relaxed restrictions on taxi licences for black entrepreneurs in the mid-1980s, many migrant Zulus saw taxi ownership as a promising economic venture. Migrants were keen to visit home more regularly and the proliferation of black-owned taxis plying the routes to KZN made this a possibility. At the same time, Philip Bonner and Vusi Ndima point out that a surge in stock theft in KZN made investment in taxis seemingly less risky than investment in livestock, and stock thieves themselves used their profits to purchase taxis. A boom in a largely unregulated industry by those on the economic margins was bound to result in fierce competition.[25] The fighting that erupted in Katlehong in 1989 and continued into 1990 initially matched the established Germiston and District Taxi Association (G & D), primarily composed of migrant Zulu owners and drivers residing in the municipal hostels, against the recently formed Katlehong Taxi Association (KATO), which drew its membership from township residents of different ethnicities. Access to preferred routes and competition for customers sparked the clash. A G & D driver reports that

> We used to fetch people inside the township and the streets were gravel then and bring them to the hospital and the KATO would operate from the hospital to town. But after the road that we were using was tarred they wanted to fetch the people from the township and ... that is how taxi violence started.[26]

Others involved in the dispute add that customers, especially young people from the townships, preferred the updated KATO taxis. 'The Zulus who were mainly from the hostel were driving old taxis and they did not have style, so township people preferred those that were driven by the township people because they were clean and new, so clearly the Zulus were not making money.'[27] In addition to more stylish vehicles, KATO courted township students by offering special 'scholar fees'.[28] Most people in the townships gravitated toward KATO,

---

[25] Bonner and Ndima, 'Roots of Violence', pp. 367–9. Taxi conflicts proliferated throughout much of South Africa in this period. See, for example, Meshack Khosa, 'Routes, Ranks and Rebels: Feuding in the Taxi Revolution', *Journal of Southern African Studies* 18, 1, (1992), pp. 232–51; Leslie Bank, 'The Making of the Qwaqwa "Mafia": Patronage and Protection in the Migrant Taxi Business', *African Studies* 49, 1 (1990), pp.71–93; and Jackie Dugard, 'From Low Intensity War to Mafia War: Taxi Violence in South Africa (1987–2000)', Centre for the Study of Violence and Reconciliation, *Violence and Transition Series*, vol. 4 (May 2001), pp. 1–46.

[26] Interview, Z50, male resident, Mazibuko Hostel, August 2006.

[27] Interview, Z81, male resident, Katlehong, August 2006.

[28] Interview with Katlehong SDU member, courtesy of Greg Marinovich, April 2009.

while hostel residents stayed loyal to migrant Zulu drivers with G & D. This divide was a crucial element in determining how the conflict unfolded. Although the initial rift was caused by business competition and national-level political organisations played no role in this fighting hostilities acquired political, ethnic and generational inflections as the violence persisted.

Despite the absence of formal ANC and Inkatha involvement, opposing approaches to protest politics figured prominently in the inception of taxi hostilities. G & D taxi men tended to stay aloof from MDM politics whereas KATO owners identified more closely with the ANC and PAC, and many KATO drivers were local high school pupils active in student politics. KATO reportedly cultivated a relationship with local youth by supporting the Congress of South African Students (COSAS), an anti-apartheid organisation that had been at the forefront of many 1980s protests.[29] G & D had poor relations with Katlehong activists who called for and then enforced boycotts and stayaways in support of national-level political objectives. Hostel-dwelling Zulu migrants

> were rarely consulted about these stayaways and were generally reluctant to take part in what seemed to be initiatives driven by youngsters ... While township-aligned KATO taxis generally observed the stayaway prohibition, G & D taxi operators carried Zulu migrants to work (or back home) and paid for their temerity by being stoned or worse.[30]

This intimidation only served to deepen the estrangement of migrant Zulus from MDM politics. KATO and G & D had different support bases within Katlehong and both groups drew on their followers as the character of the conflict expanded in step with the broader involvement of community members. Many migrant Zulus began to view the violence as an ethnic assault. A resident of Kwesine Hostel remarked that taxi violence was initially confined to rival owners and drivers but, as the fighting intensified, migrant Zulus were indiscriminately targeted by young activists: 'The children would stop taxis and check if there were Zulus in the taxi, and they could identify us by the way we look and if that person is identified as a Zulu they would be taken out of the taxi and would be beaten and sometimes a person would be killed. That was not nice, and we had meetings here at the hostel and we talked about that and we said we need to defend ourselves.'[31] One particularly gruesome incident in which a group of taxi passengers was incinerated seems to have concentrated the rage of migrant Zulus in Katlehong:

---

[29] Bonner and Nieftagodien, 'Pursuit of "Social Truth"', p. 181.
[30] Bonner and Ndima, 'Roots of Violence', pp. 370–1.
[31] Interview Z22, male resident, Kwesine Hostel, 19 July 2006.

Children used to burn taxis and we did not care really because we knew that it was taxis fighting against each other. But things changed when children started targeting the taxis from Natal only. When they started doing that it became clear that they were attacking the Zulus because people from Natal are the Zulus. They burnt two taxis from Nqutu and in one of those taxis there was a pregnant woman, Ngobese's wife. After that, things really changed because we realised that we were the victims now.[32]

The taxi war, which had acquired an ethnic dimension – township residents against migrant Zulus – became politicised as Zulu hostel dwellers directed their wrath at young township activists known as 'comrades'. Hostel dwellers attacked a primary school, killing pupils and teachers, and even invaded the local hospital to dispatch wounded comrades.[33] In May 1990, G & D taximen stormed Katlehong Secondary School, 'assaulting students and teachers with firearms, pangas and knobkerries after a house belonging to a G & D member, just down the street from the school, was burnt down by a crowd'.[34] Johannes Nkosi, who went on to become an SDU member in Thokoza, applied to the TRC for amnesty for his involvement in taxi-related violence. He was attending high school in Katlehong when G & D taxi owners attacked pupils who were driving for KATO. Many of these students associated G & D with Inkatha because the person they identified as the leader of G & D, a Mr Cebekulu, was 'well known among Inkatha circles'. Nkosi and his friends armed themselves and 'took a decision to shoot at them'. When asked if the taxi violence had a political element, Nkosi replied, 'I can say so because my schoolmates from the Letutula Secondary School, I knew that they were members of the ANC like myself, and those who were in Mr Cebekulu's side, were IFP members as I know that he was also an IFP member.'[35] George Ndlozi, who was active in student politics before joining an SDU, explained that COSAS served as the institutional conduit through which students directed violence against G & D. 'We had COSAS branches in each school, so we had – you know in these committees we had liaison officers and what have you, so the message would be passed to other schools ... So we started having defence committees in schools, defending ourselves against taxis.' These students purchased firearms from Mozambicans who also showed them how to handle the weapons. Thus equipped, groups of students 'hunted' and burned G & D taxis.[36]

[32] Interview Z41, male resident, Mazibuko Hostel, August 2006.
[33] Bonner and Ndima, 'Roots of Violence', p. 374.
[34] Mzimkulu Malunga, 'The death-toll in Katlehong's "Zola Budd" war reaches 15', *Weekly Mail*, 9 May 1990.
[35] TRC Amnesty Hearing, Johannes Dingane Nkosi, AM7960/97, 7 December, 1998, Palm Ridge, http://www.justice.gov.za/trc/amntrans/1998/9811231210_pr_981207th.htm
[36] University of the Witwatersrand Historical Papers, Missing Voices Project, SDU Interviews by Sally Sealey, A3079, Interview no. 11 with George Melusi Ndlozi, SDU

The involvement of students drew in more people as township residents, including some local police, came to the defence of the youth and casualties ran into the hundreds as the townships rallied against the hostel Zulus.[37] Nhlanhla Maake, a Katlehong resident who was part of a local peace committee that tried to negotiate an end to the fighting, traced the conflict's changing trajectory from a business dispute. After a period of intense violence between hostel dwellers and township inhabitants in late March 1990,

> the perception of the conflict had imperceptibly changed and there was no mention of the rivalry between the taxi associations, the very source of the conflict. In general conversation, the factions were now described as Katlehong residents versus hostel residents, and inevitably Katlehong against the Zulus, since the majority of the hostel dwellers were Zulu speaking people.[38]

Because some Katlehong taxi routes ran through neighbouring Thokoza, residents of that township also became involved in the conflict. As the fighting dragged on, 'The conflict was now no longer perceived as one between the residents and the "Zulus", but as between the "comrades" and the Zulus',[39] with 'Zulus' often seen as synonymous with Inkatha. Many Katlehong and Thokoza residents view the taxi-initiated violence as the precursor to the larger conflict that took hold a few months later.

Sebokeng and ANC–IFP violence

Although the Katlehong taxi conflict acquired political overtones, neither the IFP (which did not yet officially exist) nor the ANC was formally involved. Explicitly party-political hostilities on the Rand began in Sebokeng township south of Johannesburg. When the ANC returned from exile to participate in negotiations with the apartheid government, the political environment in South Africa was transformed. Perhaps inevitably, given the history of the KZN conflict, the discourse between the ANC and Inkatha became progressively provocative. In May 1990, Jay Naidoo, the general secretary of the

---

[contd] Mokoena section, Katlehong, 14 June 2004.

[37] *South*, 6 December 1990. Bonner and Ndima, in 'Roots of Violence', p. 374, place the toll at fifty dead and 350 wounded in February–March 1990. The *New York Times* claimed twenty-seven dead and over a hundred wounded in the first two weeks of March 1990; see Christopher Wren, 'In a War Over Taxis, 27 Die in a South African Township', 12 March 1990. A Katlehong resident reported thirty-five township people dead along with an unknown number of hostel dwellers in a single night of fighting in March; see Nhlanhla Maake, 'Multi-Cultural Relations in a Post-Apartheid South Africa', *African Affairs* 91, (1992), p. 586.

[38] Maake, 'Multi-Cultural Relations', p. 586.

[39] Maake, 'Multi-Cultural Relations', p. 590.

ANC-aligned COSATU announced publicly that 'Our enemy has two faces. One is that of Buthelezi and the other is that of de Klerk and the South African Police!'[40] In a perceptive article written during the transition period, Heribert Adam and Kogila Moodley argued that ANC marches and stayaways 'were supposed to demonstrate that Inkatha was not a national movement, that it could be sidelined in the forthcoming negotiations, and that Buthelezi could be "buried politically."'[41] Bonner and Ndima identify a joint COSATU/ANC call for a 2 July stayaway as the 'final moment of rupture' between Zulu migrants and ANC activists on the Rand. Dubbed the 'reign of terror' stayaway because its purpose was to protest against Inkatha's role in KZN violence, this was an anti-Inkatha campaign 'which Zulu migrant workers could not possibly join. It was at least partly in response to this call that the IFP announced its intention to relaunch itself as a countrywide political party, and initiated recruitment rallies at various townships across the greater Witwatersrand.'[42] Transvaal IFP leaders instructed their followers to go to work and resist any attempts at intimidation. The stayaway opened in the Vaal region, which encompassed Sebokeng, with a rally at which speakers called for the expulsion of IFP supporters from Vaal townships.[43] Attempts to put these words into practice by ANC youths resulted in skirmishing, and the houses of several Inkatha supporters were burnt down over the next few days. These clashes were followed by a massive IFP rally at Sebokeng soccer stadium on 22 July to mark its beginnings as a political party and, reportedly, to protest ANC violence.[44] Local township youth, assumed by their targets to be ANC backers, stoned the buses ferrying IFP supporters to the stadium. Once IFP supporters exited the stadium, fighting immediately broke out between an IFP contingent returning on foot to Sebokeng Hostel and groups of township residents. The police escorted the IFP column to the hostel, where they confronted a crowd of Xhosa hostel residents. In the subsequent battle a police officer was killed and the police withdrew, allowing the two sides to fight it out. The Xhosa hostel dwellers, supported by township youth, succeeded in denying entry to the IFP supporters who retreated and shortly thereafter occupied a nearby abandoned hostel – KwaMadala – that had been closed years previously.[45] With these developments,

---

[40] Daniel Reed, *Beloved Country: South Africa's Silent Wars* (BBC Books, London, 1994), p. 32.
[41] Adam and Moodley, 'Political Violence', p. 500.
[42] Bonner and Ndima, 'Roots of Violence', p. 375.
[43] Bonner and Nieftagodien, 'Pursuit of "Social Truth"', p. 185.
[44] Jeffrey, *People's War*, p. 247.
[45] Other than newspaper reports, very little has been written on these critical clashes in Sebokeng. This account is cobbled together from Reed, *Beloved Country*, Jeffrey, *People's War* and Jeremy Seekings, 'Hostel Hostilities: Township Wars on the Reef', *Indicator SA* 8, 3 (1991) pp. 11–15.

battle lines in Sebokeng and other Vaal townships clearly emerged. On the one side were migrant Zulus affiliated with the IFP, most of whom were hostel residents, and on the other a multi-ethnic township population that included some Xhosa hostel dwellers, understood to be supporting the ANC. The ensuing conflict in Sebokeng included the notorious Boipatong massacre.

Thokoza and the conflagration on the East Rand

News of the Sebokeng violence and the expulsion of Zulu/IFP men from the Sebokeng Hostel spread quickly and heightened tensions in Thokoza and Katlehong. Ethnically mixed hostels that were prone to divided political loyalties were particularly volatile. In early August, Xhosa residents of Lindela Hostel in Katlehong were reportedly assaulted and driven out by the Zulu population.[46] Violence quickly followed in Thokoza's Khalanyoni Hostels, which were adjacent to the Phola Park squatter camp at the bottom of Khumalo Street. These two hostels had an isiXhosa-speaking majority joined by a substantial Zulu minority. Phola Park was multi-ethnic, but primarily Xhosa. In the wake of the Sebokeng violence, many Zulus from Khalanyoni had attended a Soweto rally at which leaders from KZN whipped up anti-ANC antagonism and advised their constituents that Zulus must stick together in these dangerous times. Returnees from this rally, including visitors from Sebokeng, held a Zulus-only meeting at Khalanyoni to discuss the perceived threat facing migrant Zulus on the Rand.[47] At this point, some Xhosa hostel dwellers claim that they were threatened with violence and decided to leave Khalanyoni for Phola Park. In this atmosphere, a 12 August brawl over a woman between Khalanyoni residents, one Zulu and the other Xhosa, which resulted in the death of the Xhosa man, quickly developed into a broader ethnic conflict.[48] The deceased man's friends sought revenge the next day. They gathered support from Xhosa residents of Phola Park and returned to Khalanyoni, rampaging through the Zulu sections of the hostel, attacking Zulus indiscriminately and setting rooms alight. They were eventually repulsed in a pitched battle, which resulted in a further two fatalities. The remaining Xhosa hostel dwellers fled to Phola Park where they regrouped, leaving Zulus in sole possession of Khalanyoni. The next day Phola Park launched a massive assault on the hostels.[49] This

[46] Bonner and Nieftagodien, 'Pursuit of "Social Truth"', p. 186.
[47] University of the Witwatersrand Historical Papers, IBIIR Collection, 'Statement of Prince Mhlambi and Pola [sic] Park Committee with regard to various aspects of evidence and contextual aspects of the violence in the East Rand and its impact on Pola Park', AG2543, C18, 22 November 1991, p. 5.
[48] IBIIR Monthly Report, August 1990, p. 5.
[49] Segal, 'Human Face of Violence', p. 225; Minnaar, 'Hostels and Violent Conflict', p. 11.

was the beginning of a vicious conflict between Khalanyoni Zulus, supported by other Zulu hostel dwellers in Thokoza, and the residents of Phola Park.[50] Over days of fighting Khalanyoni was reduced to ruins. Most of the surviving Zulus took refuge in squatter camps or one of the remaining hostels. A Zulu resident of Khalanyoni described the start of the conflict:

> We were staying with other ethnic groups, we were very mixed ... What happened is I left on a weekend, and when I came back on a Monday I found the one block of the hostel had been burnt ... When it was said Mandela was coming out, the Xhosas changed ... which really created the tension amongst the Zulus and the Xhosas. I found the hostel burnt, we were divided in rooms and the rooms where the Xhosa stayed were not burnt and the ones with Zulus were burnt. Around 2p.m. the Xhosas came back – they had already left the hostel and taken their stuff to Phola Park ... they had weapons, and they attacked us ... After that, as Zulus we organised ourselves and in the afternoon we attacked them; it was a war and many people died.[51]

Both sides called for reinforcements and hundreds, perhaps thousands, became involved in the fighting. These initial conflicts served as a harbinger of the maelstrom of violence that raged for the next four years. 'That first attack in Phola Park, it was as if the world was coming to an end. Who could forget what we saw? The township was stinking because of all the dead people.'[52] For Thokoza and neighbouring Katlehong this proved to be a point of no return. Migrant Zulus rallied in their hostel strongholds expelling any who resisted the IFP's call for support, particularly Xhosa. The IFP benefitted from this violence as Zulus turned to the party for protection in a hostile township environment. Just as Xhosas and any who refused to support the IFP were chased out of several hostels, migrant Zulus residing in the townships also came under attack and returned to their rural homes, moved to other townships or sought sanctuary in IFP-run hostels. A Zulu resident of Kwesine Hostel in Katlehong remembers how the Khalanyoni violence galvanised migrant Zulus: 'Xhosas were too many at Khalanyoni and our brothers were caught off guard. You know, if you were not prepared for a fight you can easily be defeated. We learnt from them that there is a war, so we prepared ourselves.'[53]

---

[50] Reed's *Beloved Country* provides the most detailed published account of the Phola Park–Khalanyoni conflict. This episode also features prominently in oral accounts of the violence supplied by witnesses from both sides.
[51] Interview, Z11, male resident, Buyafuthi Hostel, 4 July 2006.
[52] Interview, T8, male resident, Thokoza, 22 May 2006.
[53] Interview, Z23, male resident, Kwesine Hostel, 19 July 2006.

Plate 1 Zulu hostel residents advance down Khumalo Street toward Phola Park at the start of the war in 1990 (Ken Oosterbroek, © PictureNet Africa)

Conclusion

Both the ANC and the IFP were determined to consolidate their support on the Rand and neither promoted tolerance for rivals. Instead, many ANC and IFP officials incited hatred and fear of their opponents. Add to this the state's enmity towards the ANC and its relative indifference to black casualties, and it is not surprising that violence accompanied political campaigning in several Reef townships.

The initial stages of Rand conflict illustrate some of the complexities and layers that characterised collective violence throughout the transition period. Regardless of political affiliation or ethnicity, the violence was not confined to combatants. Instead, anyone identified with the opposing side, including children and the elderly, was liable to be targeted. The ANC–IFP divide came to define the violence, but ethnic identities were also critical and local concerns not necessarily related to party rivalries often provided the impetus for fighting. Thus, depending on the context, combatants were identified *inter alia* as taxi owners, comrades, students, township residents, hostel dwellers, Zulu, Xhosa, ANC and IFP. Armed groups with no direct connection to either the ANC or Inkatha, such as the COSAS squads fighting against G & D taxi owners, operated in many townships. We also see evidence of a recurring theme in transition-era violence – the state's failure effectively to intervene in conflicts that consumed black townships and informal settlements. Policing infrastructure and resources were concentrated in white areas and, when fighting broke out in Thokoza and Katlehong, local police were not equipped to deal with the level of conflict. Despite the presence of military patrols and specialised police units, all too often state security forces were conspicuous by their absence. That said, different branches of the police, military and peacekeepers participated in transition-era violence on behalf of one side or other, or otherwise inflamed the fighting. This combination of neglect and political partisanship had a critical impact on transition-era violence. In the fighting that emerged from the taxi rivalry in Katlehong, local police got involved as community members avenging assaults on local youth rather than as state representatives upholding the law. In Sebokeng the police were accused of standing by while Zulu hostel dwellers returning from the stadium rampaged through the township. And in the Phola Park–Khalanyoni battle it was reported that Xhosa police assisted their ethnic kinsmen in attacks on the hostels, while Zulu and white police sided with the hostel dwellers. The inability of the police (and to a lesser extent, the military) to consistently function as a professional force dedicated to protecting all citizens compromised policing efforts throughout the transition period.

2 Rule of the Gun
THE ANC AND IFP AT WAR

> This violence was in layers, you remove one and the violence continues. That is why it is difficult to blame someone because there were many people fighting for different things. There were times when the SDUs were fighting amongst themselves and that exacerbated violence. There was also the issue of taxis, ethnicity, township versus the hostel, so many things were going on and one cannot pin one thing down and say this was the problem.[1]

> The reality is large elements of South Africa's township population have become ungovernable. No party or organization ... has the strength and ability to prevent these areas from falling under the rule of the gun.[2]

Whereas ANC–IFP hostilities represent the defining feature of transition-era conflict on the Rand, a diversity of armed, non-state groups operated with different political orientations, mandates, compositions and relationships with police. The most widespread of these armed entities fell under the loose heading of SDUs. These militias were associated with the ANC, but their relationships with the party varied greatly. It became clear that the ANC had little, if any, control over many SDUs, and it was never able to resolve this problem. Moreover, ANC-aligned structures fought with each other and against AZAPO and PAC activists. As IFP hostels became militarised, all male residents were expected to participate in the defence of the hostels while some younger men were slotted into special fighting units. IFP authority in the hostels was more centralised than ANC authority in the townships, but some IFP militants also engaged in violence that did not further party interests. In his examination of 'ethnic wars' in Yugoslavia and Rwanda, John Mueller argues that 'rather than reflecting deep, historic passions and hatreds, the violence seems to have been the result of a situation in which common, opportunistic, sadistic and often distinctly nonideological marauders were recruited and permitted free rein by political authorities'.[3] Similar circumstances developed in many transition-era townships. Political rivalries

---

[1] Interview, Z81, male resident, Katlehong, August 2006.
[2] *Weekly Mail*, 5 June 1992.
[3] John Mueller, 'The Banality of Ethnic War' *International Security* 25, 1 (2000), p. 43.

and objectives were paramount on the macro level, but acquisitive criminality and local antagonisms often determined conflict on the ground. The common feature shared by all these armed groups was their capacity for violence and the conviction that violence was an effective tool for navigating the challenges of this perilous period.

Self Defence Units

Origin and Composition
When violence began, township residents often banded together to defend against attacks emanating from hostels. Said one respondent, 'I think if the community did not fight, the Zulus working with the police were going to kill us all. I am telling you, this township would be history.'[4] These groups were sometimes led by existing structures like street committees or civic associations. In these early stages, the call for community defence was not always voluntary. An SDU member from Thokoza, who was sixteen when the fighting began, explains:

> I didn't have a choice that I should go and patrol the streets and everything. I was a boy in the townships and at that time I was staying alone with my mother. I was the only young man in the house, so I had to go in ... every house had to have someone ... They will come by force and take you – they will come. And if you don't go you will be seen as *impimpi*.'[5]

These initial groups were poorly armed and organised. Over time the element of compulsion was dropped as large bodies of male residents were replaced by smaller numbers of dedicated fighters – known as 'operators' – who chose to join SDUs. A Katlehong SDU commander explains the rationale:

> Not everyone was a comrade, there were people that were not really interested in politics, but when things were bad we took everyone and said everyone should participate because we were all affected. But we soon realised that we got people who were not willing to fight, and those people were going to do more damage than good and that is why we wanted volunteers. The SDUs were volunteers.[6]

Usually, the impetus to organise defensive structures began after an attack on a community or at the behest of the ANC, but in the case of Sisulu section in Thokoza an operator explains that neighbouring Phola Park combatants pressured the youth in his area to join the fight against the Zulus. This provides an example of the

---
[4] Interview, Z58, male resident, Katlehong, 2006.
[5] Interview, G1, male SDU member, Thokoza, 11 June 2004.
[6] Interview, Z82, male SDU commander, Katlehong, 2006.

difficulties of neutrality. Those who attempted to avoid allegiances opened themselves to suspicion from combatant groups, with potentially fatal consequences. When the Phola Park–Khalanyoni fighting began, a Mosotho ANC Youth League member viewed the conflict as an ethnic rather than political dispute. However, Phola Park fighters both threatened and appealed to other township residents on the grounds of political solidarity and he soon found himself embroiled in the violence.

> As you can see, we were in between. There is the hostel this side [on Khumalo Street] and Phola Park the other side. So, when both of them were beaten they would pass here. The Zulus would pass here crying saying the Xhosas are killing them and the Xhosas would say the same thing. The Xhosas started asking us why we were not involved while they were being killed. In fact, the people from Phola Park forced us to join and form the SDU ... the Xhosas swore at us, they said we were sell-outs. They said these people when they attack them, they pass by us and yet we don't do anything. They forced us to do something ... We did all this because the people from Phola Park called the meeting because they were part of the ANC. They said if we don't partake in their violence, they would kill us too. They will start by fighting in the hostel and when they are done they would come to us because we were behaving like women. That is how we got involved ... We were forced because the Xhosas were also ANC members, so we had to show solidarity. You had the slogan that says, 'an injury to one is an injury to all'; that is what we were doing there, and we had to pay the price for doing that.[7]

Many adults were at work and could not devote the necessary time for community defence, so the burden fell primarily on youngsters supplemented by unemployed adults. Youthful SDU members also noted that their parents' generation was 'too old to fight'. It seems that most combatants fell in the range of fifteen to twenty-five years of age. Some SDUs had female fighters but women and young children usually acted in a support capacity, providing food, gathering intelligence and assisting with communications. The number of members in SDU units varied significantly from under ten to more than fifty depending on the population of the area, the intensity of fighting and the degree of community support. SDUs were products of the areas in which they operated – they can perhaps be best described as neighbourhood militias.

Across the Rand, SDUs appeared in a number of guises: larger and smaller groupings, some well stocked with automatic weapons, grenades and even rocket launchers, others sharing a few firearms; some with distinct command structures and close relationships with community leaders and ANC personnel, others more makeshift and

---

[7] Interview, Z96, male SDU member, Thokoza, 21 June 2008.

answerable to no one but themselves; some integrated with MK veterans and others in conflict with these returned exiles. SDUs are typically associated with township youth, but some units were the provenance of adults, including Xhosa migrants who drew on their rural origins and connections to cope with conflict.[8] Such SDUs were prominent in Xhosa-dominated hostels and also in some of the informal settlements that had mushroomed in the late 1980s following the abolition of influx control. A handful of groups were involved in heavy fighting for the bulk of the transition period, while many were not proximate to IFP hostels and squatter camps and experienced very little combat across party lines. There was no one-size-fits-all SDU and this heterogeneity was reflected in their activities and relations to their host communities.

Political Oversight
In the mid-1980s, the ANC-in-exile urged its supporters to link with MK operatives in the country to defend themselves against the security forces. This initiative never really got off the ground but, as violence surged following the unbanning of the ANC in 1990, some afflicted communities organised neighbourhood defence schemes. In December 1990 'resolutions at the ANC's Consultative Conference committed the ANC to assisting people in setting up accountable and non-partisan SDUs'.[9] The ANC's submission to the Truth and Reconciliation Commission outlined its involvement with SDUs:

> As the violence which exploded on the Reef in July 1990 intensified, there were repeated calls by communities under attack for MK units to be deployed to defend them. The ANC (and MK Military HQ) felt that the negotiations could be jeopardised should MK become formally involved in attempts to defend people from these attacks, but approved the involvement of MK members based in communities under threat in SDU structures ...

> Various clandestine units for the training and organisation of the various SDUs were set up, and some cadres were tasked to provide weaponry where possible ... Senior ANC leaders decided that selected SDUs should be assisted in those areas of the Reef which were hardest hit by destabilisation. Selected members of MK, including senior officials from the Command structures, were drawn into an *ad hoc* structure to assist with

[8] See, for example, Philip Bonner and Noor Nieftagodien, *Alexandra: A History* (Wits University Press, Johannesburg, 2008) for a discussion of different adult and youth-led SDUs in Alexandra, pp. 370–73. A Thokoza resident noted regional/ethnic connections for Phola Park SDUs drawn from the Eastern Cape: 'In Phola Park they fetched people from the countryside to assist the same way Zulus brought their brothers from Natal.' Interview, T7, female resident, Thokoza, 23 April 2006.
[9] African National Congress, '5.3 People's Committees and Self Defence Units' in *African National Congress: Statement to the Truth and Reconciliation Commission*, August 1996, http://www.anc.org.za/content/anc-statement-truth-and-reconciliation-commission

the arming of units and to train and co-ordinate efforts in self-defence in these communities.[10]

The ANC's attempts to manage the armed formations that fought in its name were only partially successful. Part of the problem was that many communities had already established some means of collective defence before the ANC attempted to get involved. Relationships were sometimes strained because the ANC's call to communities to organise SDUs was not accompanied by tangible support. As claimed in its submission to the TRC, the party took steps to aid township residents with communal defence, but this assistance was haphazard and inconsistent. The ANC provided some units with arms, but even these groups supplemented ANC ordinance with weapons purchases. Other units relied entirely on community levies with individual households expected to contribute funds. Links with ANC structures depended on numerous variables including personal connections, the ANC's assessment of the strategic value of the township in question, the strength of local ANC branches and the willingness of local armed groups to accept ANC oversight. An SDU member from Thokoza's Sisulu section describes a trajectory of community initiative followed by ANC intervention which transformed local defenders into 'soldiers':

> When we first joined we were not joining the SDUs, we were just protecting the community. But as time went on we got a directive from the ANC that we should organise ourselves and form a unit. It became a more organised structure and that is why we were even able to fight with the police because we were now trained properly and had guns. The ANC provided us with many things, they would organise the training for us and provide us with the guns. In fact, I can say that we did something meaningful when the ANC told us to be organised. Because before we would wake up all the boys and force them to be part of us, trying to protect the community and we would have many people who were there but did not want to be there, so people like those would be the first to run when we were attacked ... When we were organised ... we became more like the soldiers.[11]

In September 1991, with no end to the political violence in sight, and at the urging of business and church groups, the major political parties negotiated the National Peace Accord. Signatories to the Accord included the NP, ANC and IFP along with lesser players (the PAC and white right-wing groups refused to sign). The key mandate of the NPA was to create structures that would monitor, mediate and,

---

[10] 'Further Submissions and Responses by the ANC to Questions raised by the Commission for Truth and Reconciliation', 12 May 1997, Manifesto: Nature of the South African Conflict, pp. 37–8, https://www.nelsonmandela.org/omalley/cis/omalley/OMalleyWeb/03lv02167/04lv02264/05lv02303/06lv02304/07lv02315.htm

[11] Interview, Z97, male SDU member, Thokoza, 21 June 2008.

ideally, reduce political violence. National, regional and local peace committees were formed with representatives from the three major stakeholders. Peace monitors drawn from all sectors of society were trained and became an integral part of local peace committees. These committees provided a forum for the combatant groups to convene at a local level to resolve differences and plan events in such a way as to avoid conflict. Regular meetings were held at which all parties could raise issues, address grievances and discuss ways to defuse tensions. The ANC took a special interest in Kathorus – the township conglomeration of Katlehong, Thokoza and Vosloorus – which was at the epicentre of the Rand conflict and the area in which the IFP, through its control of numerous hostels, had its strongest presence. As the result of a deal between the ANC and NP concerning political prisoners, Robert McBride, an MK commander on death row for his role in the 1986 bombing of a Durban bar, was released from prison in September 1992. He was assigned to the ANC's Peace Desk as its representative on the Pretoria-Witwatersrand-Vaal (PWV) region Peace Committee. His primary task was responsibility for administering SDUs with a focus on Thokoza and Katlehong. 'So, instead of being the Peace Desk, as it were, I became the defence desk or as they often joked, the war desk because I felt it necessary to give the community the capacity to defend itself.'[12] The challenges posed by organising a command structure, providing training and weapons and bringing a host of armed groups under some sort of institutional control were considerable:

> Now it's bullshit to say that the ANC established SDUs. Fuck, the ANC had no infrastructure inside at that stage to do it. People defended themselves. When I came out of prison there were about a hundred different groupings that had access to arms and, very often at risk to my own life, I enforced control and a code of conduct, where basically the people would tell me, 'no, but who the fuck are you? You've been sitting in jail. You can't come tell us things, people have been dying for the last couple of years. Who are you?' ... and basically, I had to stand up and tell them this comes from the organisation, I've consulted with the organisers.[13]

An SDU member recalls the impact of ANC intervention on community defence:

> SDUs came very late. We had already organised ourselves ... We were told by the ANC people that if we organise ourselves as SDU we will be able to defend ourselves better. The ANC was starting to take charge in the communities, and the SDUs were sort of its extension. We used to attend ANC meetings, that is when we got guidance. They also provided us with

[12] Interview, Robert McBride, Johannesburg, 21 June 2006.
[13] Interview, Robert McBride, Johannesburg, 21 June 2006.

some equipment, like the walkie-talkies ... and some of the weapons were from the ANC.[14]

Despite these successes some SDUs did not recognise the ANC's authority to dictate events on the ground, and there was little the ANC could do in such cases. Others supported the ANC and appreciated the assistance it provided but did not feel bound to obey ANC officials:

> The SDUs were part of the ANC because we as the township people were ANC. I would not say the ANC would give us directions, but they would advise us because some ANC members had knowledge on many issues ... If we felt that the advice was good for us, we would take the advice. But we were not given orders, as I have said that we were very democratic.[15]

The ANC's restrained approach to providing weapons and training alienated some SDUs which looked to the party for more robust assistance. The ANC was in a difficult position as it had officially agreed to suspend the armed struggle and did not want to appear as if it were stoking violence in the townships. Much of the moral high ground it gained over the NP and IFP during the transition period was due to the widely held perception that these two groups were overwhelmingly responsible for the township carnage. The ANC deftly managed public relations and leveraged its image as the champion of hapless township residents to advantage in political negotiations.[16] Openly ploughing massive amounts of weaponry into the townships would have compromised this advantage. However, its supporters in conflict areas pleaded with the ANC for concrete backing – particularly weapons – and the party could not afford to dismiss these appeals. The political importance of being seen to protect their hoped-for constituents was critical. McBride notes the ANC's success in this regard in Katlehong: 'The Katlehong branch of the ANC was the biggest branch in the country when I came out of prison – six thousand people. Towards the end of '93, after being able to defend the community and basically driving Inkatha back into the hostels, it had moved up to 35,000.'[17] However, the ANC's refusal to commit all its resources to the conflict proved immensely frustrating to McBride, who was trying to win a war:

> The ANC leadership didn't want the conflict to escalate so they limited the stuff they made available to us surreptitiously, so it only consisted of hand

[14] Interview, Z91, male SDU member, Katlehong, 2006.
[15] Interview, Z93, male SDU member, Katlehong, 2006.
[16] Simpson, 'Boipatong', illustrates how the ANC manipulated the massacre for political advantage.
[17] Interview, Robert McBride, Johannesburg, 21 June 2006.

grenades and ammunition. The rest of the stuff we had to go and buy from Mozambicans ... My commanders, my seniors, said 'no we don't want to escalate this situation, so you have to make do with what we have given you,' which was very hard to accept then. It was really hard, and I had some fights with people but I can see the wisdom of it now in hindsight.[18]

With McBride and Duma Nkosi, the ANC's Chairperson in Thokoza, working together, the ANC formed a central command structure for Thokoza SDUs. A violence monitor who worked closely with Duma Nkosi explained to the TRC how the Central Command operated:

The Thokoza township was divided up into [fourteen] sections ... Each section had a commander and a deputy commander which sat at the Central Command level. Also at the Central Command level the political leadership of the ANC, the South African Communist Party as well as the civics had a representation at the Central Command. Now the central – the Central Command used to meet every Tuesday at a local school. Now, the way the Central Command worked – sorry, the Central Command also had an overall commander by the name of Bonga Nkosi. It also had a secretary by the name Seko Thulo. It also had a head of logistics, Sydney Nemorani and a deputy commander, Michael Lucky Siepe. Then each section had a commander which represented the SDUs from that area. Each of those commanders that represented the [fourteen] sections had a certain amount of autonomy. Obviously when they were faced with attack they couldn't run to the central command to get orders, so basically they relied on their own commander to issue orders down to the SDU members. So when they used to meet on a Tuesday they then would report back to the Central Command the activities of the week and what had been happening ... So the Central Command didn't necessarily act as a war cabinet issuing out orders and commands to the various Self Defence Units, it was more of a co-ordinating body which co-ordinated the activities of the Self Defence Units.[19]

McBride organised training, weapons, tactics and co-ordination between units while Nkosi assisted with legal issues, burial expenses and political guidance, met weekly with the Thokoza SDU section commanders, and reported to the executive of the ANC.[20] When asked what sort of training was provided to SDUs, McBride replied bluntly, 'Military training. Training to kill an enemy.' MK veterans took SDU operators to Suikerbosrand Nature Reserve south of Katlehong to teach them how to shoot. Chichela Machitje, an MK cadre working with McBride, also oversaw military training for SDUs. MK Chief of Staff Chris Hani directed him to recruit MK returnees as instructors and the training for Thokoza SDUs took place in Vosloorus Stadium and

[18] Interview, Robert McBride, Johannesburg, 21 June 2006.
[19] TRC Amnesty Hearing, Sally Sealey submission.
[20] Interview, Duma Nkosi, Ekurhuleni, 27 June 2008.

at a high school in Vosloorus. 'What we did is from each section five members of SDU's *[sic]* were selected and those members were taken to Vosloorus Stadium and training started and it was a mix of those SDU members, MK members, trained members and internal MK members and they participated in training inside Vosloorus.'[21] The ANC also supplied handheld radios to the SDUs to facilitate communication within and between units.

The Thokoza central command effectively co-ordinated SDU activities, according to an operator from Sisulu section. 'We would be told for instance that tomorrow we are going to Slovo section because they need our assistance and sometimes we would have SDUs from Slovo section to help if we were being attacked. We did work together but the order would come from above.'[22] A Slovo operator noted the critical role of the central commander:

> There were units that were specifically there to assist other SDUs because maybe where they were stationed, there weren't many attacks and therefore they would be responsible to boost others when the need arises. And when we were given a boost, we would work very well with those units. But it had to be a directive from above not just our decision to say 'hey, you come and help us here'. The central commander would see where to deploy those units because he knew which units were in danger and needed to be supported.[23]

Katlehong SDUs received some assistance but the lack of an overarching SDU structure impeded joint operations. 'We did not work with other SDUs. We would meet when we had the meetings with the ANC because sometimes they would call us to discuss the logistics, but each SDU unit worked independently.'[24] A Thokoza SDU member from Lusaka A section who joined the SDU from Siluma View in Katlehong for an attack on Mazibuko Hostel testified that, unlike the structures in Thokoza, the Siluma SDU 'was not well organised'.[25]

Some SDUs received significant support from MK and the ANC, as reported by a former Katlehong commander:

> I can say that the SDU were a baby to the ANC because we depended on ANC for almost everything. The protocol we used was the ANC protocol, the ANC would give us guidance and support ... We used to have meetings

---

[21] TRC Amnesty Hearing, Chichela Esau Machitje, AM7634/97, 24 November 1998, Vosloorus, http://www.doj.gov.za/trc/amntrans/1998/9811241202_jhb_981124.vos.htm

[22] Interview, Z97, male SDU member, Thokoza, 21 June 2008.

[23] Interview, Z102, male SDU member, Thokoza, 23 November 2008.

[24] Interview, Z91, male SDU member, Katlehong, 2006.

[25] TRC Amnesty Hearing, Thomazile Eric Mhlauli, AM7344/97, 3 December 1998, Palm Ridge, http://www.justice.gov.za/trc/amntrans%5C1998/9811231210_pr_981203th.htm

with people like Tokyo [Sexwale] and [Joe] Modise, they would give us the guidelines on what to do and how to do it. Guns would be delivered to the head office of the ANC, so you see how connected we were.[26]

Units that had MK members seem to have fared better in accessing ANC resources. A Katlehong SDU member noted the value of the MK connection: 'They were part of us, we got the training from them because they knew how to handle a gun. In our unit we had two people who were MK, they were from exile, so we worked with them and they had knowledge on many things.'[27] Other members reported that the ANC did nothing to assist them in the fight against the IFP and security forces. Several Thokoza SDU commanders maintain that, despite the central command structure, the ANC did not offer military support to all units. The central commander of Thokoza's SDUs insisted that his unit received nothing from MK or the ANC, which 'Never offered even a beer'.[28] Another Thokoza commander complained, 'I hear the people say they was receiving the free bullets from MK. I don't even know who those MK were, where is MK. Everything I got in my section was bought from the community.'[29] A third confirmed, 'the people of MK never do anything, even the ANC, they never do anything to us, to help us.'[30]

Control and Discipline
The ANC struggled to meet the demands of its followers in conflict areas and at the same time exercise control over armed units. Placing young people on a war footing with little in the way of training or disciplinary structure was bound to lead to abuses of authority. Indeed, the TRC judged that, 'Once SDUs were established, attempts by ANC leadership to establish control failed dismally.'[31] Some SDU members took advantage of their newfound power and status to the detriment of their fellow residents. All too often community defence was accompanied by robbery, rape and general intimidation. As a Katlehong SDU member observed,

> Although we were there to restore order there were many things that happened that were out of order. Some girls were raped, and some people were wrongly accused and killed. Many things did not go well during

---

[26] Interview, Z90, male SDU commander, Katlehong, 2006.
[27] Interview, Z93, male SDU member, Katlehong, 2006.
[28] Missing Voices Project, Interview no. 29 with Bongani Caswell Nkosi, Chief Commander, Thokoza SDUs.
[29] Missing Voices Project, Interview no. 30 with Dalixolo 'Meneer' Mqubi, SDU Commander, Ext. 2.
[30] Missing Voices Project, Interview no. 20 with Moses 'Bla' Mduduzi Khubeka, SDU Commander, Phenduka section.
[31] TRC Report vol. 6, s. 5, ch. 3, 'Findings and Recommendations – Holding the ANC Accountable', p. 668.

those times but what can we say, it was a war and things were not planned properly.[32]

Many SDUs spoke of drinking and drug use that helped them cope with the fear and trauma. Violence monitor Sally Sealey reported that substance abuse was rampant. The Phenduka section SDU members

> smoked so much white pipe – marijuana mixed with mandrax – they didn't know if they were coming or going. It was the state they used to be in when they would go out and patrol and that would be the same with Extension 2. There was a lot of abuse of drugs and often it was just to be brave, to build up their nerve, but it led to excesses.[33]

Numerous SDU interviewees remarked that units removed from the front lines with Inkatha were more likely to engage in predatory acts against community members and skirmishing with neighbouring SDUs:

> All comrades are not disciplined ... Now other sections they were having plenty firearms, AKs and when you look at them, they are not involved, they are not fighting almost every day with the IFP, they are not facing them. Now those guns when they are inside your sections and you don't know what to do, they end up killing each other, they say so and so has taken my girlfriend – that's where the problem was.[34]

Even some SDUs that were at the forefront of the conflict with IFP forces were involved in deadly rivalries:

> There were disputes between SDUs like in Thokoza between Lusaka A and Lusaka B which had numerous disputes. Like one SDU accidentally killing another SDU. They'd go out for a drink or something and things would go wrong and someone would pull out a firearm. Lots of instances like that and then different SDUs would start taking sides and it would end up in a big shoot-out. There was lots of that.[35]

Discipline of errant SDU members proved problematic. The ANC drew up a code of conduct, which stipulated that only SDU members eighteen years of age and older should have access to firearms and established guidelines for the use and control of weapons, but this was never ratified by the SDUs.[36] McBride notes that while there

---

[32] Interview, Z90, male SDU member, Katlehong, June 2006.
[33] Interview, Sally Sealey, London, July 2006.
[34] Missing Voices Project, Interview no. 17 with Mandla Alfred Sibeko, SDU Ncala section.
[35] Interview, Sally Sealey, London, July 2006.
[36] Pakiso Rakgoadi, 'The Role of the Self-Defence Units (SDUs) in a Changing Political Context', Occasional Paper written for the Centre for the Study of Violence and Reconciliation (Johannesburg, January 1995), p. 6.

were mechanisms to hold SDU members accountable, punishment was inconsistent:

> A lot of people would have gotten away with a number of wrongdoings because we were unable to enforce at particular times and you had to see about keeping your eye on the big picture and not causing division on the small issues. So, in a sense it wasn't a uniform justice ... We had to pick and choose because of the circumstances, so yes some of them got out of hand and they got away with the shit that they did.[37]

With units that recognised their authority ANC structures sometimes got involved in particularly serious breaches of discipline, but in most instances unit commanders and their leadership committees (if such existed) were responsible for punishing their own members. These commanders had to balance disciplinary requirements with the imperative to maintain morale and retain members. Former commanders report that this was a challenging process because many SDUs led harrowing lives and were subject to great danger and trauma. Most members were youngsters and, given these circumstances, commanders often adopted less punitive approaches, especially for minor offences such as squabbles between members and drunkenness:

> It was difficult to discipline them because they were doing the community a favour, in a way, so we could not be too harsh. We had to bargain with them because they were there voluntarily. There were times when they will despair and want to quit ... As commanders we would try to counsel them and motivate them.[38]

SDU members judged guilty of murder were sometimes executed – 'Like if you killed someone unnecessarily, they would say "if you kill someone with a gun, you will be killed with a gun"',[39] but lesser infractions were typically dealt with through corporal punishment or suspending a member's right to carry a firearm. Discipline in Thokoza's Sisulu section was strict but fair according to a former operator:

> I remember one day ... guys in our base drank while they were on duty, X [SDU commander] beat them. The rules were there and were clearly stipulated, written down so that you can never come with an excuse that you did not know. We were not allowed to fight amongst each other because we were working with dangerous weapons and if we fought we might have used those weapons against each other and killed each other. That was a serious offence if you have been found fighting with your comrade that

---

[37] Interview, Robert McBride, Johannesburg, 21 June 2006.
[38] Interview, Z104, male SDU commander, Thokoza, 23 November 2008.
[39] Interview, Z92, male SDU member, Katlehong, 2006. See also, TRC Amnesty Committee, SDU Amnesty Decisions, AC/99/0243, 1999, Cape Town, http://www.doj.gov.za/trc/decisions/1999/ac990243.htm

you were in the same base with. We also had to report in every meeting and if you are unable to attend you had to forward an apology and give the reason why you are unable to attend. X and his executive committee were the ones who were responsible for enforcing discipline. But no one was above that structure because even those members that were in the executive committee would be disciplined if they did not behave appropriately.[40]

From the ANC's perspective, Duma Nkosi commented on dealing with militants on the ground who had little patience for diplomatic niceties. He described how, after a meeting with local IFP leader Gertrude Mzizi, the SDU representatives at the meeting were outraged at his perceived 'softness' in the face of IFP provocation:

When we came back there were chaps who weren't happy because they think I let the woman shout at me and I don't say anything. Now they think the chairperson of the ANC is soft and they have an issue with me. So, I have to call them to a meeting and say, 'listen what problem do you have?' They say, 'You're not talking back' and I say, 'No, it's none of your business how I communicate' ... When they feel unhappy and think I'm not representing them well they may even want to be conflictual, so when I go to that meeting I have to carry my weapon. When I go there I must really demand to be listened to. And if they actually get very noisy I must be able to pull out my weapon and say, 'No, if you want to fight we can fight.' It gets to that point. The point is that it's a military environment if you want to bring discipline.[41]

Rogue commanders presented a greater challenge and there was little the ANC could do to bring such units to heel. According to Robert McBride, 'tribally aligned SDUs' sometimes had tense relations with local youth. They also proved a challenge for ANC officials, like McBride, tasked with bringing SDUs under centralised direction:

They could listen to you as a youngster in their midst and they could nod their heads and you could link it to political issues. When they go back into the shacks, they're doing their own tribal thing again. So, those dual allegiances, one to the ANC and their community and another one to their tribe, was a problem.[42]

Phola Park SDUs resisted ANC direction. After concluding that, 'The Phola Park SDU has little or nothing to do with defence and much more to do with blatant aggression and also serves as a guise for criminal activity', the Goldstone Commission of Inquiry's 1992 investigation into violence in Thokoza recommended that the SDU be

[40] Interview, Z96, male SDU member, Thokoza, 21 June 2008.
[41] Interview, Duma Nkosi, Ekurhuleni, 27 June 2008.
[42] Interview, Robert McBride, Johannesburg, 21 June 2006.

dissolved.[43] Whereas unit commanders in Phola Park tended to be ANC sympathisers or even members, Reed concurs that they did not answer to the ANC and several 'were more renowned for their criminal activities than their political zeal'.[44] The ANC admitted, in a submission to the TRC, that the Phola Park SDUs were beyond its control.[45] In Thokoza's Extension 2, the SDU was infamous for terrorising the community and executing people they designated as *izimpimpi*, criminals and witches. An SDU member from a neighbouring section reported that his unit had a serious conflict with the Extension 2 group:

> The unit that came from Extension 2 and my unit had a fight, a very serious fight, maybe our fight lasted for six days. The person who intervened in that fight was our mayor Duma Nkosi because he was staying there in Extension 2. We accused them of many things. They killed people claiming that they are witches. They killed people who they said were criminals. They killed some people in Extension 2 and chased out some others who came to our section. We went and inquired what was wrong with those guys and they told us they were criminals and we must expect that we will be attacked for harbouring criminals. And we said no, if maybe someone is a criminal, correct matters must be taken just to discipline that person, not to kill him. That's when our fight with those guys started and we fought for six or seven days.[46]

The local ANC chapter called meetings to urge the Extension 2 operators to exercise greater restraint. According to a local ANC official, the young men would *toyi-toyi* (a militant dance developed among MK in exile) and fire their weapons on the way to the meeting and threaten the ANC contingent when it questioned their actions. This official attributed the problem primarily to the leadership of an out-of-control commander, and the situation was only resolved when the commander ordered the killing of the mother of one of his members as a witch and was, in turn, killed by that member.[47] In Sebokeng, an SDU commander known as 'Skosana' was similarly executed. He was implicated in murder for hire and extortion and, finally, his own unit turned on him. According to one of his comrades, 'Skosana was supposed to be ANC, but really he was answerable to no one. The power structures in Sebokeng and the whole of the Vaal were terrified of him.' Such was the fear he inspired that Sebokeng residents

---

[43] *Report of the Committee of Inquiry into the Phenomenon and Causes of Violence in the Tokoza Area, Under the Chairmanship of Mr M.N.S Sithole.* Presented to the State President by R.J. Goldstone, Chairman of the Commission of Inquiry Regarding the Prevention of Public Violence and Intimidation, 17 November 1992, p. 28.
[44] Reed, *Beloved Country*, p. 67.
[45] TRC Amnesty Hearing, Michael Phama, Day 1, AM3155/96, 21 June 1999, Johannesburg, http://sabctrc.saha.org.za/documents/amntrans/johannesburg/53500.htm
[46] Interview, G2, male SDU member, Thokoza, 16 July 2006.
[47] Interview, male ANC official, Thokoza, 19 May 2005.

widely celebrated his gruesome execution. 'After being shot, and half dead, he was loaded (according to witnesses) into a van, taken to his mother's home where he was mutilated and his head crushed with a huge stone. He was finally set alight in the house, which now stands partially destroyed.'[48]

Weapon Supplies
Community support was crucial in terms of supplying food and shelter and especially financial contributions for arms purchases. It was only with the financial backing of township residents that SDUs were able to buy the AK47s (and ammunition) that became their weapon of choice. Some even managed to purchase rocket launchers for use against the hostels. Firearms came from a variety of sources, including directly from the ANC. Even when the ANC did not supply the weapons, key personnel, like McBride, operated as brokers for sales and transported weapons to conflict-ridden townships. McBride reports that he took advantage of Peace Accord personnel and vehicles to smuggle weapons. He was dismissive of the Peace Accord's ability to reduce violence and contemptuous of its strict neutrality and advocacy of gun-free zones. He went to NPA meetings to gather intelligence, and then used his position to have some of his subordinates employed as peace monitors:

> I had people driving the peace monitoring cars – they were my people – so they would carry weapons for me into the townships ... No one stops the car with the dove [emblem of the Peace Accord] on it, so go through a roadblock, greet the policeman, say how's things and bring the stuff in.[49]

Giving evidence before the TRC in October 1999, McBride estimated that he supplied Kathorus SDUs with between twenty and forty AK47s, six Makarov pistols, approximately fifty grenades and assorted ammunition, with some of these munitions coming from Ronnie Kasrils.[50] A year later he reported to the TRC that he provided weapons to these SDUs 'on various occasions'.[51] McBride was by no means the only ANC official involved in procuring and delivering military ordinance to SDUs on the Rand:

> Some of our weapons came straight from the ANC. It was 1992 when weapons were delivered right on my street. They were in a blue drum, a drum that was usually used to store oil. There were eighteen rifles and

[48] *Saturday Star*, 9 January 1993.
[49] Interview, Robert McBride, Johannesburg, 21 June 2006.
[50] TRC Amnesty Hearings, 7 October 1999, Durban, http://sabctrc.saha.org.za/hearing.php?id=53741
[51] TRC Amnesty Hearings, AM7726/97, 3 October 2000, Johannesburg, http://sabctrc.saha.org.za/hearing.php?id=54509

ammunition in that drum. The weapons that the ANC gave us came from Robert McBride and Winnie Mandela.[52]

Along with Winnie Madikizela-Mandela, a number of operators and township residents named Chris Hani as a weapons supplier. Ronnie Kasrils also appeared before the TRC to discuss his involvement in arming SDUs.[53] According to McBride different departments within the ANC, including MK intelligence, ran guns into the townships.[54]

When SDUs were first formed and weapons were not readily available, some units borrowed firearms from local criminals, but as the conflict continued weapons flooded into the Rand. Mozambicans – Frelimo and Renamo ex-combatants in particular – were the foremost suppliers of automatic weapons and would, for a fee, instruct buyers on the use and maintenance of AK47s. Phola Park had a substantial Mozambican population and was a well-known arms depot. Although SDUs from across the Rand bought weapons and received training from Phola Park, proximity made it especially popular with Thokoza units. A Sisulu section member remembers, 'Phola Park was the main place where we got the guns.'[55] Victor Mngomezulu, an SDU Commander from Phenduka section, corroborated this statement, adding that both Winnie Madikizela-Mandela and Chris Hani delivered weapons to Phola Park.[56] Reed claims, 'Phola Park acquired the largest concentration of illegal firearms in the country.'[57] MK veteran Stephen Makhura confirmed Phola Park's status as an armed camp. When he returned from exile in 1992 he moved to Phola Park, where he trained SDUs and was allocated a shack. Makhura was impressed: 'Even militarily, the place was feared by the previous rulers of this country. We had all assortment of weapons … It was a base, a guerrilla base.'[58] Several state security force personnel were killed in battles with Phola Park SDUs and ISD veterans confirmed that the police treated Phola Park with extreme caution.

Several MK members made their home in Phola Park and the SDUs also had ex-Frelimo and even SADF veterans. With this concentration

---

[52] Interview, G2 male SDU member, Thokoza, 16 July 2006.
[53] For Madikizela-Mandela's and Hani's involvement see interview Z95, male SDU member, Katlehong, 2006; interview T8, male township resident, Thokoza, 22 May 2006; Missing Voices Project, Interview with no. 1 with Victor Mngomezulu, SDU Commander, Phenduka section. For Kasrils, see TRC Amnesty Committee Hearings, AM7634/97, 24 November 1998, Vosloorus, http://sabctrc.saha.org.za/hearing.php?id=53075.
[54] Interview, Robert McBride, Johannesburg, 21 June 2006.
[55] Interview, Z97, male SDU member, Thokoza, 21 June 2008. Numerous other interviewees identified Phola Park as a major weapons supplier.
[56] Missing Voices Project, Interview no. 1 with Victor Mngomezulu, SDU Commander, Phenduka section.
[57] Reed, *Beloved Country*, p. 67.
[58] TRC Amnesty Hearing, Stephen Donald Makhura, AM0014/96, 16 November 1998, Welkom, http://sabctrc.saha.org.za/documents/amntrans/welkom/52973.htm

of firepower and military experience, Makhura reported that it was a common occurrence for comrades elsewhere to ask for their assistance: 'We sometimes undertook missions to go and defend other places, for example, Ermelo, Ratanda, Thembisa, Meadowlands and other places.'[59] Ernest Sotsu, an ANC-aligned strongman in Sebokeng, reported that isiXhosa-speaking hostel dwellers in Sebokeng obtained guns from Phola Park on the basis of shared connections to the Transkei.[60] A Phola Park SDU member remembers initially buying AK47s from Mozambican residents of Phola Park but, when that supply was exhausted, sending a group to Maputo to buy enough weapons to arm all the resident operators.[61] A Katlehong operator reported to the TRC that he and a colleague travelled to Mozambique where they bought AK47s, other rifles, pistols, grenades and ammunition, which they smuggled back into South Africa and handed over to their section commander.[62] Guns and ammunition were also purchased from hostels, where certain hostel inmates took an apolitical approach to arms dealing. SDU buyers or ANC brokers could not source weapons from hostels against which they were fighting but were able to make purchases from hostels that were less directly involved in the violence. Thokoza SDUs bought from hostels in nearby Vosloorus, and Daveyton hostel fifty kilometers northeast of Thokoza was also a reliable supplier according to a Thokoza SDU commander. When asked if the sellers were Zulu or Xhosa, he replied that they were Zulu, but 'They were just businessmen. They don't care about who kill who. Who's the ANC or who's the IFP, they just selling the guns, taking the money.'[63]

Other ANC Armed Groups
SDUs were the primary armed groups affiliated with the ANC, but the conflict transcended the townships and people came together in diverse settings to deal with the violence. For the most part, employed ANC and IFP supporters did not jeopardise their jobs by engaging in violence at work and respondents sometimes commented that factories or other places of employment offered a refuge from the conflict. However, violence occasionally spilled into the workplace. Zandisile Kondile was convicted for murder after a skirmish at Langeberg factory in Boksburg. His lengthy testimony to the TRC describes the spiral of violence directly preceding the events that led to his arrest. Kondile was an ANC member and a shop steward with the ANC-aligned Food and Allied Workers

[59] TRC Amnesty Hearing, Stephen Donald Makhura.
[60] Reed, *Beloved Country*, pp. 62–3, 67.
[61] TRC Amnesty Hearing, Michael Phama, Day 1.
[62] TRC Amnesty Committee, Sipho Japhta Maduna, AM5475/9702, 18 February 1999, Central Methodist Church, Johannesburg, http://www.doj.gov.za/trc/decisions/1999/ac990348.htm
[63] Missing Voices Project, Interview no. 30 with Dalixolo 'Meneer' Mqubi, SDU Commander, Ext. 2.

Plate 2 Thokoza SDU members in action, 1990s (© Joao Silva)

Union (FAWU). The factory workforce was comprised of both ANC and IFP supporters and Kondile claims that Inkatha workers continually intimidated other employees, especially FAWU members, to join the IFP. When people resisted, the IFP employees resorted to violence. Kondile traces the beginning of his involvement in the conflict to the abduction of two ANC and FAWU co-workers by Inkatha supporters who subsequently murdered one of the men. The fortunate escapee identified his abductors as IFP stalwarts who worked at the factory. At this point, Kondile reported that the shop stewards approached factory management, the police, COSATU, FAWU and the ANC to appeal for assistance and protection. Much to their disappointment, FAWU and the ANC refused to provide them with weapons, and neither the police nor management responded positively to their requests for protection. Seeing no other option, the shop stewards called a meeting of FAWU workers, convinced them of the need for proactive measures and collected funds with which they bought four AK47s and two handguns:

> We decided that we should give them a taste of their own medicine. They were hunting us down, they knew where ... each and every one of us lived. Some of our members were killed in their houses or along the way to their places, so we decided that we should also hunt them down, look for them in their houses. If we see them along the way we should shoot to kill.

Their first mission was to kill an alleged *impimpi*. This fellow employee was a Xhosa man they believed had defected to Inkatha and was supplying their enemies with information. Kondile and some of his comrades murdered him in his home. Shortly after this assassination Kondile was riding a bus to work when he witnessed IFP supporters shooting at two shop stewards on the grounds outside the factory, one of whom was killed. He proceeded into the factory where he met with other shop stewards and decided to mount a revenge attack. 'We went out of the office and we told ourselves that we were going to kill anything and everything that had to do with Inkatha, whether it was women or men.' It was risky to bring firearms to work so Kondile armed himself with a bayonet from his locker and led the shop stewards straight for a group of Inkatha workers. A general melee ensued and Kondile stabbed two men before one of the IFP contingent produced a pistol and shot him in the foot. The police arrived and 'saw that there were some dead bodies lying all over the factory floor'. Kondile was identified by a supervisor as a principal in the violence and was arrested on the spot.[64]

Train violence was one of the more perplexing and terrifying aspects of transition conflict. On some occasions, armed men opened fire on passengers with no obvious regard to political affiliation or ethnicity. However, the ANC–IFP rivalry was often apparent on trains. Supporters from both sides of the political divide commandeered train carriages and attacked other passengers. Some groups armed themselves specifically to deal with the threat of train violence. Mohale Motlokwa was convicted of murdering two IFP train passengers in 1993. At the time, he was an ANC chairperson in Katlehong, a NUMSA shop steward and an SDU member. In his appeal for amnesty he explained that ANC-supporting train passengers were frequently attacked by IFP supporters. Motlokwa belonged to a group of ANC commuters who referred to themselves as the 'train sector'. They chanted ANC slogans and attempted to mobilise support for ANC-aligned unions during their train journeys. Following various incidents of train violence, including one in which Motlokwa was shot, the train sector held a meeting at which members decided to contribute funds to purchase arms. This meeting marked the formation of an armed group of ANC supporters distinct from SDUs, whose purpose was to combat IFP militants on trains. Motlokwa was arrested following a conflict in which he claimed an IFP crowd aggressively interrupted ANC passengers' *toyi-toying* and chanting. An ANC supporter was stabbed in the ensuing scuffle prompting Motlokwa to fire repeatedly. Two IFP men were hit and the rest fled at the next stop. Motlokwa testified that 'after the train had proceeded, we took the two deceased and threw them outside the train because we were not able to *toyi-toyi* with the corpses in the train'.[65]

[64] TRC Amnesty Hearing, Zandisile Patrick Kondile, Langeberg Factory incident, 12 October 1998, http://www.justice.gov.za/trc/amntrans/1998/98101215_jhb_joha1.htm
[65] TRC Amnesty Hearings, Mohale Oscar Motlokwa, AM3135/96, 22 March 2000, Pretoria, http://sabctrc.saha.org.za/hearing.php?id=54097

Inkatha armed structures

SPUs were the IFP's version of SDUs, but much of the fighting was done by hostel and squatter camp residents as opposed to specialist units. During the initial stages of the Thokoza conflicts those who stayed were mobilised to defend the hostels and avenge the assaults on Khalanyoni Zulus. The beds of those who abandoned the hostels 'were taken by young unemployed rural migrants, many coming with the objective of fighting and looting'.[66] Parts of KZN had been embroiled in political hostilities and stock theft–related conflict for several years, and these new arrivals were schooled in violence: 'People from Qudeni, Msinga and Hlazekazi played a leading role in the violent episodes because gunfighting was their daily bread.'[67] According to the commanding officer of ISD Unit 6, fighters transported from KZN posed particular difficulties for police working to contain the violence:

> The biggest positivity of it was that the Zulus were confined in the hostel. You could manage that situation. As long as you could keep them in the hostels you had peace but the minute they came out of the hostels, you had trouble. And you would contain them in the hostel, but they would send groups out from Natal in *kombis* [mini-buses] and then you'd pick up fighting far away from the hostels and these Zulus in the *kombis* would make havoc in areas where there were no Zulus and then afterwards you would find out that people would say the Zulus attacked them. But we were at the hostels, how the hell could the Zulus get out and attack? And it was these Zulus in *kombis* coming down from Natal. They were retaliating because some of their buddies were killed. And where they came into the townships you start picking up bodies.[68]

Hostel militants assumed leadership and residents had little choice but to take up arms when called upon.[69] A Katlehong hostel resident recalls:

> You could not avoid violence, we needed to fight. We were grouped by *indunas* to prepare us for a war, so you see even if you did not want to fight you could not refuse because it would be like you used other people to fight for you and even die for you.[70]

---

[66] Bonner and Ndima, 'Roots of Violence', p. 377.
[67] Bonner and Ndima, 'Roots of Violence', p. 377. A study of Soweto hostels in the conflict also indicated that young men recently arrived from KZN were instrumental in the militarisation of hostel life and took a leading role in the fighting. See Babylon Mgcina Ka Xeketwane, 'The Relation Between Hostels and the Political Violence on the Reef from July 1990 to December 1993: A Case Study of Merafe and Meadowlands Hostel in Soweto' (M.A. dissertation, University of the Witwatersrand, 1995).
[68] Interview, Hein Kilian, ISD Unit 6 Commanding Officer, 2017.
[69] Xeketwane reported the same process in Soweto hostels in 'Hostels and the Political Violence', p. 134.
[70] Interview, Z52, male resident, Mazibuko Hostel, 2006.

Coercion was central to at least some mobilisation efforts as related by one of Sitas' informants:

> There is the call to come to the meeting ... it does not come from strangers, the strangers are marching up and down on the other side chanting ... it comes from your own people who call you by name, they ask you to come for the nation is crying... the comrades are killing your brothers. The cowards are chased, or they are killed.[71]

At the time, much was made in the press of fearsome Zulu regiments, known as *impis*, decamping from the hostels to wreak havoc in the neighbouring townships. Indeed, this is exactly what happened in the 1992 Boipatong massacre. Police, residents and journalists all commented on the lethal nature of mass attacks from the hostels which resulted in substantial casualties, often of non-combatants:

> When the *impis* went on a rampage there was that whole Zulu thing about not leaving any living household thing alive, chickens, dogs, the whole thing, kids. Nobody else killed kids, the *impis* killed children, infants. Nobody else killed babies in that war. The traditional thing was that when you take out a house you take out every living thing in that house and that's what they tried to do.[72]

Hostel inmates reported that visiting Inkatha officials held meetings to encourage residents to take the offensive against their township adversaries. 'Now, when the violence threatens the hostel, the chief *induna* calls a meeting of his subordinate *indunas* and orders are issued for the formation of tribal regiments to patrol the complex. When the *impis* have been created it is easy for them to go on attacks in the townships.'[73] The concentration of thousands of men in the hostels, along with the hierarchical nature of hostel leadership and the cultural connections to a martial past which legitimised the carrying of 'traditional' weapons, marked a clear separation from township combatants:

> You've got this huge grouping of people, they're utterly controlled ... they're armed and ... willing to kill. Besides that, they have a kind of military discipline – if you see them moving down the street towards you chanting and then they go down on their haunches five metres away from you as one and then they go backwards and then come forwards, but they come one more metre forward this time and then down and then the same

[71] Sitas, 'New Tribalism', p. 245.
[72] Interview, Greg Marinovich, Johannesburg, 4 July 2006.
[73] *Weekly Mail*, 26 June–2 July 1992. Residents of Meadowlands Hostel in Soweto also reported that large scale attacks on the townships were organised by visiting IFP officials, including leaders of the Inkatha Youth Brigade. Xeketwane, 'Hostels and the Political Violence', pp. 133–4.

thing again. The ANC never had anything close to that kind of coherent thing.[74]

Neither the IFP nor the residents themselves had the means to equip all hostel dwellers with firearms and, when large war parties left the hostels, most were armed with spears or clubs. In Thokoza and Katlehong, where some SDUs acquired quantities of automatic weapons early in the violence, such attacks were phased out in favour of confrontations between smaller groups of well-armed fighters. For the IFP this meant SPUs. The IFP utilised the violence to consolidate its presence in the hostels. The victimisation of migrant Zulus in the surrounding townships bolstered fears of an ethnic onslaught and lent credence to the IFP's claim that it was the only organisation on the Rand devoted to the welfare of migrant Zulus. IFP office holders represented hostel residents on peace committees, negotiated with the security forces, held rallies to boost the morale of migrant Zulus on the Rand and, when the violence intensified, facilitated the delivery of Red Cross food parcels and other supplies. And, just like their ANC counterparts, IFP officials delivered weapons and organised armed units in the hostels and IFP-controlled informal settlements.

Unlike SDUs, for which there is a significant amount of source material, comparatively little is known about the inner workings of SPUs on the Rand. The IFP chose not to participate in the TRC so the Commission was unable to cast much light on the structures, composition and activities of SPUs. And, whereas many Thokoza and Katlehong former SDU operators were willing to meet with and be interviewed for this study, the SPU veterans who were contacted refused to participate. Thus, the information on SPUs is limited to hostel dwellers' insights on these combatants and the testimony of a few imprisoned SPU members who defied the IFP's ban on the TRC to gain amnesty for offences for which they had been convicted.

It seems that most SPU members were unemployed young men who could serve as full-time combatants:

> We did have the SPUs. They are the ones that protected us, they were here with us. Our leaders came and told us that we need to have people who will help us in this violence, and younger people were selected because they wanted people who still have energy, not people like us who are old.[75]

These young men were grouped together by hostel leaders closely connected to the IFP. 'The SPUs were boys that we sent for training so that they could fight for us. We realised that the other side had trained people who could use guns properly while on our side we were

---

[74] Interview, David Storey, Johannesburg, 26 May 2006.
[75] Interview, Z2, male resident, Buyafuthi Hostel, 10 June 2006.

not trained. The *indunas* were responsible for the selection of those boys.'[76] Several hostel residents reported that SPUs left the hostels to be trained.[77] Some SPU members were provided with rudimentary instruction by others in the hostel and do not appear to have received additional training. Zwile Chamane was one of a handful of SPUs who applied to the TRC for amnesty. When Khalanyoni was destroyed he took refuge further up Khumalo Street in Mshayazafe Hostel where he was recruited as a combatant:

> One of the *indunas* with whom we had fled Khalanyoni met with me and others and we discussed the dying of many Inkatha members as well as the burning of their houses in the township and we discussed this so that this *induna* whose name was Mkhondo advised that we should ensure the safety and protection of our members. That is when I got this firearm [AK47] from the same Induna.

Mkhondo showed Chamane and other SPU fighters how to operate an AK47.[78] In some cases, military preparation seems to have been even more *ad hoc*. A Katlehong SPU recalled that hostel residents contributed R50 to *indunas* for arms purchases and that, 'When they come back with the guns, they just distribute it to anybody who was willing to carry a gun.'[79]

The centrality of *indunas* in the militarisation of the hostels is stressed in numerous interviews and also emerges in TRC testimony. Mzobona Hadebe was the IFP Secretary for the Heidelberg Region, worked at Escort Bacon Factory and lived in Ratanda Hostel, southeast of Katlehong. He applied for amnesty for his role in a 1992 grenade attack on a bus carrying ANC supporters. Hadebe claimed that the assassination of a hostel *induna* by ANC people, along with workplace intimidation of IFP supporting employees by ANC colleagues at the bacon factory, precipitated the attack. He describes a meeting at the hostel during which the attack was planned:

---

[76] Interview, Z3, male resident, Buyafuthi Hostel, 10 June 2006. Other interviews indicate that *indunas* were instrumental in organising hostel defence and the SPUs.

[77] The TRC uncovered evidence of a significant SPU training project in KZN and estimated that five thousand to eight thousand members received instruction in 1993 and 1994. It seems likely that some of the SPUs serving on the Rand were trained in KZN. See TRC Report, vol. 5, ch. 6, subsec. 16, p. 235, http://sabctrc.saha.org.za/reportpage.php?id=12822; TRC Amnesty Hearing, Mr Hlongwane, AM54696, 21 April 1998, Durban, http://sabctrc.saha.org.za/hearing.php?id=54696; TRC Amnesty Hearing, Thulani Mzokhona Myeza, AM54702, 26 March 1998, Durban, http://sabctrc.saha.org.za/hearing.php?id=54702.

[78] TRC Amnesty Hearing, Nicholas Zwile Chamane, AM0188/96, 7 September 1999, Johannesburg, http://www.justice.gov.za/trc/amntrans/1999/99090609_jhb_990907jh.htm

[79] Don Foster, Paul Haupt and Maresa de Beer, *The Theatre of Violence: Narratives of Protagonists in the South African Conflict* (HSRC Press, Cape Town, 2005), p. 256.

Rule of the Gun: The ANC and IFP at War

The death of Mgababa makes us aware that we are being killed and we are getting finished and we should make some plans to also attack the ANC because they were intensively attacking us. Then we decided to have a plan and we sat down and discussed as to how we were going to attack the ANC ... We decided that maybe we should attack one of their buses so that we can send a message to them to show them that we are also brave and prepared to fight them. Therefore, Thokozani Biela who was our chairperson selected two Indunas, saying that they will be responsible with selecting people who were going to carry out that plan, the plan to attack the ANC. The Indunas went aside and discussed this issue amongst themselves ... When they came back they said we have people who are going to attack the ANC people. We have already selected them. When we leave this meeting we will go and inform them. That was the final agreement. And we dispersed.[80]

Money was collected in the hostels and from IFP supporters in townships and squatter camps to finance arms purchases. In addition, township residents not affiliated to the IFP who lived close to the hostels were coerced into paying a weapons tax.[81] However, with a much smaller population base than the surrounding townships, the IFP could not depend on these contributions as its sole means of acquiring weapons. IFP officials like Themba Khoza, the leader of the Transvaal province Inkatha Youth Brigade, liaised with state police personnel to obtain firearms and ammunition. Eugene de Kock headed C10, an SAP counter-insurgency unit that worked out of a farm known as Vlakplaas. Under de Kock's command C10 was involved in assassinations of anti-apartheid activists. In addition, de Kock revealed to the TRC that he and his officers supplied Khoza with AK47s, shotguns, hand grenades and ammunition on a regular basis between 1990–92.[82] These weapons were passed on to combatants in the hostels. A Mazibuko Hostel resident expressed appreciation that, 'Khoza was working very hard for the hostel and he would organise things for hostel dwellers so that they can be able to protect themselves.'[83] Given the government's consistent and long-standing demonisation of the ANC as terrorists, it is hard to believe that Vlakplaas was the lone security force group supplying weapons to IFP fighters on the Rand. The only evidence on record of security force provision of weapons to the hostels is de Kock's testimony, although an ex-SPU member stated that a 'Defence Force' armoured vehicle delivered thirty to thirty-five R5 rifles to his Katle-

---

[80] TRC Amnesty Hearing, Mzobona Leonard Hadebe, 2 February 1999, Nelspruit, http://www.doj.gov.za/trc/amntrans/1999/99020105_nel_990202ne.htm

[81] See for example, IBIIR/Peace Action, *Before we were good friends: An account and analysis of displacement in the East Rand Townships of Thokoza and Katlehong*, April 1994, p. 10 for the reported amounts that residents were forced to pay.

[82] TRC Amnesty Decision, Eugene Alexander de Kock, AM0066/96, AC/2001/225, http://www.doj.gov.za/trc/decisions/2001/ac21225.htm

[83] Interview, Z50, male resident, Mazibuko Hostel, 2006.

hong hostel.[84] While there was no equivalent to MK, the IFP had a pool of combatants trained by the state. In 1986, Inkatha sent two hundred supporters for clandestine military training by SADF special forces in the Caprivi Strip of then South West Africa (Namibia). These fighters became notorious for their involvement in KZN violence against UDF and ANC supporters, but it is also possible that some of them made their way to the Rand. Robert McBride claims that 'the main guy behind the violence from the Inkatha side', a resident of Buyafuthi Hostel, had been a Caprivi trainee.[85] One SPU leader at Soweto's Meadowlands Hostel who termed himself a 'defence adviser' reportedly served as an MK cadre in Tanzania, East Germany and Angola before returning to South Africa and defecting to Inkatha.[86] In addition, it was rumoured that ex-Renamo fighters from Mozambique worked for the IFP as snipers in Katlehong.[87]

In some circumstances competition for employment overlapped with politicised conflict. This seems to have been the case leading up to the IFP grenade attack at Ratanda referenced above. The dispute apparently began during a mid-1992 strike at the Escort Bacon factory by FAWU members. IFP supporters employed at the factory claimed the conflict began because the ANC tried to force all workers to join the FAWU-initiated strike.[88] Factory management responded to the strike by bringing in scab labourers who happened to be members of UWUSA, an IFP-affiliated union. The scabs were housed in the same company hostel as the striking workers and within a short period, UWUSA/IFP supporters had evicted all others from the hostel.[89] The conflict then extended to the workplace. In his TRC submission, Mzobona Hadebe stated that IFP supporters were instructed to threaten and assault ANC employees at the factory. He testified that an UWUSA organiser held a meeting of IFP employees at the hostel in which he urged them to 'attack ANC Fawu members and drive them out of the company so that only Zulus or IFP members can remain'. According to Hadebe, 'We did just that and even now, people who are working in that company are IFP only.' Once ANC supporters were chased from the factory, unemployed men from the hostel filled the vacant positions.[90]

Some hostel residents resented the ascendance of youthful SPUs: 'Youth were no longer so submissive. They dictated to elders, especially over war issues.'[91] Segal's interviews led to her to conclude that,

[84] Foster, Haupt and de Beer, *Theatre of Violence*, pp. 256–7.
[85] Interview, Robert McBride, Johannesburg, 21 June 2006.
[86] Bill Keller, 'Island of Fear: Inside a Soweto Hostel', *New York Times Magazine*, 20 September 1992.
[87] Interview, Robert McBride, Johannesburg, 21 June 2006.
[88] Minnaar, 'Hostels and Violent Conflict', p. 23.
[89] Bonner and Nieftagodien with Mathabatha, *Ekurhuleni*, p. 191.
[90] TRC Amnesty Hearing, Mzobona Leonard Hadebe.
[91] Bonner and Ndima, 'Roots of Violence', p. 377. Gibbs also reports that older men

'The violence has thus to some extent upset the balance of gerontocratic rule as the younger hostel dwellers have taken the lead in organising the violence.'[92] A Thokoza IFP official confirmed that some SPUs were 'loose cannons' who acted on their own initiative.[93] However, in this insular, more hierarchical environment in which all were under siege by township combatants, infighting and predatory activity by the SPUs against migrant Zulus does not appear to have been as much of an issue as SDU rivalries and abuses of township residents. A Peace Accord official who spent time with both camps described a beating administered by an IFP official to young IFP members accused of raping a peace monitor: 'She went, she found those guys and she flogged them to within an inch of their lives. Now that the ANC didn't do. I'm not saying there was no discipline, but it was a different ball game from what was happening with the Inkatha guys.'[94] It seems as if the authority of *indunas* placed limits on SPU waywardness as opposed to some SDUs that openly defied ANC leaders.

ANC-IFP hostilities served as Kalyvas' 'master cleavage' in transition violence as SDU and SPU militants faced off in many townships across the Rand. However, conflict transcended this divide with a proliferation of armed groups emerging in the militarised environment of the larger war. The next chapter explores the 'rule of the gun' outside the confines of the ANC-IFP rivalry.

[contd] in the hostels were sometimes intimidated by younger militants. Timothy Gibbs, 'Inkatha's young militants: reconsidering political violence in South Africa', *Africa* 87, 2 (1994), pp. 362–86.
[92] Segal, 'Human Face of Violence', p. 202.
[93] Interview, female IFP official, Johannesburg, 21 June 2004.
[94] Interview, David Storey, Johannesburg, 26 May 2006.

3 Rule of the Gun
VIOLENCE ON MULTIPLE FRONTS

The previous chapter described how SDUs – formally and informally aligned with the ANC – were the foot soldiers in the war against the IFP and clashes with state security forces. However, this was only one axis along which armed violence was conducted. This chapter identifies others: internecine violence within the ANC; battles which pitted the ANC against non-Charterist liberation movements; and forms of violence which wove together politics and crime in complex patterns.

ANC internecine violence

Violence within and between ANC-affiliated structures, such as SDUs, MK veterans, African National Congress Youth League (ANCYL) members and different civic associations, surfaced throughout the transition period. The ANC was acutely aware of the severity of these conflicts and was active in attempting to resolve many of them. A 1993 ANC Peace Desk report includes a section devoted to 'Intra-Violence' that lists nineteen areas on the Reef that were experiencing conflicts. The Peace Desk report noted that, 'In the absence of hostile attacks in various areas ... the observance in them is the increase on Intra-Violence.'[1] These conflicts took several forms and were often attributed to 'power-mongering amongst comrades'. In Brits (north west of Johannesburg) rival factions of the ANCYL were at each other's throats as 'one group had lost elections and started mobilising against those elected'. An ANCYL-MK conflict in Sharpeville led the Peace Desk to bemoan that, 'MK and Youth League members ... hunt and kill each other with weapons of destruction.' Diepkloof in Soweto featured an ANCYL–COSAS rivalry and warring ANC-affiliated civics in Orlando caused the deaths of 'key activists and promising leaders in the area'. In one of several clashes in which 'tribalism' was said to be a factor, hostilities in Daveyton between 'Amabutho and members of the Youth League' claimed many lives. Amid the ANC–IFP conflict in

[1] University of the Witwatersrand Historical Papers, Local Disputes Resolution Committee, 1992–93, Annexure D, ANC Peace Desk, 'Report to the 4th Regional Conference', 29–31 October 1993, AK2832 A-C9, p. 19.

Alexandra, the ANC was called on to mediate fighting between rival SDUs.[2] A generational struggle in Khutsong between ANC members led to 'lots of conflict'.[3] The ANC often claimed that problematic groups had been infiltrated by criminals, police informers and third force agents seeking to undermine the party. This may well have occurred on occasion, but most internecine violence was rooted in local power struggles. Three case studies illustrate the local dynamics at play.

Phola Park
As we have seen, Phola Park SDUs played a notable role in the conflict in Thokoza and across the Rand as combatants and arms suppliers, and were censured by the Goldstone Commission for alleged criminal activities. In addition, some of these SDUs were at the heart of a struggle that deeply divided the community and resulted in the death of a prominent local activist. Phola Park's war with Khalanyoni and the other nearby hostels had attracted much media attention. Community leader Prince Mhlambi, an educated, English-speaking resident with a flair for publicity, advocated for Phola Park with the media, the police, various NGOs and government departments. The political climate was changing during the transition period and Mhlambi gathered support for development assistance, including the provision of formal housing and services. He headed a Residents' Committee that worked with NGO Planact to come up with a proposal to transform the 3500 shacks of Phola Park into a permanent urban settlement with all the requisite amenities, including home ownership for residents. On behalf of Phola Park, Planact approached the Independent Development Trust (IDT), a recent government creation tasked with developing informal settlements. The IDT funded the entire 21-million-rand project.[4] Unfortunately, not all Phola Park residents supported the development scheme or the Residents' Committee. Phola Park, as a war zone, was not an attractive prospect for development so Mhlambi had been working to improve relations with the security forces. He brokered an agreement with the ISD that their officers should wear name tags, their vehicles should be painted with identification numbers and patrols should check in at the Resident's Committee office on the way in and out of Phola Park. An ISD officer involved in these negotiations reports that, in return, Mhlambi promised to turn in weapons to the police.[5] When he failed to do so, the agreement fell apart and Mhlambi lost credibility, especially in the eyes of militants.[6] From the outset, the

[2] ANC Peace Desk, 'Report to the 4th Regional Conference', pp. 20–3.
[3] Interview, Sally Sealey, London, July 2006.
[4] Reed, *Beloved Country*, p. 69
[5] Interview, Hein Kilian, ISD Unit 6 Commanding Officer, 2017.
[6] Reed, *Beloved Country*, p. 74. See also Lindsay Bremner, 'Development and Resistance: The Lessons for the Planners of Phola Park', *Urban Forum* 5, 1 (1994) and Davin Bremner, 'The Thokoza Peace Process' in L. Douwes-Dekker, A. Majola,

SDUs, who were in perpetual conflict with security forces, were critical of Mhlambi's overtures to the police. And, by 1992, these SDUs were a law unto themselves. As Reed described:

> The sixteen section commanders of the SDU had become despots in Phola Park. Those who questioned their decisions were denounced as police spies, *impimpi*. The punishment for an *impimpi* was to be locked inside an abandoned freight container overnight, awaiting trial ... If at the end of the trial, the women were shooed away and the children told to go and play football, everyone knew the sentence was death.[7]

Some of the Xhosa migrants in Phola Park had little interest in improved housing if it meant they had to pay service charges. Like hostel dwellers, these rurally oriented men had no desire to invest extra funds in urban lodging. The bulldozing of Phola Park to erect homes was antithetical to their interests. Many of these men were SDU operators. Mozambicans, residing illegally in Phola Park, stood to lose their unregulated sanctuary if the development project proceeded as planned. They, too, had close connections to the SDUs. Many SDUs were involved in criminal activities and 'In the new Phola Park, with its orderly patterns of streets, high-mast lighting and numbered houses, there would be nowhere to hide from the police.'[8]

In March 1992 an SDU faction accused the Residents' Committee of siphoning off development funds for their personal use and colluding with the police and forced them out of Phola Park at gunpoint, reportedly killing two. SDUs then assumed control of Phola Park and 'imposed a "protection" levy of R23 on each member of the settlement'.[9] Mhlambi escaped and went into hiding but gathered support from ANC heavyweights for his reinstatement. Reed claims that both Chris Hani and Tokyo Sexwale visited Phola Park to campaign for Mhlambi's return but to no avail, as SDU leaders refused to consider it. The *Weekly Mail* reported that in the aftermath of the coup,

> Members of the old committee now have their names on a hit-list and this month one of the ousted members was pulled off a bus, allegedly by members of the rebel group, and shot dead. Since then senior ANC leaders have held a series of fruitless talks aimed at getting the rebel group to disarm themselves. At one stage the MK leadership was so desperate that it considered sending in an armed detachment to do the job.[10]

(contd) P. Visser and D. Bremner (eds), *Community Conflict: The challenge facing South Africa* (Juta & Co. Limited, Cape Town, 1995).
[7] Reed, *Beloved Country*, p. 75.
[8] Reed, *Beloved Country*, p. 76.
[9] Bremner, 'Development and Resistance', p. 34.
[10] *Weekly Mail*, 29 May–4 June 1992.

To make matters worse, Phola Park SDUs passed a death sentence on Mhlambi who was tracked down and executed in Thokoza in November 1992 along with the three other passengers in his car. His murder only escalated the violence. 'The coup leaders in Phola Park themselves became victims of a coup. Most were killed. Some fled and were assassinated in Mandela Park, another squatter settlement nearby.'[11] Amid this violence, the development scheme collapsed and the conflict with hostel dwellers and security forces continued. Development workers with extensive involvement in Phola Park judged that, by late 1992, the settlement was, 'untouchable for outsiders, unpredictable for residents, unsafe for the security forces'.[12]

Trouble in the Vaal
The Vaal townships south of Johannesburg witnessed some of the worst internecine violence. In Sebokeng, where the ANC–IFP violence on the Rand had begun, a lethal feud between rival SDUs and ANC-affiliated structures ran parallel with the larger conflict. By the ANC's estimation this conflict claimed the lives of thirty 'key and industiors *[sic]* activists and leaders' in 1992 and 1993.[13] Local ANC leader Ernest Sotsu was at the heart of this dispute. Sotsu had grown up in the Transkei but moved to the Vaal Triangle area and played a leading role in the Vaal Civic Association during the political protests of the mid 1980s. He fled back to the Transkei as the security forces cracked down on protest leadership and joined MK as an organiser and recruiter. He was arrested in 1986 while visiting his wife in Boipatong, sentenced to five years in prison for subversive activities and deported to the Transkei to serve his jail time. Sotsu returned to the Vaal after being amnestied by Transkei leader Bantu Holomisa (his former cell mate) in 1989.[14] His MK connections left him well placed to build an armed following during the transition period.

Two hostels in Sebokeng, the Sebokeng Hostel and kwaMasiza, housed Xhosa migrant workers loyal to the ANC. Sotsu had moved into the Sebokeng Hostel after his wife, daughter and grandson were killed and two of his sons wounded during a 1991 attack on his home in the township of Boipatong (notorious IFP-affiliated criminal Khetisi Kheswa was implicated in this attack; more on this below). By mid-1992 these two hostels were embroiled in fighting between a faction loyal to

[11] Reed, *Beloved Country*, p. 78. For struggles between SDU commanders in Phola Park see TRC Amnesty Hearing, Bhekindile Davis Ndwangu, AM7055/97, 7 December 1998, Palm Ridge, http://www.justice.gov.za/trc/amntrans/1998/9811231210_pr_981207th.htm and TRC Amnesty Hearing, Michael Phama, Day 2, AM3155/96, 22 June 1999, Johannesburg, http://sabctrc.saha.org.za/documents/amntrans/johannesburg/53501.htm
[12] Davin Bremner, 'The Thokoza Peace Process', p. 135.
[13] ANC Peace Desk, 'Report to the 4th Regional Conference', p. 16.
[14] Reed, *Beloved Country*, pp. 30–2.

Sotsu and another linked to NUMSA shop steward Jeffrey Ndamase. That Sotsu's energies were concentrated on this rivalry rather than the conflict with IFP, even though his family had been slaughtered by IFP militants, speaks volumes to its intensity. Even amid the ongoing ANC–IFP conflict, the violence was substantial enough to attract media attention and compel the ANC to initiate a commission of inquiry. The two hostels housed thousands of Iron and Steel Corporation (ISCOR) workers, most of whom were represented by NUMSA. A disagreement between NUMSA shop stewards and rank-and-file workers represented one divide in this conflict with the other, related, breach setting returned exiles, including many MK members, against established leaders in local ANC and civic structures. The *Weekly Mail* reported that

> the latter are apparently threatened by the skills the MK members acquired abroad and are attempting to isolate them for fear of losing their positions. Such tension may have been defused were it not for the fact that defence groups, loyal to either side and armed to the teeth, have entered the fray.[15]

Sotsu, who allegedly commanded the loyalty of some two hundred MK veterans in Sebokeng, claimed that local defence units spurned MK leadership and resisted MK attempts to assist with organisation.[16]

The ANC's investigation, headed by Pius Langa, followed a June 1992 intervention by Nelson Mandela and Cyril Ramaphosa. They had met representatives of the various ANC branch leaders and NUMSA officials in an attempt to stem the bloodshed, which had claimed at least ten lives during the previous week and had seen several assassinations of shop stewards before that.[17] The Commission of Enquiry held meetings in Johannesburg, Durban and Port Elizabeth starting in July 1992 and received oral and written submissions from ANC and NUMSA members resident in both hostels as well as elsewhere in the Vaal, along with the ANC regional command and the National Executive Committee of the ANC. The report was signed and presumably submitted to the ANC in February 1993. It found that the dispute originated within the ISCOR workforce, as many hostel residents were disgruntled with the NUMSA shop stewards:

> There was a lack of clarity on the part of Iscor workers, with regard to the position of shop-stewards. Specific questions were in relation to their terms of office and their accountability as well as the right of workers to remove them from their positions in terms of the NUMSA Constitution should the need arise. For instance, it was reported that NUMSA shop-stewards seemed to have been appointed for life, having served from 1986–90 without

[15] *Weekly Mail*, 5 June 1992.
[16] *Christian Science Monitor*, 15 June 1992.
[17] *Weekly Mail*, 12–18 June 1992.

elections. This caused great dissatisfaction among workers and created a schism generally between workers on the one hand and shop-stewards on the other.[18]

The Commission was unable to obtain a detailed account, but part of the problem seemed to be a particular workplace arrangement proposed by ISCOR and endorsed by shop stewards but opposed by the majority of workers. Shop stewards, including Ndamase, who kept pushing for this scheme were labelled sell-outs. This tension was reportedly aggravated by the intervention of Sotsu, who called a meeting to discuss the role of shop stewards in the political structures of the Vaal. Two competing narratives emerged from this meeting. Sotsu supporters claimed that, as a senior and respected comrade, Sotsu discussed the demarcation of the roles played by different structures and advocated separation of these roles. For example, NUMSA was not an ANC preserve so a PAC official could serve in NUMSA provided the individual confined himself to workplace issues. The contrary account held that Sotsu

> made a vitriolic attack on NUMSA and the institution of shop-stewards and from that time daggers were drawn between Sotsu supporters on the one hand and NUMSA and the shop-stewards on the other. According to this version the burden of Sotsu's talk was that NUMSA must not operate in hostels but only on the factory floor.[19]

The result of this meeting was that two opposing armed camps emerged, one headed by Sotsu and backed by returned MK and some ISCOR workers, the other led by Ndamase representing shop stewards and their followers as well as some members of the Sebokeng ANC branch. The conflict was further complicated by the involvement of SDUs and the collection of funds for arms purchases. Sotsu was said to have solicited funds from Sebokeng Hostel residents, but no weapons appeared and 'the complaint is that either that money was misappropriated or the arms were purchased and diverted to supply more favoured individuals'.[20] The *Weekly Mail* highlighted a NUMSA demand

> that members of the defence unit, who are based at the kwaMasiza Hostel and work closely with a group of returned MK exiles, accept the political leadership of the local shop stewards' committee and account for money that has allegedly gone missing after the pro-MK unit imposed a levy on hostel dwellers supposedly for the purpose of buying arms and ammunition.[21]

---

[18] University of the Witwatersrand Historical Papers, Local Disputes Resolution Committee, 1992–93, Report: 'Vaal Commission of Inquiry', AK2832 A-C9, p. 3.
[19] Local Disputes Resolution Committee, 'Vaal Commission of Inquiry', p. 4.
[20] Local Disputes Resolution Committee, 'Vaal Commission of Inquiry', p. 5.
[21] *Weekly Mail*, 29 May–4 June 1992.

As the conflict progressed, the hostels split into warring factions with SDUs playing a leading role:

> The current position is that there are two DUs operating in the Sebokeng Hostel, as follows: there is one for Blocks 4 and 5, which is Ndamase supporting and another for block 2 which supports Sotsu. KwaMasiza Hostel has one DU. There is no free movement between the blocks; the DUs are at war. With regard to KwaMasiza, allegiances are not clearly divided in terms of blocks, residents are mixed. It has been said that that makes it easy for a person from one faction to move to another flat and kill a member of the other faction.[22]

The Commission expressed alarm that there was no centralised management of the SDUs. It was not clear to them who the commanders were, to whom the SDUs were accountable, what level of co-ordination existed between SDUs, and to what degree SDUs were linked to MK. The rival SDUs appear to have answered only to Sotsu and Ndamase, who the Commission identified as 'the two principal characters in the conflict'. This was very much an internecine battle, as 'both are regarded by those working with them at least as ANC comrades who are prepared to die for the ANC'.[23] Several recommendations were put forth regarding the role of shop stewards and the lines of communication between different ANC structures, but the greatest emphasis was on control of SDUs. The Commission urged that the Sebokeng and kwaMasiza SDUs be disbanded and disarmed and stressed that 'there needs to be overall control if the DUs are not going to be allowed to slide to anarchy. There must be an overall authority, which will also be in a position to disarm those who do not toe the line.'[24] This, of course, was the crux of the problem. When SDUs followed their own script, the ANC had very limited means to rein them in. This remained a challenge for the transition period and beyond.

Sotsu's connections to MK also raises the more general issue of conflict between returned MK veterans and local SDU members. Many SDUs across the Rand worked closely with MK and MK veterans were integrated into some SDUs. However, reports circulated, especially in Sharpeville and Sebokeng, of clashes between these two constituencies. In these cases it seems that MK veterans regarded SDUs as untrained thugs, while SDUs rejected the authority of MK outsiders to dictate to them. As with the hostel SDUs in Sebokeng, the IBIIR judged that, 'the nine SDUs in Sharpeville are not answerable to any structure'.[25] Some of these SDUs were, however, linked to the ANCYL,

---

[22] Local Disputes Resolution Committee, 'Vaal Commission of Inquiry', p. 6.
[23] Local Disputes Resolution Committee, 'Vaal Commission of Inquiry', p. 7.
[24] Local Disputes Resolution Committee, 'Vaal Commission of Inquiry', p. 11.
[25] University of the Witwatersrand Historical Papers, IBIIR, Memorandum: 'Crisis in Sharpeville', [undated, but written after September 1993], AG2543 3.1-3.42.

and these combined groups took offence when MK veterans refused to accompany them on joint patrols. MK was encouraged by the ANC to lend their expertise to SDUs but

> The Vaal group said they and other cadres in their area were reluctant to get involved with SDUs beyond the level of consultation. Attacks orchestrated by undisciplined youths, they said, were often badly planned and arbitrary, exposing them to the perils of police crackdowns in a messy war with many enemies and few rules.[26]

To make matters worse, some residents and MK veterans attributed an increase in criminal violence to the SDUs. These residents appealed to MK soldiers to deal with out-of-control SDUs. 'The end result of this situation was that residents were pitted against each other in the form of two camps. Those that supported MK and those that did not.'[27] This included other ANC-affiliated structures like COSAS. Some of the SDUs aligned with MK so that neighbouring SDUs lined up on opposite sides of this increasingly rancorous divide. In February 1993 an MK deputation in Sharpeville is said to have confronted the local ANC Branch Chairperson, Siza Rani, demanding that ANCYL members disarm and that if weapons were not surrendered in the next three days, 'MK would launch a full-scale offensive on Rani and the entire Youth League'.[28] A Youth League activist, Oupa Manete, was shot dead on the day of the deadline, and his brother organised the 'Germans' gang to avenge his death. The Germans were composed of sixty or so youth, including many ANCYL members at odds with the ANC. In addition to feuding with MK, the Germans were accused of extorting money and generally terrorising residents in Sharpeville's Matthew Goniwe section. The Germans clashed with Slovo section MK veterans and, according to the IBIIR, 'countless deaths' resulted. It was rumoured that some police backed the Germans because they were fighting MK.[29] The ANC brokered numerous meetings and peace agreements beginning in July 1993, but continuing violence, including clashes at the meetings, derailed these efforts. For example, 'On 3rd August the reconciliation process was dealt a severe blow when an MK commander, Joshua Khumalo, also known as "Chipper", stabbed a COSAS member while the meeting was in session in full view of the leadership and other participants.'[30] A follow-up report by the IBIIR in January confirmed that the violence was ongoing and concluded that,

[26] *Weekly Mail*, 15–22 May 1992.
[27] IBIIR, 'Crisis in Sharpeville'.
[28] Richard Wilson, *The Politics of Truth and Reconciliation in South Africa: Legitimizing the Post-Apartheid State* (Cambridge University Press, Cambridge, 2001), p. 178.
[29] IBIIR Monthly Report, October/November 1993, pp. 23–4.
[30] IBIIR, 'Crisis in Sharpeville'.

'Although we welcome the public castigation of the SDUs by the ANC, we are far from convinced that the ANC has applied itself properly or sufficiently to resolving conflict between SDU factions or between SDUs and the ANCYL.'[31]

MK veterans' dissatisfaction with the conditions of return may have contributed to their involvement in unsanctioned violence according to the *Weekly Mail*:

> While many MK cadres have been absorbed into regional structures, others complain that leaders who rose to prominence in the United Democratic Front era are clutching onto their positions, leaving no space for the returnees ... The recent attempted assassination of Vaal activist Bavumile Vilikazi was perhaps testimony to such frustration. Many MK soldiers have accused Vilikazi of 'blocking positions' for them.[32]

As with errant SDUs, the ANC struggled to restrain such disaffected elements.

Katlehong Killings

Our third case of internecine conflict between ANC supporters took place in Katlehong on 7 December 1993, when the SDU from Moleleki section, Extension 2 executed seven ANCYL members ranging in ages from fourteen to eighteen, along with one adult ANC member.[33] SDU respondents repeatedly claimed that SDUs furthest removed from the front lines with the IFP were more prone to infighting and preying on their communities. Moleleki Extension 2 did not border any of the hostels and had competing centres of power in the SDU and the local ANCYL. The SDU was composed of men in their thirties and forties, most of whom were isiXhosa speakers with rural roots. The ANCYL cohort was younger, predominantly urban born and drawn from different ethnic groups. In the absence of significant conflict with the IFP to unite them, these two bodies vied for local influence and eventually turned on each other. The ANCYL accused the SDU of being anti-democratic and exclusive because it was comprised of Xhosa adult males who self-selected as SDU members instead of being put forward by the community.

[31] University of the Witwatersrand Historical Papers, IBIIR Memorandum: Update on Sharpeville, 16 January 1994, AG2543 C21; IBIIR Monthly Report December 1993/January 1994, p. 33.

[32] *Weekly Mail*, 15–22 May 1992.

[33] The following account is drawn from Vanessa Barolsky, 'The Moleleki Execution: A Radical Problem of Understanding' (PhD dissertation, University of the Witwatersrand, 2010). There is also an extensive TRC archive dealing with this event, as thirteen SDU members applied for amnesty. They were denied amnesty as it was ruled that the massacre was a revenge killing without political motivation. Following the TRC process five SDU members were subsequently convicted of murder and received life sentences.

Some residents also objected to the SDU's dictatorial nature, as it imposed a curfew without consulting community members and enforced the curfew through violence.[34] In turn, the SDU considered the youngsters unfit to assume leadership roles in the community and demanded that they submit to SDU authority. The ANCYL was not prepared to defer to the SDU and mounted their own patrols. Thus, the relationship between the two groups was already fractious before the killing of an ANC activist on 6 December, which served as the immediate impetus for the mass execution. ANC local official Bulelwa Zwane was gunned down the night after a meeting at which she had cautioned against the formation of another SDU in Block F of Extension 2. ANCYL members suspected the existing SDU was responsible for the shooting and, along with some outraged community members, the ANCYL set off to find the culprits. They converged on the house of SDU Deputy Commander Malusi Kiyana, known as 'Blanko', where three ANCYL members forced their way in and opened fire, killing Blanko instantly. Vanessa Barolsky describes the aftermath of the shooting:

> Goods from the spaza shop that Blanko operated from his home were taken by some younger Youth League members, which when later found in their possession by SDU members provided 'evidence' of their criminality and involvement in Blanko's death and became the basis for their later abduction and execution. After the spaza shop was looted, Blanko's shack was set alight. The remains of his charred body were found in a sitting position on a chair, propped outside against the ruins of his shack.[35]

A neighbouring SDU member had witnessed the attack and, when his colleagues gathered at Blanko's house, his identification of ANCYL members as the killers precipitated a hunt that led to the abduction of fourteen youngsters. Most of the ANCYL members apprehended by the SDU had not been present at Blanko's death but were nonetheless herded into an open shack in Block F, where they were put on public display. Such was the distrust of the police and the fear of being labelled as an informer that, although the ISD came to collect the bodies of Blanko and Zwane and were within sight of the shack where the captives were being held, no one alerted them or otherwise contacted the authorities. A father who came to plea for his fourteen-year-old son's release was then also captured and subsequently executed. 'While the youth cowered in the shack, SDU Commander Njebe Ndondolo arrived with a list of names of the youth who were to be executed, comprising members of the ANCYL who patrolled the township rather [than] those instrumentally involved in Blanko's

[34] Lekgoathi and Ndlovu, 'Political violence in the PWV region', p. 990.
[35] Barolsky, 'The Moleleki Execution', p. 8.

killing.'[36] Several captives were then released because their names did not appear on Ndondolo's list, and the remainder were condemned as criminals. On the morning of 7 December, ten ANCYL members and one father were marched into an open field on the boundary of Extension 2. One was given a gun and told to shoot the others. He was then released. The rest were shot and mutilated, although two survived and escaped once their assailants abandoned the bodies in the field.

This massacre constitutes yet another example of the 'rule of the gun' ethos that prevailed in many Rand townships during this period. State authority was not recognised, and new possibilities had opened for the exercise of local authority, albeit in dangerous and often contested environments. Despite its significant support and moral authority, the ANC was unable to fill the void in local governance, especially in townships riven by ANC–IFP and other hostilities. This struggle to establish local authority was exacerbated in the case of Moleleki because it 'was a new township, only established in November 1992, one year before the execution, and its structures of internal governance remained fragile, fluid, its leadership contested'.[37] And although the ANC loomed in the background as the most powerful liberation movement and a possible government in waiting, its local influence was often relatively limited. As Barolsky observes for Moleleki, 'despite the fact that both sets of protagonists in the conflict were ANC members, neither the SDU nor the ANCYL approached the ANC for assistance to help address the division between the organisations prior to the execution'.[38]

Evidence of fighting between IFP members on the Rand is almost non-existent. This may reflect the greater internal cohesion of the IFP and the need for its supporters to close ranks as the hostels were under siege and migrant Zulus were persecuted in the townships. ANC supporters, by contrast, were far more numerous and belonged to many diverse groupings, thereby greatly increasing possibilities for conflict. Almost certainly, however, the insularity of the IFP has prevented such incidents from coming to light. ANC structures were more open to the press and many had close relations with violence monitoring groups. The ANC also co-operated with the TRC; thus, violence between ANC supporters was more likely to be publicised. An amnesty application to the TRC does reveal that IFP supporters were not immune from internal conflicts. IFP member Phakamani Ndinisani was forced out of Phola Park and then Khalanyoni Hostel by politicised violence and settled in Zonkizizwe squatter camp, which was also caught up in ANC–IFP fighting. The IFP drove ANC supporters out and, in this, IFP preserve Ndinisani emerged as a youth leader. The IFP chair in Zonkizizwe, referred to only as Ndebele, came

[36] Barolsky, 'The Moleleki Execution', p. 14.
[37] Barolsky, 'The Moleleki Execution', p. 5.
[38] Barolsky, 'The Moleleki Execution', p. 216.

under suspicion because he was unable to account for the money that he had collected from residents for firearms and ammunition. Ndebele was replaced and a new committee was elected, which led to a schism in the squatter community as Ndebele refused to surrender his position and marshalled the support of some followers. The two groups began fighting, with Ndinisani on the side of the recently elected faction. Ndinisani testified that he planned to kill Ndebele, whom he believed was responsible for the death of two of his friends and because he suspected him of working for the ANC. He used his AK47 to rake a shack he mistakenly believed to be inhabited by Ndebele and instead killed a stranger and wounded three others. He was arrested shortly thereafter, and applied for amnesty from prison.[39] This cannot be the only incidence of conflict within the IFP, but internecine ANC violence on the Rand was clearly more common, more protracted and more destructive.

ANC–PAC/AZAPO violence

During the turbulent 1980s as various movements, coalitions and organisations mounted campaigns against apartheid, Charterist groups aligned with the ANC sometimes battled with other national liberation movements outside the Charterist fold. Similar conflicts on the Reef took place throughout the transition period with Bekkersdal township on the West Rand being particularly hard hit. The *Weekly Mail* traced the origins of this violence:

> The trouble began early last year [1990] when the ANC began to actively recruit members and make inroads into what has been predominantly an Azapo/PAC stronghold since the early 1980s. When ANC stalwart Thapello Seoka returned to his hometown after [twelve] years on Robben Island early last year, he motivated the youth to form the Bekkersdal Youth Congress (Beyco) ... When Beyco was launched in February the 'Azapos' allegedly launched an attack at the meeting, which led to retaliation, murders on both sides and a spiral of revenge and retribution ... While both groups may in principle be opposed to the government and imposed local authorities, the desire for political control effectively blurs all common goals.[40]

As the conflict in Bekkersdal dragged on it transcended the ANC/AZAPO divide, although most casualties seem to have been AZAPO members. A Beyco 'warlord' was identified as a leading figure in the violence. He was said to work closely with local councillors who

---

[39] TRC Amnesty Committee, Phakamani Alex Ndinisani, AM5906/97, 13 March 2001, Cape Town, www.doj.gov.za/trc/decisions/2001/ac21090
[40] *Weekly Mail*, 8–14 February 1991.

provided him with land which he used to settle retrenched miners in return for their support in the conflict.[41] The notorious Basotho 'Russians' gang also became involved, both to protect fellow Basotho as the violence threatened all residents of Bekkersdal and as guns for hire in the conflict. Over time, the IFP, other criminal elements and black police were implicated in the violence on both sides and, 'while the conflict may have started as a political struggle for control of Bekkersdal, it has become little more than an anarchic mess'.[42]

ANC and PAC student organisations seem to have been particularly prone to conflict with reports of bloody clashes surfacing in several areas. An SDU member in Katlehong dated his involvement in violence to his student days where, as a ANCYL member, he fought against the Pan Africanist Student Organisation (PASO). He claimed that PASO was allied with gangsters 'and we as the ANC youth league were against criminal activities so we had to fight them, and many people died'.[43] Violence between PASO and ANC-aligned COSAS in KwaThema on the East Rand was sufficiently substantial to merit a formal Commission of Enquiry. The Enquiry traced the origin of the conflict to COSAS supporters interrupting the attempted launch of PASO at a local high school in June 1993. A COSAS member objected to school staff that, 'one cannot tolerate two organisations operating in the same school'.[44] PASO persisted with its plans and many students needed to be hospitalised after the ensuing brawl. In the next few days 'a number of students lost their lives and many were injured'.[45] The violence continued sporadically for years, with occasional peace agreements that lasted only fleetingly. The conflict was still ongoing at the time of the Enquiry in 1997.

The Vaal also experienced ANC–PAC conflict. PAC supporters reported that clashes took place over boycotts and stayaways unilaterally called by ANC bodies without community consultation and then violently enforced – sometimes by necklacings. Commenting on the violence, Barney Desai, the PAC's secretary for publicity and information maintained that

---

[41] *City Press*, 11 November 1990.
[42] *Weekly Mail*, 8–14 February 1991. The TRC also references the conflict in Bekkersdal. TRC Report, vol. 3, ch. 6, subsect. 96, p. 721, http://sabctrc.saha.org.za/reports/volume3/chapter6/subsection96.htm
[43] Interview, Z95, male SDU member, Katlehong, 2006.
[44] University of Witwatersrand Historical Papers, IBIIR Kwa-Thema, *Commission of Inquiry into Incidents of Violence in Kwa-Thema presented to the Honourable Premier of the Province of Gauteng*, January 1997, by Advocate Clive van der Spuy, AG 2543, C-12, p. 31.
[45] University of Witwatersrand Historical Papers, IBIIR Kwa-Thema, *Commission of Inquiry into Incidents of Violence in Kwa-Thema presented to the Honourable Premier of the Province of Gauteng*, January 1997, by Advocate Clive van der Spuy AG 2543, C-12, p. 29.

tension always arises between the PAC and the ANC when the ANC starts claiming hegemony over whole territorial areas for itself, despite the fact that there may be other organisations there as well. We have experienced massive intimidation and violence being perpetrated against our members, who have had to respond. Although the ANC claims to be a party of democracy, on the ground its supporters do not acknowledge democracy.[46]

Although nowhere near the scale of the ANC–IFP conflict, violence between ANC-aligned groups and other anti-apartheid organisations persisted throughout the transition period.

Crime and political conflict

Differentiating between criminal and political violence represents one of the foremost challenges in the analysis of transition-era conflicts. Attacks that were ostensibly politically motivated were often accompanied by looting, for example, and the murder of a personal or business rival across the political divide defies simple classification. Much of the time there was no clear distinction, as some political militants robbed, raped and killed for personal advantage, and criminal figures aligned themselves with political groups for protection, to acquire a measure of legitimacy and to gain support for their illegal activities. In return, the gangsters were expected to fight for the organisation to which they were affiliated. Apartheid police had long made use of criminal and vigilante groups against anti-apartheid activists and some police continued to target ANC and PAC supporters, sometimes in alliance with the IFP. The lawlessness that characterised the civil conflict provided opportunities and created space for criminal groups to operate in conjunction with politicised violence.

Two of the most notorious criminal figures on the Rand worked closely with the IFP and elements within the police. Victor Khetisi Kheswa, dubbed the 'Vaal Monster', was implicated in dozens of killings before his July 1993 death in police custody. Mbhekiseni Khumalo, family man, self-appointed Archbishop of the Light of God Church of Zion and local business owner, headed a group that inspired terror in Thokoza.[47] According to testimony supplied to the TRC, Khumalo and his accomplices were guilty of murder, attempted murder, armed robbery, extortion, arson, theft, sale of stolen property and possession of unlicensed firearms. Partially because the violence was multi-layered and exceedingly difficult to isolate and define, but

---

[46] *The Citizen*, 10 September 1992.
[47] Much of the material on Kheswa and Khumalo is taken from Gary Kynoch, 'Crime, Conflict and Politics in Transition Era South Africa', *African Affairs* 104, 416 (2005), pp. 493–514.

also because much of the police involvement was covert, the evidence regarding the activities of Kheswa, Khumalo and their associates is far from comprehensive. However, the following patchwork accounts provide an impression of the interplay between personal feuds, acquisitive criminality and politicised hostilities.

The Vaal Monster
Kheswa was a young man, only twenty-eight at the time of his death, and his Sebokeng neighbours reported that he had been on a criminal path since early adolescence when he started stealing cars and selling marijuana.[48] Kheswa's conversion from apolitical criminal to IFP militant was precipitated by a clash with local comrades in 1990. By this time Kheswa was the leader of a gang of car thieves and apparently fell afoul of comrades at the forefront of an anti-crime initiative. In a meeting with the comrades Kheswa was accused of various offences and was shot after he refused to surrender his firearm. He escaped, despite being wounded, and the strife between these comrades and Kheswa's gang became entrenched. Outnumbered and outgunned, Kheswa aligned himself with IFP members residing in KwaMadala Hostel. At the time of his death, the IFP listed Kheswa as the chairman of its Sebokeng branch.[49] The benefits of IFP membership were immediately apparent, as Kheswa's house was guarded by armed IFP militants. With the backing of the IFP Kheswa embarked on an offensive against the comrades, which led to the death of Christopher Nangalemebe in January 1991.[50] Nangalembe and Kheswa had been openly feuding for some time and, when Nangalemebe's corpse was found in a rubbish dump on 6 January, Kheswa was the prime suspect.[51] A funeral vigil was planned for Nangalemebe, and Sebokeng residents claim that Kheswa's gang warned Nangalemebe's family and the community against attending.[52] The vigil went forward on 12 January and threats were made good as a large group of men attacked the mourners with AK47s and hand grenades, slaughtering forty-eight people. It was widely believed that Kheswa's gang, supported by IFP hostel dwellers, was responsible for the massacre. Enraged ANC supporters retaliated by burning down the houses of Kheswa and two of his gang members. Kheswa and his family then moved into KwaMadala Hostel.[53] Kheswa's

[48] *Star*, 18 July 1993.
[49] *Star*, 18 July 1993.
[50] IBIIR Monthly Report, June/July 1993, p. 25; *Star*, 18 July 1993.
[51] *Business Day*, 16 January 1991; *Sunday Star*, 18 July 1993; University of Witwatersrand Historical Papers, IBIIR, 'Confidential Report on Sebokeng Vigil Shootings', 18 January 1991 AG2543, C20, p. 2.
[52] *Sunday Star*, 18 July 1993; IBIIR, Kheswa file, AG2543, C20.
[53] University of Witwatersrand Historical Papers, IBIIR, 'Confidential Report on Sebokeng Vigil Shootings', 18 January 1991, AG2543, C20, p. 14; *City Press*, 14 July, 1991. Kheswa was not a singular criminal figure in the IFP hostels as residents of

notoriety continued to grow as he was linked to several high-profile killings, including the murders of Ernest Sotsu's relatives, an attack on the Sebokeng beer hall in which thirteen people died and a shooting incident at the Erika Tavern that resulted in five additional deaths.[54] Sotsu had been hired by COSATU to assist in the inquest of the night vigil massacre and reported that Kheswa had visited his home several times to dissuade him from pursuing this matter. Indeed, Kheswa was charged with intimidation for these visits. On 3 July 1991, when Sotsu was attending an ANC conference in Durban, armed men invaded his home and killed his wife, daughter and grandson. Two other grandchildren, who survived despite being shot, identified Kheswa as one of the attackers. He was subsequently arrested but never convicted of the murders.[55] Operating out of the KwaMadala Hostel, Kheswa was constantly in trouble with the law and received a six-year sentence for illegal possession of an AK47 in September 1991. He served four months before he was released pending an appeal.[56] Kheswa was often seen in the company of police and the local ANC was convinced that he was a police agent. In an affidavit submitted to the TRC, Vaal police officer Masoli Mahlatsi stated that Kheswa and his gang members received special treatment when they were detained and that Kheswa often boasted that he and his gang worked with the police.[57] Kheswa's death in custody reinforced suspicions that he was eliminated to cover police complicity in township killings. At the time of his death, Kheswa had lost his appeal and it was thought that his police handlers feared he would give evidence against them rather than serve out his sentence. Kheswa was also under investigation for murder and faced a much longer sentence if convicted. He died while in the custody of Detective Sergeant 'Pedro' Peens. According to a TRC investigative report, 'Peens and two of his colleagues booked Kheswa out for investigation from Vanderbijlpark police station on 6 July at 19h05.'[58] He was pronounced dead on arrival at the hospital the next afternoon. A murder docket was opened against Peens and his two colleagues, who

---

(contd) Soweto's Merafe Hostel reported that young militants operating out of the hostel were involved in local car-jacking rings. Xeketwane, 'Hostels and the Political Violence', p. 146.

[54] *City Press*, 14 July 1991.
[55] University of Witwatersrand Historical Papers, IBIIR, 'Briefing documents on the murders of Constance, Margaret and Sabata Sotsu on July 3, 1991', AG2543, C20 and IBIIR, Kheswa File, AG2543, C20 pp. 2–3; *Weekly Mail*, 19 July 1991; *City Press*, 14 July 1991.
[56] *Sunday Times*, 18 July 1993.
[57] TRC Report, vol. 2, ch. 7, subsect. 7, p. 600, http://sabctrc.saha.org.za/reports/volume2/chapter7/subsection7.htm
[58] University of Witwatersrand Historical Papers, 'Boipatong Inquiry, General Description of the Incident', TRC Investigative Report Submitted by Jan-Ake Kjellberg, (n.d.), http://www.historicalpapers.wits.ac.za/inventories/inv_pdfo/AK2672/AK2672-C2-3-006-jpeg.pdf

were immediately suspended, but charges were dropped following a post mortem by a state pathologist which declared that Kheswa died of natural causes. The state examination found that Kheswa's heart had stopped beating due to a viral infection and the Attorney General judged that there was no need for an inquest.[59] 'However, the findings were disputed by an independent pathologist who found that Kheswa died from "unnatural causes" which included acute suffocation, electrocution, hypothermia and toxic substances.'[60] In his statement to the TRC, Masoli Mahlatsi indicated that, on the day Kheswa was taken away by Peens, he was threatening to expose his relationship with the police. It is perhaps worth noting that shortly after Kheswa's death, a member of his gang was killed after having been run over by a car driven by Peens.[61] Kheswa's story highlights the possibilities of criminal involvement in political hostilities and the role of police in subverting law and order in these circumstances.

The Archbishop
Unlike Kheswa, there is no evidence that Khumalo was involved in criminal activities prior to the start of politicised violence in Thokoza. Rather, Khumalo's emergence as a violence entrepreneur can be traced to his leadership of an anti-crime campaign, specifically targeting a local gang led by a young man known as 'Mugabe'. Interviews with township and hostel residents from both sides of the political divide suggest that Khumalo's vendetta was precipitated by his daughter's abduction and rape by the gang. Khumalo claimed that the feud began after Mugabe attempted to extort money from him and take his daughter from his home.[62] By all accounts, the Mugabe gang was a scourge in Thokoza and Khumalo's fight against Mugabe was initially supported by both the police and the local ANCYL.[63] ANC sources report that the alliance with Khumalo fell apart because Khumalo and his male relatives began indiscriminately assaulting township youth. At that point, the ANCYL turned against Khumalo and refused to return the weapons he had lent them. An IFP official claims that the ANC condemned Khumalo because he was Zulu and known to have Inkatha connections.[64] Whatever the cause of the rupture, once Khumalo faced off with ANC supporters, he and his remaining followers were supported

---

[59] *Star*, 31 August 1993; *Citizen*, 31 August 1993; *Sowetan*, 12 July 1993.
[60] *City Press*, 22 August 1993.
[61] TRC Report, vol. 2, ch. 7, subsect. 7, p. 600, http://sabctrc.saha.org.za/reports/volume2/chapter7/subsection7.htm
[62] *Sowetan*, 24 December 1992.
[63] University of Witwatersrand Historical papers, IBIIR, Memorandum on the Activities of Mbhekisini Khumalo, 24 February 1993, AG 2543 3.1-3.42; TRC Amnesty Hearing, Sipho Steven Ngubane, AM7295/97, 3 December 1998, Palm Ridge http://www.justice.gov.za/trc/amntrans%5C1998/9811231210_pr_981203th.htm
[64] Interview, female IFP official, Johannesburg, 21 June 2004.

by the IFP. Khumalo had reportedly been a member of Inkatha since the 1970s, but it was conflict with ANC supporting youth that cemented his relationship with the IFP. The TRC found that, 'the gang appeared to have been fundamentally integrated into the organisational hierarchy of the IFP. It was the IFP leadership who initiated political projects and directed their execution.'[65] An SPU member claimed that he and other SPU fighters were instructed by *indunas* to guard the Khumalo home because Khumalo was a well-known IFP strongman.[66]

A convergence of interests developed as the Khumalo gang was accused of targeting ANC supporters who also happened to compete with Khumalo in the taxi and grocery store sectors.[67] The association with Inkatha reportedly proved profitable as the Khumalo gang played a leading role in the campaign to cleanse ANC supporters from the neighbourhoods adjacent to the hostels. Gang members intimidated residents into abandoning their homes and then confiscated the furniture and electrical goods left behind by fleeing families.[68] These activities did not go unopposed, as area ANCYL members who had turned against Khumalo launched at least two grenade attacks on the Khumalo home and engaged the gang in shootouts.[69] Khumalo's wife was gunned down in January 1993 in Thembisa where she had taken refuge after repeated attacks on their Thokoza house. Although rumours abounded that Khumalo was responsible for her death, he insisted that she was killed by comrades.[70] A former SDU member corroborates Khumalo's account: 'The mission came out that she must be killed because we couldn't kill him. He was always with the police and he was well armed and protected, so his wife was killed in that way ... We could not get to Khumalo, so someone had to die.'[71] To exact revenge Khumalo allegedly ordered his gang to attack a tavern frequented by ANC supporters, some of whom happened to have competing business concerns. Several people were killed in the Ngema Tavern massacre, and victims were relieved of their possessions. The testimony of the gang members involved led the TRC Amnesty Committee to conclude that the motive for the attack 'was either business rivalry or robbery or both'.[72]

[65] TRC Report, vol. 3, ch. 6, p. 715, http://sabctrc.saha.org.za/reports/volume3/chapter6/subsection94.htm
[66] TRC Amnesty Hearing, Nicholas Zwile Chamane.
[67] TRC Amnesty Hearing, Themba Stephen Zimu, AM1806/96, Ngema Tavern Killing, 6 September 1999, Johannesburg, http://sabctrc.saha.org.za/documents/amntrans/palm_ridge/53670.htm
[68] University of Witwatersrand Historical Papers, IBIIR TRC, Section 29 Hearing, 'In Camera', 'Khumalo Gang', AG2543, A13, pp. 75, 101.
[69] TRC Amnesty Hearing, Sipho Steven Ngubane.
[70] University of Witwatersrand Historical Papers, IBIIR, Memorandum on the Activities of Mbhekisini Khumalo, 24 February 1993, AG 2543 3.1-3.42.
[71] Interview, G1, male SDU member, Thokoza, 11 June 2004.
[72] TRC Amnesty Decisions, Thembu Zima, Thulani Tsotetsi, Mzwake Khumalo,

Khumalo was also accused of involvement in the September 1991 assassination of Sam Ntuli, General Secretary of the Civic Associations of the Southern Transvaal and a popular ANC figure. Khumalo gang members testified that the Archbishop colluded with Inkatha officials in the assassination because of Ntuli's role in organising stayaways that adversely affected Khumalo's taxi business.[73] The TRC Amnesty Commission, noting that Ntuli was on good terms with Inkatha leadership at the time of his murder, judged that the 'pecuniary interests of some taxi owners or business people were the main reason for the assassination'.[74] Ntuli's death further inflamed political tensions and more than twenty people were killed in two incidents following his funeral. Mourners returning from the Ntuli funeral attacked drivers and passengers at an Inkatha-affiliated taxi rank and a separate group of funeral-goers was fired on by several people using AK47s.[75] If the Amnesty Committee was correct, a primarily criminal act had severe political repercussions.

Along with their ties to the IFP, the Khumalo gang had extensive police connections. The Murder and Robbery Squad in Benoni reportedly attended barbecues at different houses owned by gang members and supplied the names and car registration numbers of people they wanted killed to the Archbishop, whose men would carry out the murders. In return, the police provided the gang with weapons and protected them from prosecution and their ANC enemies. Khumalo claimed before the TRC that he had around-the-clock protection from the ISD and other police for several months during 1992. When the Commission observed that such service was highly unusual and asked Khumalo why he qualified for protection, he attributed his good fortune to divine intervention.[76] An SPU member stated that his unit shared guard duties of Khumalo's home with soldiers and police.[77] Khumalo was arrested numerous times on different charges but does not seem to have been convicted of any offences.[78] During a 1993 appearance in Alberton Court on charges of arson, murder and attempted murder, Khumalo informed the court that, he, his sons and brother had 'been involved in several wild shoot-outs with comrades and residents of Thokoza since June last year'. He was refused bail but 'magistrate TJ

[contd] Mbekhiseni Khumalo, 2000B, AC/2000/0198, http://www.doj.gov.za/trc/decisions/am00b.htm

[73] TRC Amnesty Hearing, Themba Stephen Zimu.
[74] TRC Amnesty Decisions, Thembu Zima, Thulani Tsotetsi, Mzwake Khumalo, Mbekhiseni Khumalo, 2000B, AC/2000/0198, http://www.doj.gov.za/trc/decisions/am00b.htm
[75] Sithole Report, pp. 18–26.
[76] University of Witwatersrand Historical Papers, IBIIR TRC, Section 29 Hearing, 'In Camera', 'Khumalo Gang', AG2543, A13, p. 430.
[77] TRC Amnesty Hearing, Nicholas Zwile Chamane.
[78] University of Witwatersrand Historical Papers, IBIIR, Memorandum on the Activities of Mbhekisini Khumalo, 24 February 1993, AG 2543 3.1-3.42.

Green ordered that the Khumalo house in Mdakane Street, Thokoza should be placed under police guard while he remained in custody'.[79] SDU member Sipho Ngubane stated that Khumalo was on intimate terms with the locals at Thokoza police station. Ngubane related the story of his arrest following a conflict with Khumalo's people:

> When I got to the Thokoza Police Station, the policemen that we got there were clearly working hand in hand and collaborating with the Khumalo gang. Khumalo was prancing around, walking up and down as if he owned the place and he knew the people. They took me to the back of the police station. You go past the charge office, and I was put into some cells in there. I was never asked any questions. Whilst I was still in the charge office, I heard Khumalo telling the police that, 'These dogs need to be killed' and he would come back at 1:00 a.m. to pick us up to go and kill us. So they took us into these cells. I think we were awaiting our death under the hand of Khumalo. Khumalo was back within [thirty] minutes of having left us there. He had a box with him which had Hunters Gold [alcoholic cider] inside, or cans of Hunters Gold. He had brought some alcoholic beverages to the policemen who were at the charge office.

Fortunately for Ngubane he was released due to the intervention of an uncle who was a kinsman of one of the resident officers. 'That is how I was able to be taken out of that cell at about 8:00p.m., because my uncle, who's a Tshabalala, had spoken to that policeman who is also a Tshabalala.'[80] The case of the Khumalo gang speaks to the complexities of the politicised violence in Thokoza. Khumalo did not start out as a gangster, but a personal affair triggered his involvement in the larger conflict, which in turn presented opportunities for profiteering. For its part, the IFP was quick to welcome an armed cohort to assist in the war with comrades and had no qualms about allowing the Khumalo gang free rein to plunder the townships. Unlike Kheswa, Khumalo's police connections enabled him to survive the conflict.

SDUs and Crime
On the ANC side, SDU and MK criminality was an ongoing problem. At the beginning of the conflict, before firearms were readily available, some SDUs borrowed weapons from criminals to fight the IFP and police. This largesse did not come without conditions. Phenduka section Commander Victor Mngomezulu explains:

> And in Tambo and Slovo, we didn't have much guns. And since we know that the parents, most of them were running away, some of them were in Spruitview and other things. So the money was not there to buy the guns and other things. So before we have people that were gangsters, we used

[79] IBIIR Monthly Report, March 1993, p. 32.
[80] TRC Amnesty Hearing, Sipho Steven Ngubane.

to go and borrow the guns from them. They were from – in our section, for example, like Kapas Gang. We go there and then they borrow us the guns, then we can fight. Sometimes they even ask our guns to do their things and we have no choice because they give their guns to us to defend.[81]

Mngomezulu added that his members would also acquire funds to purchase weapons by robbing and killing known IFP people. 'We identified the guys that are having money from the IFP ... so we will know that at this time this guy will come from this direction to that direction. Even tomorrow, he will come at this direction ... So we shoot them.' He estimates that his unit targeted and killed fifteen IFP supporters in this manner.[82]

The *Weekly Mail* devoted several stories to the criminal excesses of SDUs in 1992. The paper reported that 'some of these out-of-control cells operate in much the same way as township gangs to impose personal power and fiefdoms over areas they live in – except that they use the name of Umkhonto we Sizwe and the prestige of being former freedom fighters to legitimate their activities'.[83] It also observed that ANC efforts to control SDUs and MK cadres 'have failed dismally'.[84] Even the IBIIR, which was generally sympathetic to the ANC, criticised the movement for failing to take action against rebellious SDUs.[85] ANC officials stated that they were 'alarmed that certain individuals, who claim allegiance to the ANC and its allies, are acting completely outside the mandate and policies of these organisations'.[86] In Sasha Gear's study of challenges facing ex-combatants in South Africa, former Thokoza SDU members claimed that some groups were forced to commit crimes to fulfil their role as community defenders:

> According to their reports, SDUs in some sections of the township were more reliant on crime than others. The necessity for members to use crime for financing SDU activities largely depended on the composition of the respective community during the violence. In some sections community members were able to finance SDUs through donations. In others, SDU members were left on their own to defend the properties when others had fled the violence. Especially in the latter scenario, SDUs resorted to crime to feed and arm themselves.[87]

[81] Missing Voices Project, Interview no. 1 with Victor Mngomezulu, SDU Commander, Phenduka section.
[82] Missing Voices Project, Interview no. 1 with Victor Mngomezulu, SDU Commander, Phenduka section.
[83] *Weekly Mail*, 8–14 May 1992.
[84] *Weekly Mail*, 5–11 June 1992.
[85] IBIIR Monthly Report, December 1993/January 1994.
[86] *Weekly Mail*, 15–22 May 1992.
[87] Sasha Gear, 'Wishing Us Away: Challenges Facing Ex-Combatants in the "New" South Africa', Violence and Transition series, vol. 8 (Centre for the Study of Violence and Reconciliation, Johannesburg, 2002), Violence and Crime section, p. 29.

A former SDU member who contemplated criminality explains:

> Me and my friend we once took the guns with us to school to try and rob other people ... our commander used to tell us that we must not do that, but the situation we would find ourselves in sometimes it would force us to think along those lines because we would find ourselves without money. You know the money from the community was not that much and we had to do many things, and most of us we were smoking and we did need money especially on holidays.[88]

An MK veteran made a similar observation regarding returned cadres who resorted to crime: 'The problem of MK banditry is linked to the material insecurity that exiles face upon their return to the country.'[89]

In January 1994, the IBIIR recommended that SDUs on the East Rand be phased out. After describing a series of executions ascribed to SDU members, the IBIIR stated that terrified communities felt helpless to do anything about the SDU scourge:

> A cloak of silence exists when it comes to exposing the illegal activities of SDUs. Despite a general objection by residents to SDUs anarchy and violence and the desire for them to be held accountable and brought back under community control, many are too afraid to say anything for fear of risking their own lives.[90]

The problem the ANC faced was its dependence on SDUs not only as front line combatants in the conflict with Inkatha, but as a critical component of its on-the-ground political presence in embattled communities. Recall Robert McBride's claim that SDU successes against IFP hostel dwellers in Katlehong were instrumental in building a strong ANC branch in the township. The ANC's Peace Desk judged that, 'If it wasn't because of the SDU's *[sic]*, the ANC would long have been crushed out, in many townships today. The life line of the organization is in the hands of the SDU's *[sic]*.'[91] ANC officials might negotiate with problem units, but they had to tread carefully. In many instances, the ANC lacked the capacity to disarm SDUs and it feared alienating armed groups that could turn against party supporters. Better to negotiate with such groups, exercise patience and try to temper their excesses while keeping them in the ANC camp. The story of the Toaster Gang in Thembisa served as a cautionary tale of comrades-gone-bad who aligned with the IFP. According to the TRC:

---

[88] Interview, Z96, male SDU member, Thokoza, 21 June 2008.
[89] *Weekly Mail*, 29 May–4 June 1992.
[90] IBIIR Monthly Report, December 1993/January 1994, pp. 32–5.
[91] ANC Peace Desk, 'Report to the 4th Regional Conference', p. 16.

The Toaster gang, which was allegedly responsible for considerable violence in the township of Tembisa, consisted largely of former 'comrades' who had been pushed out of the political circle of the ANC. The gang specialised in car hijackings. As the township community began to mobilise against the activities of the gang, it was forced to find a new home. The Vusimuzi hostel offered the ideal refuge, both physically secure and providing the possibility of a new political identity. The gangs' facility for violence was effectively utilised by the Inkatha Freedom Party.[92]

Conclusion

Rand townships had been contested terrain for decades between apartheid security forces, various anti-apartheid groups, criminal gangs and vigilante outfits. The 1980s uprisings and massive state repression in many townships had further eroded the rule of law, and the unbanning of the ANC in 1990 opened the doors for a proliferation of armed conflict. This and the preceding chapter have detailed how the ANC–Inkatha conflict, which had been raging in parts of KZN since the mid-1980s, spread to the Rand; how some ANC-aligned groups clashed with PAC and AZAPO rivals; and how ANC structures fought among themselves for local advantage. Different groups relied on violence to police their own members and resolve disputes with rivals, and criminal opportunists capitalised on the political turmoil. The state's longstanding practice of neglecting civil policing in black areas, twinned with desperate rearguard actions by elements within the security forces to weaken the ANC prior to democratic elections, exacerbated the violence. However, police and military units played very different roles in the unfolding conflicts and the changing political environment shaped security force involvement. The following chapter examines this aspect of transition-era violence.

---

[92] TRC Report, vol. 3, ch. 6, subsect. 93, p. 712, http://sabctrc.saha.org.za/reports/volume3/chapter6/subsection93.htm

4 State Security Forces and Township Conflict

There was one constant in the chaos: the certainty that, wherever murders were committed and for whatever reason, police would be blamed. ... I do not remember visiting a single site of massacre in South Africa – and there were scores of them – where police were not alleged to have been involved. Eyewitnesses veered wildly between obvious fiction and possible fact, and many seemed unable to distinguish between third-hand hearsay and firsthand observation. Certainly, all of them believed police had been involved; far fewer actually had any evidence of it ... Neither I, nor any journalist I know, ever saw policemen fighting alongside Inkatha Party members. But it was never hard to tell which side they were on.[1]

Perhaps the most controversial aspect of transition-era conflict was the differing interpretations of the role that state security forces played in this violence, including the impact of 'third force' elements. The ANC, violence monitoring groups, human rights organisations and segments of the South African and international media consistently painted a picture of military and police working to manipulate the transition to democracy by provoking violence and assisting the IFP in its conflict with the ANC. The government denied the existence of a state-directed third force and maintained that any anti-ANC operations were the work of errant units and individuals acting without government approval. Negotiations to establish a new constitution and agreement on democratic elections proceeded alongside heated exchanges between the government and the ANC over third force allegations and security force partiality.

It is beyond the scope of this study to gauge the extent of security force transgressions or to assess NP responsibility for covert operations. But it provides a ground-level examination of police and military involvement in these conflicts at an unprecedented level of detail. A key finding is the diversity of security force engagement. A Security Branch operative at Vlakplaas, a police officer based at a township station, an SADF soldier rotating through a township posting and an Internal Stability Division (ISD) member working in a conflict zone had disparate roles and experiences. This occupational difference was

[1] Patti Waldmeir, *Anatomy of a Miracle: The End of Apartheid and the Birth of the New South Africa* (W.W. Norton & Co., New York, 1997), p. 180.

further complicated by the race of security force members, their political perspectives and the rapidly shifting political atmosphere. Many township residents, especially ANC supporters, believe that white police backed the IFP. The ISD provided the sharp edge of township policing in the areas most affected by politicised violence, and these units were predominantly white. ISD veterans deny that they assisted the IFP in any way but acknowledge that their relationships with the township communities they policed were often contentious and that they were effectively at war with the SDUs. Vlakplaas and other covert units that actively supported the IFP employed black police and soldiers, including turned ANC and PAC militants known as 'askaris', but their leadership was entirely white. By contrast, most township police, including some station commanders by this period, were black and the SADF deployed many black soldiers on township duty, especially in the later stages of the conflict. Black police serving in the townships had often been targets for anti-apartheid militants through the 1980s, but the prospect of an ANC government emboldened some black officers to support ANC-affiliated groups more openly after 1990. This, along with their vulnerability to IFP attacks and SDU retribution in some communities, contributed to their collaboration with SDUs in the fight against the IFP. Both IFP and ANC followers in Thokoza and Katlehong stated that SADF soldiers tended to favour the ANC and sometimes even worked with SDUs against IFP militants. Media reports indicate similar situations in other Rand townships. While political allegiances and biased conduct were not reducible to the race of security force personnel or any other single factor, different security forces were confronted with a fluid political environment that introduced opportunities and constraints.

Political change and security forces

The long history of animosity between the security forces and the ANC, coupled with decades of racist, oppressive policing undoubtedly influenced security force actions in the transition era. White South Africans and the security forces in particular, had been conditioned by relentless government propaganda to accept that the ANC, abetted by the communist powers, constituted the foremost danger to white South Africa. It was unrealistic to expect that all soldiers and police would suddenly embrace the notion of impartiality once the ANC was unbanned. Commissioner of Police Johan Van der Merwe's reflection indicates police dissatisfaction with political leadership and the ANC's standing:

De Klerk had no insight into the kind of battle the security forces had to wage. The ANC refused to renounce violence and to reveal its arms caches all over the country. We were expected to expose the underground activities of the ANC but at the same time treat it as the government's equals.[2]

As the transition era progressed, however, the government was forced to rein in security force units engaged in covert operations against the ANC and to make concessions to its primary negotiating partner on some security issues.

The ANC persistently condemned the NP, both at home and abroad, for sponsoring township violence, and the government was under great pressure to demonstrate that this was not the case. President F.W. de Klerk claimed that the ANC slandered the security forces to score political points and maintained that any covert operations were the work of outliers rather than a key pillar of a government orchestrated strategy to weaken the ANC prior to elections. His relationship with the security forces has been the subject of much scrutiny, but regardless of the extent of his awareness of and approval for covert operations, the pressures of the negotiation process compelled de Klerk to act against high-ranking police and military officers suspected of continuing underground campaigns against the ANC. The NP had staked its future on a successful political settlement and in September 1992, following the Boipatong and Bisho[3] massacres that threatened to derail negotiations, the government and the ANC signed a Record of Understanding that committed both parties to bilateral negotiations to establish a new constitution and a framework and date for elections. Ellis outlined de Klerk's predicament:

> So far had his authority diminished that he now needed the ANC, and particularly the personal support of Mandela, to support the writ of the state and to prevent a slide into anarchy or even civil war. But to secure Mandela's support required a fundamental change in National Party strategy, which had previously been based on the notion of eroding the ANC's power and building an alliance with Inkatha. After the Bisho massacre, the government's whole political strategy was comprehensively and rapidly switched. On 26 September 1992, the National Party and the ANC signed a Memorandum of Understanding which implicitly confined Inkatha to the margins.[4]

In December 1992, in the wake of a de Klerk-initiated investigation, the State President dismissed twenty-three generals suspected of having

---

[2] Giliomee, *The Last Afrikaner Leaders*, p. 307.
[3] The Bisho massacre took place in the Ciskei homeland on 7 September 1992, when an ANC march to force the resignation of military leader Brigadier Oupa Gqozo, who refused to allow the ANC to campaign in Ciskei, was fired on by Ciskei Defence Force soldiers. Twenty-eight marchers were killed.
[4] Ellis, 'South Africa's Third Force', p. 290.

a hand in unapproved clandestine operations: 'de Klerk had now hitched the National Party to the ANC and was demonstrating his determination to act against covert units which had constituted the Third Force and which had until now been making war on the ANC'.[5] The Goldstone Commission uncovered damning evidence of illegal, covert activities principally by Vlakplaas and Military Intelligence. As a result, Vlakplaas was closed in 1993 and it became increasingly difficult for covert operators to persist with their campaigns. With the establishment of the Transitional Executive Council (TEC) – and its Sub-Councils on law and order, stability and security, intelligence and defence – multi-party oversight was extended into these areas, further restricting the opportunities for illegal operations. The workings of the TEC also forced the government to make important concessions such as the disbanding of the notorious 32 Battalion, the withdrawal of the ISD from East Rand townships and its replacement with the National Peacekeeping Force (NPKF). The ANC promoted all these developments, and none of them would have been conceivable prior to the transition period.

Police, journalists and violence monitors also noted the local impacts of a changing political environment. The National Peace Accord, for all its limitations, created local peace committees, which liaised with police and military representatives. These representatives at least paid lip service to the idea of working with the communities they policed and could not completely ignore the concerns raised in these forums. Political party and community representatives, and Peace Accord officials, were sometimes able to get the police and military to work with them to address security issues. David Storey describes how, when he received information that an attack was being planned, such co-operation could reduce the levels of violence:

> I would talk to the police and the army and sit down and work out an operational plan with them and they would prioritise that area so that if a group of SDU guys show up and they see three armoured vehicles in that area they would turn around and go home. They would be pissed off and they may go somewhere else but that particular event which may have led to or sparked something else was dealt with effectively.[6]

Despite Phola Park's fractious relationship with the security forces, its leadership was still able to negotiate with the police:

> In 1991 the Phola Park Residents' Committee began a series of peace meetings with the Riot Unit [ISD] and the South African Defence Force. ... Riot Unit representatives agreed that policemen should wear name tags and paint identification numbers on all the vehicles. A system was devised

---

[5] Ellis, 'South Africa's Third Force', p. 290.
[6] Interview, David Storey, Johannesburg, 26 May 2006.

whereby police vehicles would check at the Residents' Committee office on their way in or out of Phola Park. Brigadier Venter, who shook hands on the deal was enthusiastic. 'We're inventing community policing for the rest of South Africa ... Solving problems together,' beamed Venter.[7]

Even though this agreement did not last, it indicates the degree to which police could not impose their will and act with impunity to the same extent as they had done in the past. Specific Peace Accord provisions addressed police conduct when engaging with crowds, including illegal gatherings, and it was agreed that, even in the face of unruly crowds, 'the least degree of force should be used' and rather, 'persuasion, advice and warnings should be used to secure co-operation, compliance with the law and the restoration of order'.[8] Several ISD veterans reported that the policing climate changed in the transition years. They were subjected to increased oversight and required to exercise greater restraint when carrying out their duties. 'After 1990 when Mandela was released, and the ANC was unbanned ... we were in the same role, but we were closely monitored. They scrutinised every move that we made because now all these political guys were walking around, Inkatha on the one hand and ANC on the other hand.'[9] As the transition period unfolded, the ISD was instructed to take a less confrontational approach to crowd control:

> In the beginning of the '90s with the ANC you had a sense that things were working, and you could feel that the sense was coming from the top down where they do gatherings you won't break them up anymore. You could feel the politics were changing. You didn't just go out there and give them three minutes to disperse. That was earlier in the 80s, but in [the transition period] that didn't happen.[10]

This is not to suggest that security force abuses and support for Inkatha disappeared, for they clearly did not, only that the move towards democracy introduced new conditions to which different security force units were required to adapt.

Township police

Vulnerabilities
Black police, who made up the majority of officers stationed in townships, had been in a difficult position for decades. Many township resi-

---

[7] Reed, *Beloved Country*, pp. 73–4.
[8] Julian Brown, *South Africa's Insurgent Citizens* (Jacana Media, Johannesburg, 2016), p. 110.
[9] Interview, Hein Kilian, Unit 6 Commanding Officer, 2017.
[10] Interview, ISD6, Unit 6, 2017.

dents viewed them as sell-outs to the white government, a sentiment that intensified during the 1980s unrest when militants often targeted black officers. In the war-torn townships of the 1990s, their situation was even more complex; they were not equipped to handle this scale of conflict and, as township residents themselves, many black police were caught up in the ANC–IFP violence. The long-term neglect of township policing infrastructure had concentrated police resources in white areas, and this left no option but for specialised units unconnected to township police – the ISD supplemented by the SADF – to assume primary responsibility for suppressing civil conflicts and violence. It became increasingly dangerous for regular police to patrol in many areas and, in the worst, township officers were effectively confined to their stations. An SAP officer based in Thokoza commented that, shortly after the violence began in 1990, 'we couldn't drive with these unprotected vehicles in the township and then the only thing that we were doing, we would only go and report on duty, sit at the police station to assist those who are coming in'.[11] ISD veteran Nick Howarth noted that, although the Thokoza police station was sometimes deserted, he did not blame the local SAP. 'If I were them I would also have closed it and gone home. It was war out there and they were only equipped with soft-skinned Toyoya Hilux 1800 bakkies [pick-up trucks] without bullet proofing.'[12] When local police did venture out of the station they were easy targets for well-armed militants, and they were also exposed in their homes. A Katlehong police officer describes their predicament:

> All situations were difficult, but for me when I was on duty I felt vulnerable because I had to wear that police uniform and automatically I would be the enemy of everyone, both township people and the hostel people and I knew that I could be killed. That is why we would always be in a group. We could not go in pairs we really had to be a group, at least that way we could protect each other. It was difficult because we were perceived as informers by some members of the community, but those who knew us defended us ... We really had to show our loyalty to earn that trust and obviously you could not convince everybody, that is why many police houses were burnt down.[13]

According to an ISD officer, it was impossible for regular police to function in the East Rand's polarised conflict zones:

---

[11] Missing Voices Project, Interview no. 18 with Inspector Charles Dlamini, SAP Thokoza.
[12] Nick Howarth, *War in Peace: The Truth about the South African Police's East Rand Riot Unit, 1986–1994* (Galago Books, Johannesburg, 2012), p. 101.
[13] Interview, Z85, male police officer, Katlehong, 2006.

There was no ways they could patrol the streets, no ways they could do it unless they were full-on ANC. They would have been killed instantly. That said, if they were ANC they wouldn't have been able to go anywhere near the hostels. They just couldn't do their job properly. I mean they would open up every now and then and then things would blow up and they would be out again. I felt for them. I wouldn't want to have to do that job ... And these guys just wouldn't come in to work and I can't blame them. I mean one morning we found a burnt-out police vehicle in Mpiki Street in Katlehong so we called the police station, but no one answered. Drove around the area and found a guy down by the bottom, by the *spruit* [stream] and there was one policeman walking dragging his mate who he had been handcuffed to and they were both naked. The one was dead, and he'd just dragged him out of this *vlei* [marsh]. He was also left for dead ... The guys who'd done that to them, they were SDUs. That's the kind of thing that happened to township police when they were working.[14]

Working for a white-controlled organisation contributed to the insecurity faced by black police. In the words of a Soweto officer, 'People hate us because there are things we do on the orders of our white superiors who, at the end of the day, go back to their homes and leave us here alone.'[15] A municipal police officer from Katlehong explained,

> The violence was terrible and ... we were in a very difficult position because people expected us to protect them but we could not as our hands were tied. We were getting orders and could not do otherwise ... We really lived in fear because we could easily be targets as we were employed by the government which was perceived as perpetuating the violence and taking sides ... I was always worried about my safety and the safety of my family.[16]

The IBIIR also recorded that 'Black policemen are angry that they are being targeted for assassination in the townships because of the actions of their white seniors.'[17]

The deployment of the ISD was sometimes a direct response to the targeting of local police. This was the case in Alexandra in 1993:

> Police have withdrawn their normal patrols in Alexandra township, north of Johannesburg, after the murder of its members this month. Police spokesman Colonel David Bruce said as a result of the four murders the SAP would not patrol the township in normal police vehicles or on foot until the danger to policemen had passed ... Instead, the Alexandra police would have to rely on the Internal Stability Division to maintain a policing visibility and escort them on duty. 'Until the Alexandra community accepts its responsibility regarding support and protection of the police, the SAP

---

[14] Interview, ISD1, Unit 6, 2015.
[15] *Weekly Mail*, 17–23 July 1992.
[16] Interview, Z85, male police officer, Katlehong, 2006.
[17] University of the Witwatersrand Historical Papers, IBIIR, 'Memoranda on Reef Violence', 16 August 1993, AG2544 3.3-3.7.

will not be able to render an effective and efficient policing service to that community.'[18]

The ANC took a different view, alleging that black police were deliberately sidelined from having any role in investigating incidents of politicised violence, which were the sole purview of white-led units. As a result, 'The local black police are seen as having no authority and lacking the power to act properly as a police force.'[19] Not surprisingly, few residents looked to the local SAP for assistance in settings where the ISD and SADF were the dominant security force presence. An NGO report commented on the ineffectiveness of local policing in Thokoza: 'In Phenduka [section] widespread intimidation took place in broad daylight. Loudhailers within earshot of the Thokoza Police Station called for the expulsion of non-IFP members from the area. People were shot dead and houses burnt and looted within a stone's throw of the Thokoza Police Station.'[20] In 1993, the IBIIR characterised the Thokoza station as 'totally inadequate. There is no investigative wing. The police station is powerless. More often than not their telephone is not working. If one is fortunate to get through there is a lack of transport and they are unable to come to your rescue.'[21] A few months later, also referring to Thokoza, *The Star* declared,

> Something has gone badly wrong when a police station serving 230,000 people crammed into a 7 sq km stretch of township badland receives fewer than [thirteen] criminal complaints a day. ... [This] reflects the extent to which routine contact between township dwellers and the police takes place through armoured vehicles of the unrest-fighting Internal Stability Division (ISD), which operates independently of the local police.[22]

Allegiances
Township police navigated the challenges of the transition period according to political allegiances, safety considerations, community and ethnic loyalties and the need to keep their jobs. Many retreated as far as possible from involvement in politicised violence beyond adherence to orders, while others were active in a variety of ways. Given the historically antagonistic relationship between the SAP and

---

[18] *The Citizen*, 27 December 1993.
[19] University of Witwatersrand Historical Papers, *Memoranda on the Ongoing Violence and the Failure by the Security Forces to Prevent the Violence, Protect Residents and Bring the Perpetrators of the Violence to Justice*, Submitted on Behalf of the ANC (PWV), ANC (Vaal) and Vaal Council of Churches (n.d.), Submission to the Goldstone Commission, p. 13, http://www.historicalpapers.wits.ac.za/inventories/inv_pdfo/AK2672/AK2672-B14-2-001-jpeg.pdf
[20] IBIIR/Peace Action, *Before we were good friends*, p. 28.
[21] University of the Witwatersrand Historical Papers, IBIIR Thokoza, 'Briefing on the Violence in Thokoza since 22 May 1993', AG2543 C26.
[22] *The Star* 22 January 1994.

black South Africans, especially in urban areas, it is not surprising that many township and hostel residents continued to view police with suspicion and hostility. At the same time, some township respondents demonstrated an awareness of the plight of black police whose agency was limited due to their positions at the lower end of the SAP hierarchy. 'Black police would try to protect us and they would give us some tips on how to defend ourselves but they did not have power because they were controlled by Afrikaners.'[23] With the prospect of an ANC victory in the transition period, some black police who identified with the liberation struggle assisted ANC supporters and specifically the SDUs through the provision of guns, ammunition and intelligence.[24] A Thokoza IFP official certainly believed this to be the case, and not just in terms of street level officers: 'when time goes on some top ranking commanders within the police they could realise that the ANC would be in power and they wanted to be friends with them so they could take care of themselves. And the victims were us.'[25] The changing trajectory of police involvement during these years was described by a Katlehong resident: 'There were police that understood the struggle and ... in the 90s there were police who risked their jobs and supported the township people. I think they were tired of what was happening, and they did not want to watch their people dying. Some even helped us with organising weapons.'[26] An SDU member adds, 'We cannot put police under one umbrella. There were police that were fighting us, and there were police that were helping us ... The relationship was complicated, but the police that we worked with we worked with them very well.'[27] For some officers, safety considerations probably trumped professional obligations and political leanings. In many areas SDUs were the foremost armed power and, for police living in these townships, working with SDUs offered the best opportunity to secure their own welfare and that of their families. Acting against SDUs could put them in jeopardy of retaliation. Furthermore, Inkatha attackers did not discriminate and it was in the best interests of police living close to the hostels to assist in community defence. In Katlehong's Siluma View section,

> We had a lot of policemen and they really helped us a lot. They had access to all sides, so they could take guns from the hostel people and tell us that it was safe to attack them. They also needed to protect their families and

[23] Interview, Z69, female resident, Katlehong, 26 May 2007.
[24] See for example, Missing Voices Project, Interview no. 20 with Moses 'Bla' Mduduzi Khubeka, SDU Commander, Phenduka section; TRC Amnesty Hearing, Thomazile Eric Mhlauli.
[25] Interview, female IFP official, Johannesburg, 21 June 2004.
[26] Interview, Z60, male resident, Katlehong, 2006.
[27] Interview, Z90, male SDU member, Katlehong, 2006.

houses, and that is why we were not that much affected in this section compared to other sections, because we had many policemen who were part of the community.[28]

For many residents, policing was overtly racial. An SDU member explains:

> There were police that were on our side, especially from the township, while there were police that were our enemy, and those were white police. So, the relationship was complicated in the sense that police were not the same, we worked with some police and we worked against some police. What was sad was that black police were juniors and white police were senior and they would give those black police orders to kill us and sometimes they would have to obey those orders because it was part of their job, but secretly those that were on our side would come and give us tips.[29]

Ethnic partisanship also came into play at times. Although officers at the Thokoza police station were criticised for their passivity in the face of township violence, it seems that in the conflict's initial stages they played a leading role in a major assault. Both ANC and IFP respondents remember Xhosa police accompanying Phola Park militants in a 1990 attack against a Thokoza hostel. Hostel residents interviewed by Lauren Segal described this event in detail, summarised here by Reed:

> Xhosa policemen sympathetic to their clansmen in Phola Park were a key part of that night's operation. They entered Mshayazafe [hostel] early in the evening and told the hostel dwellers that the police were planning a raid that night. They advised them to stash their armaments ... Meanwhile the war party from Phola Park, numbering [one hundred] men, was joined by an additional [fifty] men from Tokoza township. They were accompanied by Xhosa-speaking policemen, who were in charge of the night shift while their Zulu speaking colleagues were off duty ... Hostel-dwellers were awoken by automatic gunfire aimed into their rooms from the outside windows. As they fled into the hostel yard they were cut down by gunmen who had entered the hostel ... The Xhosa-speaking policemen were fighting shoulder to shoulder with the Xhosa blanket men, gunning down the hostel residents in the yard.[30]

---

[28] Interview, Z86, male resident, Katlehong, 2006.
[29] Interview, Z57, male SDU member, Katlehong, 2006.
[30] Reed, *Beloved Country*, p. 55. Lauren Segal's informants in 'Human Face of Violence' and others reported that this attack was on the adjacent hostel, Madala. As Mshayazafe and Madala are part of the same complex, the confusion is understandable. The general account of this attack is corroborated in interviews conducted for this study, as well as in *The Heart of Hope: South Africa's Transition from Apartheid to Democracy*, O'Malley Interviews 1985–2005, 'Interview with Thokoza Hostel Residents', 18 December 1990, https://www.nelsonmandela.org/omalley/index.php/site/q/03lv00017/04lv00344/05lv00389/06lv00507.htm

The fighting lasted until early morning when Zulu officers reported for duty and, suspicious at the absence of their Xhosa colleagues, decided to check the hostels. A hostel dweller claimed that, 'The Zulu police took us out of our rooms to go and fight ... The couldn't let us be butchered by Xhosa policemen and their brothers.'[31] Reports of police partiality focus primarily on the race of police officers, the activities of specialised units like the ISD and general complaints about police preference for the IFP, but ethnic policing may have been more widespread than generally assumed. A Zulu resident of Thokoza's Madala Hostel provided his perspective:

> To be honest with you police were divided, and I understand why. I would do exactly what the police people did. I left the township and stayed here because I was a Zulu, they say blood is thicker than water. So, because police did not constitute one ethnic group, division becomes normal when there is a war. There were police that were on our side and some were on the other side.[32]

Internal Stability Division

The ISD was the most recent manifestation of the riot units dating from 1980 that were formed to deal with political 'unrest'. Janine Rauch and David Storey provide the following characterisation:

> The units were para-military in nature (by way of training, operational understanding and culture), and brutal in the enforcement of bans on political protest. They operated within a policy paradigm that accepted and supported the lethal use of force. This, combined with the authorities' complete intolerance for protest action, meant that they frequently used maximum force.[33]

In response to the rising tide of violence the government announced the formation of the ISD in 1991 as 'a specialized public order component separate from the rest of the SAP'.[34] By 1994 there were forty ISD units stationed throughout South Africa with some seven thousand members. Unit 6 was responsible for fourteen East Rand townships, including Katlehong and Thokoza. It was based in Dunnottar (between Nigel and Springs) but had several satellite stations in different townships. When the ANC–IFP conflict began in earnest in mid-1990,

[31] Segal, 'Human Face of Violence', p. 228.
[32] Interview, Z25, male resident, Madala Hostel, 8 August 2006.
[33] Janine Rauch and David Storey, 'The Policing of Public Gatherings and Demonstrations in South Africa, 1960–1994' (Centre for the Study of Violence and Reconciliation, Johannesburg, 1998), http://www.csvr.org.za/wits/papers/papjrds.htm
[34] Rauch and Storey, 'The Policing of Public Gatherings'.

Unit 6 had approximately two hundred regular members, most of whom were white, augmented by black constables known as 'specials' who did not receive the same training and were equipped only with shotguns. Unit 6 was occasionally backed up by Unit 19, a mobile reaction unit based in Pretoria that was dispatched to different hotspots around the country. In addition various SADF outfits, including 32 Battalion, which had achieved notoriety fighting in Namibia and Angola, and other ISD Units were temporarily posted to the East Rand to work with Unit 6. Like their predecessors, the ISD was a paramilitary force equipped with armoured vehicles and assault weapons. And, whereas they sometimes worked with SADF patrols and co-operated with SAP units such as Murder and Robbery and Special Branch, they had 'no structural relationship with local police commanders'.[35]

Because riot units had been responsible for suppressing the unrest of the 1980s, they were unpopular in the townships. Township residents were not apt to welcome police who had participated in the sort of operations described by a Unit 19 veteran:

> It was 1988. We were working in Pietermaritzburg at that stage and we got shipped out on the Sunday, it was going to be the first Sunday that we were going to get off in two or three months or something like that. We were really looking forward to that day and then that morning we got the call that we had to go to Kokstad [small town in southern KZN]. They had attacked some of the black policemen the day before and also stoned one of the police vehicles. So, we got shipped out to Kokstad and emotions were high, some guys had made arrangements to see loved ones and it was all cancelled. I'm not saying it justifies it, I'm just trying to create the picture. The guys were despondent. And when we got to Kokstad, it was our job to go into the houses, search people and remove everybody between the ages of fourteen and fifty-five so we could do fingerprinting, police scans and take photos of everybody and start records. And the army put a cordon around the outside and we went in and started searching and halfway through it tensions started flaring up on both sides and a couple of incidences happened and the guys were very rough and were manhandling people. We got the job done and a couple of people ended up in hospital. And that night we called a curfew and said that's it, ten o'clock everybody in their houses, we don't want people on the streets.[36]

The following account, which took place on the eve of the transition period, graphically illustrates why many township residents feared and resented the riot units:

> On the day that Nelson Mandela was released we were at Jan Smuts airport. We were expecting that Mandela was going to come. It was being said in

[35] Rauch and Storey, 'The Policing of Public Gatherings'.
[36] Interview, ISD3, Unit 19, 2017.

the media that he was going to leave from Pollsmoor or wherever it was and come to Jan Smuts. And there were thousands of people waiting. We were there, the riot unit, dog units and other policemen in long rows keeping the people back from the main part of the airport. I was there with my shotgun. I didn't have a whip because I'd lost it, or somebody stole it. And they said, 'Listen, Mandela's not coming.' He'd decided he was going to stay another few days. So, 'You guys need to disperse.' The colonel got on the speaker, 'You need to disperse in five minutes, or we're going to disperse you.' And somebody in the dog unit misinterpreted these words and the dogs went off. The riot unit said, 'Right, we're in.' We went around the dog units and we just started dispersing people and it was all hell breaking loose. I was watching guys, people falling and people getting the shit knocked out of them and I thought, 'Well, I'm losing out on this, what the hell am I going to do?' So, I turned my shotgun around and the first person I saw, 'smack' with the butt end of my shotgun, which broke, the whole butt broke. The person that I hit stumbled and then kept on running. I looked on in amazement. That was my memory of that day. As I say, pure aggression.[37]

Once the ANC was unbanned and the transition period began, the ISD's primary job on the East Rand was to police public gatherings, to search for and confiscate illegal weapons (particularly firearms), to prevent conflicts from erupting and to separate combatants and protect bystanders when violence did occur. ISD personnel and vehicles monitored rallies and marches to maintain public order. Large operations, usually with SADF support, were undertaken to search hostels and informal settlements for weapons. Sometimes, ISD patrols were assigned to hotspots like Phola Park to pre-empt further conflict. The most common aspect of ISD policing, however, was reactive. Every shift, ISD sections would patrol the different townships in armoured vehicles and respond to whatever trouble came up. If major incidents occurred, reinforcements from all over the East Rand would converge to provide backup. Once the ANC–IFP conflict took hold, the ISD also became responsible for the grisly task of collecting the dead. Mortuary vans would not venture into the conflict-ridden townships so picking up corpses was left to the ISD. In Katlehong and Thokoza the body count reached such dimensions that ISD patrols were issued with special trailers to load bodies.

Township Perceptions
Respondents held a range of opinions on the partiality of the SAP, but there was a near consensus on the ISD's political inclinations. From the very beginning of the Rand conflict, the ANC and its supporters complained that police sided with the IFP and as the conflict progressed the ISD were cast as the worst offenders in this regard. A black officer stationed in Thokoza who had previously served with a

[37] Interview, ISD5, Unit 6, 2017.

Plate 3 Police load bodies into a trailer following a night of fighting in Thokoza, 1993 (© Philip Littleton, Getty Images)

riot unit in KZN reported, 'most of the time when we were working our white colleagues would never shoot or fight at the IFP groups but when the ANC comes definitely they were the ones who would be in the forefront and they were happy to shoot'.[38] The IBIIR portrayal of the East Rand ISD echoed the views of many township residents:

> The ISU were regarded as biased and were often accused of operating above the law targeting political, community leaders and particularly members of self-defence units. A number of community leaders and residents claim that the ISU had exacerbated an already violent situation and were not carrying out their primary task of making the East Rand secure from attacks. Consequently, communities relied on SDUs for much of their security, which inevitably led to direct conflict with the ISU.[39]

The IBIIR's criticism of the ISD also noted its reputation for using excessive force: 'It would seem that a particular breed of man is attracted to this unit – one that thirsts for so-called "action" and one that is prepared to shoot and not ask questions.'[40] In high conflict areas ISD patrols worked almost exclusively from armoured vehicles. A local journalist who accompanied an ISD patrol in Katlehong was critical of its drive-and-blast method of policing:

[38] Missing Voices Project, Interview no. 18 with Inspector Charles Dlamini, SAP Thokoza.
[39] University of the Witwatersrand Historical Papers, IBIIR, Memoranda, ISU, SADF and the NPKF, Undated [but almost certainly April 1994], AG2543 3.1-3.42.
[40] IBIIR, 'Reef Violence', p. 5.

I did not feel afraid or vulnerable while I was with the police. The Casspir is wonderful protection. However, I felt deeply troubled; there was too much 'fun', no arrests and little attempt to exercise the law by confiscating dangerous weapons. When police arrived at a clash, with groups fighting or where squatters were attacked, they would fire birdshot, rubber bullets and teargas into the distant crowd, and then hare off to another conflict where they would fire another salvo. They would return to the first scene fifteen minutes later and shoot at any group still gathered there.[41]

The ISD had primary responsibility for patrolling Phola Park and the mistrust on both sides was palpable. After an incident in which four police officers were shot in January 1991, a peace monitor/observer assessed the relationship between residents and the police:

The SAP believed that they had been ambushed. Phola Park residents believed that they had been defending the community. Because any incident takes place within the context of the ongoing dysfunctional relationship, there doesn't seem, to me, to be any objective truth or reality concerning any particular incident. Both sides will build a story around their version of a particular event, and the larger context of a war between the community and the police will remain the same.[42]

Reed also noted the depth of residents' scepticism towards the police:

There were constant rumours of attacks, particularly at weekends. People became paranoid. If the police patrolled the camp, searching for guns, Phola Park concluded that they were being softened up, disarmed in preparation for a Zulu attack. If the police stayed out of Phola Park, the silence grew deafening, and people drew the same conclusion but for the opposite reason: an attack was on the way because the police were leaving the coast clear for the Zulus.[43]

The ISD was excoriated by township residents for its perceived Inkatha bias and its brutality in dealing with township residents. Respondents for this study repeatedly claimed that ISD units sometimes accompanied IFP fighters when they attacked the townships and the ANC insisted that the ISD aggravated township violence. A pronounced animus existed between the ISD and SDUs. When discussing the criminal excesses of some SDUs, a Thokoza resident placed the blame on the ISD: 'There was stability unit, the worst police. They made the youth wild because they were hunting them down like animals. And if they arrested one, we knew he would not live.'[44]

---

[41] *Business Day*, 14 September 1990.
[42] University of the Witwatersrand Historical Papers, IBIIR, 'Report from Davin Bremner to Goldstone Commission', 25 March 1992, C26.
[43] Reed, *Beloved Country*, p. 53.
[44] Interview, T5, male resident, Thokoza, 20 March 2006.

Plate 4 MK leave a message for police in Phola Park, 1990s (by permission of ISD Unit 6)

An NGO report on violence in Thokoza and Katlehong stated that evidence gathered 'gives the distinct impression that the ISU has a clear programme to eliminate members of the self-defence units'.[45] Despite the deadly conflict with the hostels, a Thokoza SDU commander declared, 'The war it was difficult ... but IFP was not strong enough for us. To my knowledge, the IFP was not so strong enough. The people who keep us busy was Stability. It's those people who make the war more difficult.'[46] A veteran from Thokoza confirmed, 'They were here to shoot, they weren't here to stabilise anything. If you see a white man, you know they are coming to attack. None of our members here in this section were killed by IFP, only by ISU.'[47] SDU operators often made specific mention of race when referencing the ISD:

> Although there were police that you could see were doing their job there was this unit called Stability Unit. Those ones their mission was to finish black men. The Stability Unit its job was just to kill us. They would even take our comrades and throw them in the hostel so that they would be killed by IFP people, what kind of police are those?[48]

Another announced, 'I was very scared of the Boers, those people were cruel, the Stability Unit. That was the only thing I was scared of.'[49]

[45] IBIIR/Peace Action, *Before we were good friends*, p. 6.
[46] Missing Voices Project, Interview no. 30 with Dalixolo 'Meneer' Mqubi, SDU Commander, Ext. 2.
[47] Interview, G3, male SDU member, Thokoza, 16 July 2006.
[48] Interview, Z98, male SDU member, Thokoza, 21 June 2008.
[49] Interview, Z93, male SDU member, Katlehong, 2006.

Robert McBride stopped short of claiming that the ISD actively assisted the IFP in armed operations but maintained there was a consistent pattern of partiality: 'If there is an engagement between us and Inkatha and we're getting the upper hand, then [the ISD] would intervene, but if Inkatha was giving us a bit of a hiding they would just stand on the side and allow it to happen.'[50]

ISD assistance during IFP attacks against ANC supporters was never proven but, as noted during the conflict, such rumours thrived 'on the conspicuously easy relationship between police and hostel dwellers'.[51] In contrast to the SADF, which the IFP believed was pro-ANC, IFP spokesperson and Katlehong hostel resident, Jeffrey Sibiya, commented that the ISD, 'have shown greater sympathy for us. They protect us. They recognize us as people'.[52] Many hostel residents confirmed that the ISD was well disposed towards them and several recalled an ISD intervention to stop an SADF assault on Buyafuthi Hostel. 'I remember when the SADF attacked us it was December ... it was Stability Unit that came to our rescue. If it was not for the Stability Unit we would have all died.'[53] The ANC pressured the government at every turn to pull the ISD out of the townships, including a September 1993 call to Kathorus residents: 'Under the slogan "In Defence of Our Lives!", residents of Thokoza, Vosloorus and Katlehong were urged to stay away from work on Monday 2nd September to march on an ISU centre in Vosloorus and to demand the removal of the ISU.'[54] Just as the ANC campaigned for the removal of the ISD, IFP leadership on the Rand praised the neutrality of the ISD and opposed the proposed withdrawal. The ANC prevailed and the ISD was replaced on the East Rand by the SADF at the beginning of February 1994.

Veterans' Accounts
Former members of Unit 6 and Unit 19 describe the ISD's primary task in the transition period as keeping opposing factions from killing each other and clearing the townships of illegal weapons. No matter their support from township residents and political parties, township militants carrying AK47s and other firearms were breaking the law and contributing to violence, and they needed to be dealt with. A veteran's recollection of responding to an incident in Phola Park encapsulates the collective feeling that, 'We were only there to curb the violence.'

[50] Interview, Robert McBride, Johannesburg, 21 June 2006.
[51] Bill Keller, 'Patrolling South Africa's Hardest Beat', *New York Times*, 19 January 1994.
[52] Bill Keller, 'Patrolling South Africa's Hardest Beat'.
[53] Interview, Z10, male resident, Buyafuthi Hostel, 4 July 2006.
[54] Jeffrey, *People's War*, p. 410.

The one night I drove in there and there was a lot of shooting going on and you don't know why they're shooting. Are they getting attacked? Are they shooting each other? You don't know, you just hear the shots. But you go ... There was no question about it. You don't sit back and leave them, that never happened with us. You'll call in and the unit will respond immediately but it will take an hour if not longer because they're sitting out there in Dunnottar and Casspirs are not the fastest vehicles in the world. But you have to go in because it's your job. A lot of people could die if you don't do that. I mean the ANC was ruthless but Inkatha took no prisoners and if they go into a built up area, it's a problem because everybody dies. They didn't ask questions, 'Are you ANC, are you this or that?' Whoever is there dies. They go like a wave through the place.[55]

Without exception, these men contemptuously dismissed allegations that they ever actively supported the IFP. They describe a chaotic environment in which patrols reacted to the conflicts they encountered. A veteran posted at the Katlehong satellite station recalls how his section dealt with major skirmishes:

The only thing they [commanding officers] told us was to prevent the shit from happening. If there's clashes or whatever, get in between them. And if it's tear gas or shooting or whatever you do, just get them apart... Obviously, when the shit hits the fan the unit gets called in and they will reinforce you. But I mean you're driving through this hell and you're alone and you're twenty years old. You can scream on the radio but it's just you and your guys ... You called for help, but until the help gets there you're alone and you deal with it. And then you shoot both sides. There was no, 'I'm choosing the ANC', or anything like that. If I see a guy with a weapon, doesn't matter which side he was, he was done for.[56]

Veterans conceded, however, that their relationships with ANC supporters, especially SDUs, were more antagonistic than those with the IFP and hostel dwellers. ANC 'terrorists' had undertaken an armed struggle against apartheid rule, whereas Inkatha had rejected armed resistance. The riot units that preceded the ISD had been on the front lines suppressing ANC-instigated protests throughout the turbulent 1980s, and the unbanning of the ANC and the onset of political negotiations was a shocking development for many of these officers. Unit 6's commander explained:

It was a hell of a thing to adapt to. I mean, we were hunting them. If you find a guy like Joe Slovo or any of those guys in the streets you would have arrested him, or ten to one even shot him. And all of a sudden, these guys are all walking around in the streets. For us to adapt, it was very difficult. I mean Mandela was sitting next to me once in a Casspir. I picked him up one

[55] Interview, ISD6, Unit 6, 2017.
[56] Interview, ISD6, Unit 6, 2017.

night with his wife. They both sat with me in my Casspir. Here I was riding with this guy who was in my eyes one of the biggest terrorists that ever lived. I was educated to the fact that he was a terrorist and he was sent for life to Robben Island and the same with Tokyo Sexwale and all those guys. They were known enemies to us and now the enemies were walking in the streets. It was a very difficult thing, but we had to adapt to it.[57]

A veteran insisted,

> We would never have assisted Inkatha in any way, but our sympathies swayed that way without a doubt. So, if I caught an Inkatha guy and an ANC guy doing the same thing I probably would have been more lenient on the Inkatha guy because he doesn't want to kill me.[58]

Another added, 'Look, we were definitely anti-ANC and more pro towards Inkatha, but you couldn't trust any of them. I never trusted any of them.'[59] Media reports that the ISD aided Inkatha were intensely frustrating for these men, who labelled such portrayals as 'propaganda' and 'total bullshit'. In Unit 6, 'Our commander carried out the orders that he was given but he never, ever spoke one word against the ANC. The only thing that ever came out during the briefings was to curb the violence – keep them apart as much as we can.'[60] This commander repudiated all allegations of partiality:

> I can tell you in all honesty that we weren't biased, and I can prove my point by all the raids we did on the hostels. We raided those hostels continuously, so if we were biased why would we do that? We raided those hostels on a weekly basis. That must answer anybody's question because if we were biased we would have left them alone in the hostels, so they could do whatever they want with their weapons. And we actually took three layers of barbed wire and cordoned off hostels 4, 5 and 6 [on Khumalo Street]. They were surrounded by barbed wire to prevent them from going out and killing people and coming back. Only the entrances were open and if we were biased towards Inkatha why would we do that? Our job was to maintain peace and if we raided a place and got a lot of weapons that was payment for our effort.[61]

Veterans maintain that conflict followed the course it did because hostel dwellers respected them, whereas the SDUs and ANC supporters were confrontational. These accounts often differentiate between the compliance of IFP supporters versus aggressive ANC 'mobs'.

---

[57] Interview, Hein Kilian, Unit 6 Commanding Officer, 2017.
[58] Interview, ISD1, Unit 6, 2015.
[59] Interview, ISD3, Unit 19, 2017.
[60] Interview, ISD6, Unit 6, 2017.
[61] Interview, Hein Kilian, Unit 6 Commanding Officer, 2017.

> The Inkatha guys were more disciplined. You could go and speak to them. They were disciplined. I mean I walked into a hostel at Vosloorus. I had to leave my weapon there. My guys were standing outside the hostel on the Casspirs. I walked in there like this [hands out to the side] all the Zulus were there, and the *induna* was there and when he spoke they all sat down, and you could hear a pin drop. And I went to him and I told him this is who I am, this is what's happening. 'If I pick up one more body outside this hostel, I'm going to close down this place. Nobody will come out and nobody will get in. You will starve in here. I don't want any more bodies.' Because every day we picked up bodies outside the hostel. And the *induna* listened, and he spoke to the people and they never moved, they never said anything, and I walked out of there without my weapon. I felt like Piet Retief, really. But that was the end of it, we never picked up bodies outside that hostel again.[62]

In some cases, these assessments were tied to ethnic characterisations:

> Zulus are far more disciplined as far as I'm concerned than any other race and this we learned from experience. ... the head *induna* would say something, and those guys would just sit now. And they don't go [makes a prolonged whining sound] like the Xhosas or Sothos where you can't get a flippin word in. This oke speaks and if they don't heel he hits them with a knobkerrie. This is just how they work. Naturally we related because we said we're getting somewhere with them. When you talk to them and say, 'listen you okes can't do it' and they say 'ja, but these okes attacked us and whatever' and we say 'sorry, just don't do it, go home'. They did go home and would do things at their own places but at that moment they listened. So, we felt like we were getting somewhere. It was obviously a different story with the ANC, the Xhosas, the SDUs, they would just not fricking listen, they would taunt you. And we would go, 'No, no, no, you don't do that, you don't go there because now you're going to pick up trouble.'[63]

When trouble arrived, the ISD had a decisive edge: 'We were well trained, and we were well protected in the vehicles. The Casspirs were our saving grace.'[64]

> If you wanted to engage us, you got trouble. We were issued with birdshot for our shotguns, but we had R1s, we had LMGs, we had uzis, we had H & Ks, we were armed to the teeth. And some of them you left in the vehicle, some you took. You always took a backup, your 9 mil was the backup of the backup. So, you'd have a shotgun and sharp point ammunition or shotgun and R1 or a shotgun and an uzi, and a shotgun and an H&K or a shotgun and an LMG.[65]

[62] Interview, Hein Kilian, Unit 6 Commanding Officer, 2017.
[63] Interview, ISD2, Unit 6, 2015.
[64] Interview, ISD6, Unit 6, 2017.
[65] Interview, ISD2, Unit 6, 2015.

Despite these advantages, ISD patrols were often attacked and veterans related that these assaults came almost exclusively from ANC-controlled areas. This was another critical difference in their relationships with the IFP and ANC. 'You've got four thousand Inkatha guys marching down Khumalo Street ... but they would never shoot at us. I could climb out at night between thousands of them to move to another vehicle. And they would do nothing. Do that at Phola Park and you would be dead.'[66] Patrols through ANC territory invited a different response:

> Every night, every night they would shoot at us and I'm not talking about just one shot. I mean they would let rip at you. In the early days it wasn't that often but I'm talking the later days when all you would hear was ping, ping, ping and you hear the AK shooting. We had petrol bombs and grenades thrown at us. We had hatches, a porthole that opened and that didn't close properly so that if a grenade goes off that blast could come through that little gap next to where the guy sits, and it could blast shrapnel in there. And there were times when they put wires across the road. Most of the Casspirs had a wire cutter but we received the old Koevoet [SAP paramilitary force that operated in Namibia] Casspirs and they were made for bush warfare, so they didn't have the wire cutters and they would stretch wires across the road so at night if a guy sits on top it can take him out.[67]

These veterans were scornful of accusations that ISD patrols hunted down SDUs, stressing that they only responded to SDU attacks:

> I used my firearm only when I was being shot at or when I was having petrol bombs thrown at me and I was a commander, so I made sure the guys in my section did the same thing. I'll tell you I was married with children and I didn't need that kind of shit, I didn't need that legal stuff in my life and I wouldn't have wanted to do it anyway. There would have been no way we would have attacked a group of people just because we felt they were going to attack us. It was always the other way around. We were never gunning for anybody.[68]

Another veteran insisted that their animosity towards SDUs and the ANC was driven primarily by SDU attacks on ISD patrols:

> Did you have a hate towards the ANC? I mean, of course because they're shooting at you every night but I'm not going to go out there and hunt and kill people unless they're shooting at me. Not because they're wearing a T-shirt. If you have a gun in your hand I'm going to take you down, but not

---

[66] Interview, ISD6, Unit 6, 2017.
[67] Interview, ISD6, Unit 6, 2017.
[68] Interview, ISD1, Unit 6, 2015.

because you're wearing a T-shirt. I have no problems with that. Nobody had a problem with that.[69]

The ISD sometimes confronted IFP fighters but the relationship was far less antagonistic:

> We would sometime go days without end without sleeping so we'd just catch a bit of a nap whenever we could and the best place to catch a nap was inside the hostels. You'd go and park your vehicle inside the hostels because you knew you weren't going to be attacked.[70]

The ISD was the primary force responsible for pacifying conflict-ridden townships, and there is a pervasive sense in veterans' recollections of being under-resourced and overwhelmed by the demands of the job. Part of the issue for Unit 6 was the number of widely dispersed townships they were required to police:

> All the units didn't have all the action we had. We were the burning point in the country for many years. This was the pot that boiled all the time because we had fourteen townships and you sit there with Katlehong, Thokoza, Vosloorus and then KwaThema, Tsakane, Duduza and then Thembisa and Daveyton and they're all big townships and they're all under the East Rand. The East Rand had this bulk of townships and even small places like Balfour and Leandra and Ratanda in Heidelberg. They all had major problems at some stage. That's what made Unit 6 unique compared to other units, that had one or two townships when we had fourteen. So, once you get things under control in Katlehong and Thokoza the next minute you've got problems in Thembisa, the next minute you've got problems in KwaThema, Tsakane, Duduza.[71]

To compound the difficulties of being responsible for multiple townships spread over a substantial area, 'We didn't have the equipment we needed, and we didn't have the personnel we needed. I don't know why because we were the busiest unit in the country and we were probably the most understaffed and under-equipped.'[72] At times, the sheer scale of the violence was too much for the ISD patrols to handle:

> In Khumalo Street, there was a big *veldt* [open field] between Phola Park and the other hostels after they demolished the one hostel [Khalanyoni] and there they would clash. There was nothing you could do. You'd just shoot tear gas as much as you can to try to get these people away from each other and call for help but by the time help gets there it's over and then everyone

[69] Interview, ISD6, Unit 6, 2017.
[70] Interview, ISD1, Unit 6, 2015.
[71] Interview, Hein Kilian, Unit 6 Commanding Officer, 2017.
[72] Interview, ISD1, Unit 6, 2015.

is just picking up bodies. Even if you had twenty vehicles there it wouldn't stop. It wouldn't be enough sometimes because there would be four or five thousand people just on the Zulu side. And they come up there towards Phola Park and anyone they catch, it's over. Anything outside the hostels was free game for them.[73]

Most of the veterans interviewed believed that the ISD's presence vastly reduced the body count in Thokoza and Katlehong, as well as in other East Rand townships. At the same time, virtually all concerned parties agreed that, even with occasional military support, the presence of the ISD was not sufficient to deal with the scale of violence that engulfed so many Rand townships.

Vlakplaas and the 'Third Force'

Accusations of security force partiality – primarily in support of the IFP – were ubiquitous. They ranged from charges that a government-approved third force of security force operatives was stoking the violence, to claims that some police officers continued to view the ANC as the enemy and took independent action against ANC officials and supporters. The IBIIR listed a typical complaint with regard to the SAP's Crime Intelligence Service officers in Thokoza who 'constantly arrest ANC activists and then show them a photograph of MK members in the area and demand to know their whereabouts'.[74] The Goldstone Commission and the TRC uncovered extensive evidence of SAP Security Branch and SADF Department of Military Intelligence support for Inkatha, primarily in the KZN conflict.[75] The most blatant covert operations on the Rand that have come to light are those of Eugene de Kock's unit operating out of Vlakplaas. De Kock's extensive confessional exposed a consistent pattern of supplying weapons, cash and other goods to IFP officials on the Rand who were registered as informants. De Kock was convinced that his assistance to the IFP 'was in line with the general feeling among police members', and he was confident that he would secure the approval of his superiors for this course of action.[76] His association with Transvaal IFP leader Themba Khoza began shortly after the ANC was unbanned and, in the initial meeting, he provided Khoza with a shotgun, a large quantity of ammunition and

---

[73] Interview, ISD6, Unit 6, 2017.
[74] IBIIR Thokoza, 'Briefing on the Violence in Thokoza'.
[75] For an overview of the security forces' relationship with Inkatha structures in KZN see, Mary de Haas, 'Violence in Natal and Zululand: The 1990s' in *The Road to Democracy in South Africa*, vol. 6, part 2, South African Democracy Education Trust (Unisa Press, Pretoria, 2013), pp. 876–957.
[76] Eugene de Kock, *A Long Night's Damage: Working for the Apartheid State* (Contra Press, Johannesburg, 1992), p. 235.

hand grenades. 'This was the beginning of supplying arms [including machine guns, AK47s and explosives] to the IFP.'[77] Many of these weapons were delivered to Khoza and IFP officials Humphrey and Victor Ndlovu who distributed them to hostel dwellers on the Rand.[78] Vlakplaas operatives also covered for Khoza after he was arrested with AK47s used in an IFP attack. With the assistance of local police, they removed the weapons from SAP forensics custody. 'The idea was to clear Khoza and the IFP by showing that the weapons had not been used in the shooting. After the weapons had been altered they were returned to the forensics division.'[79] Vlakplaas also used slush funds to pay Khoza's bail and worked with local police to have the charges against Khoza dropped. The TRC recorded that:

> During September 1990 Van der Gryp (third Applicant) arrested Themba Khoza, a leader within the Inkatha Freedom party ('IFP') for the unlawful possession of arms and ammunition. He filed a statement in this regard. Conradie (first Applicant) then a major attached to the Security Branch in Vanderbijlpark then disclosed to Jacobs (second Applicant) of the Murder and Robbery Squad in Vanderbijlpark that Khoza was an important source of information to the Security Branch. They jointly decided that steps had to be taken to protect Khoza. Jacobs amended the statement and requested Van der Gryp to sign it, which he did.[80]

The IFP's close relationship with Security Branch may provide at least a partial explanation for IFP militants' reluctance to attack the ISD and other police. The IFP did not have the same historical animosity with the SAP as did ANC-supporting activists, but it is also not difficult to imagine that Security Branch instructed its IFP contacts that weapons provision depended on those weapons not being used against police – especially white police. An ISD veteran reflected on the possible implications of Security Branch support for the IFP:

> From what I've learned since with what Eugene de Kock and his guys were doing, they were supporting Inkatha quite actively so I'm assuming that was spilling over. At the time, it was a bit of a mystery because we would fire on [IFP militants] them. I mean if they were attacking we would fire on them and they would pull a couple of shots back but we would drive them out with force and they wouldn't come back with some kind of vengeful attack or anything like that. That was strange.[81]

---

[77] de Kock, *Long Night's Damage*, p. 235.
[78] TRC Amnesty Decision, Eugene Alexander de Kock. The largest consignments from Vlakplaas to the IFP, including truckloads of heavy weaponry, went to KZN.
[79] de Kock, *Long Night's Damage*, p. 241.
[80] TRC Amnesty Committee, AC/2001/118, Cape Town, 2001, http://www.doj.gov.za/trc/decisions/2001/ac21118.htm
[81] Interview, ISD1, Unit 6, 2015.

As Vlakplaas came under increasing scrutiny in the transition period, de Kock claims that weapon supplies to the IFP were discontinued after 1992. However, he kept providing arms to the IFP in a private capacity after Vlakplaas was disbanded in 1993. De Kock then joined the IFP and assisted with military training in KZN. And while gunrunning to Rand hostels may have dried up after 1992, Vlakplaas operatives were reportedly involved in a 1993 plan to help organise SPUs at all IFP-controlled hostels on the Rand. Both de Kock and the TRC claimed that these activities were undertaken with the full knowledge of de Kock's superiors in the Security Branch and some members of other SAP units clearly co-operated with Vlakplaas. As stated by de Kock, 'I received my orders from generals in the South African Police. They in turn ... got their instructions from the highest levels of government'.[82] Given the network of connections that existed between the IFP, Security Branch and Military Intelligence it would be naïve to think that security force assistance to the IFP on the Rand was limited to Vlakplaas. As far as Vlakplaas police actively assisting Inkatha attacks on the Rand, de Kock, who freely admitted to numerous assassinations, denied that his people ever took part in any IFP operations and, despite consistent allegations of white men participating in IFP attacks, no incontrovertible evidence of this has been produced.[83]

South African Defence Force

Although SADF troops had been deployed in many townships during the 1980s, they did not have the same history of enmity with township residents as the SAP – especially the riot units. And, given the hostility between many communities and the ISD in the transition era, the SADF was frequently viewed as a more palatable alternative to the police. This was sometimes attributed to racial dynamics, as many SADF units in the townships were predominantly black. In the midst of intensive ANC–IFP fighting in Alexandra township in 1992, many residents exulted at the arrival of the SADF.

> When truckloads of black soldiers from 21 Battalion in Sasolburg began to pour in at about 5 pm, the crowds welcomed them like heroes. Women toyi-toyied in the streets and people leapt about with clenched fists. The soldiers waved as though being honoured in a ticker-tape parade. 'The black SADFs are helping us. They don't want this corruption. But the Boers in their Casspirs are shooting at us. When the soldiers are there they are too scared to shoot,' said 'Chris', who would not give his surname.[84]

---

[82] de Kock, *Long Night's Damage*, p. 249.
[83] de Kock, *Long Night's Damage*, p. 241.
[84] Philippa Garson, 'The War on the Corner of Third', *Weekly Mail*, 3–9 April 1992.

Many respondents in Thokoza and Katlehong commented on the SADF's partiality. Hostel dwellers condemned the soldiers for persecuting them, while SDUs and non-combatant township residents applauded the SADF's confrontational approach to IFP militants which sometimes included active support for SDUs. Different SADF units were rotated into Thokoza and Katlehong during the transition period with the SADF having a base in Thokoza from 1991. Until February 1994, however, when the SADF assumed primary responsibility for security in these two townships, the military served in a support capacity to the police, primarily the ISD. IFP supporters listed a litany of complaints against the SADF, including general assessments such as, 'We were all shocked because we thought SADF should come to stop violence, but they did the opposite and killed us. Everyone here in the hostel knows about that.'[85] More detailed descriptions of specific actions include disarming hostel dwellers travelling through the townships and the killing of IFP leader Jeffrey Sibiya:

> I remember this other day, we were from the rally and we were in the train. The SADF, you know those soldiers were full of shit, so the SADF searched us, they took all the weapons we had, even the sticks. Okay, the next station we were told that the train line is cut off, so the train cannot go to Kwesine [station next to the hostel]. Now that meant we had to walk inside the township, without weapons, and when we were going to the rally in the morning the township people were saying you must never come back. It was like all this thing was planned, they knew that the soldiers would search us, and they cut off the train line so that we pass by them and they kill us. I remember getting off that train, I wished that there can be a straight bullet that can hit me and I will just die on the spot, because I knew that if we pass by the township people they might catch me and burn me and that was my worst fear.[86]

> There is this incident where we were attacked by the soldiers SADF, they attacked us at night and we all know that soldiers do not belong to political parties, but they came here and killed us at night ... it was like it is a circus, the way the soldiers were shooting. I was sleeping flat on the floor, we had our leader Sibiya who called the police and we were saved by the police because they came and threw the light and the soldiers stopped shooting. The following day SADF came and wanted to search in our rooms, and Sibiya refused and told them that we did not trust them. He was not scared of them and they had guns, but he was able to tell them in their face that they would not get in our rooms unless they come with the police and he called the police and the police arrived. When he was going to the police to tell the police what had happened, the soldiers shot him in front of everyone, us and the police, and he had done nothing, he died on the spot.[87]

[85] Interview, Z7, male resident, Buyafuthi Hostel, 24 June 2006.
[86] Interview, Z45, male resident, Mazibuko Hostel, July 2006.
[87] Interview, Z9, male resident, Buyafuthi Hostel, 4 July 2006.

Several hostel dwellers reported that the SADF executed Sibiya and the IFP complained at the time that this was the case. Themba Khoza declared that, 'The army has continued where MK and the self-defence units failed – to eliminate the IFP leadership. This is an election war against us.'[88] SAP officers investigating the shooting alleged that Sibiya was gunned down in cold blood while attempting to negotiate. Of course, the soldiers' account was different. The SADF stated that Sibiya was killed during a gunfight that occurred during an arms raid on Buyafuthi Hostel.[89]

The IFP opposed the February 1994 replacement of the ISD with the military on the East Rand, citing what it considered to be a history of persecution at the hands of the SADF in these townships and insisting that the SADF was packed with black soldiers, including MK veterans, loyal to the ANC.[90] IFP official Hennie Bekker protested that substituting SADF units for the ISD represented 'the final abdication of the National Party and Government to the ANC–communist alliance'. By contrast, the ANC labelled this move 'a major victory for the people'.[91] As the SADF strength increased to three battalions by early February, the townships were saturated with troops and the level of violence dropped, but the relationship between the soldiers and IFP hostel residents became increasingly tense. Inkatha leaders denounced the SADF occupation whereas the ANC held a rally to welcome the troops. Patrolling soldiers were aware of the different reception. A reporter accompanying an army patrol recorded their reaction as they moved past a hostel: '"Every night they shoot at us," said Pvt. David Ramapaeane, [twenty-one] years old, shrugging nervously. "The Zulus don't like us." As they crossed into an African National Congress block, the soldiers relaxed, and the private said, "Here, we don't get problems."'[92]

Township perspectives on the SADF varied depending on the units in question. In general, soldiers were not viewed in the same negative light as many police, especially the ISD. Some SDU members reported that they regularly fraternised with black soldiers posted in Thokoza:

> The soldiers were from different units and they were deployed, there was a camp right inside the middle of Thokoza location. I don't know if they were redeployed after six months or seven months or whatever but some of the soldiers were in favour of us whereby they would come to our bases and ask us if we had enough ammunition and they gave us their packs, their food packs and some of them got liquor and sat down with us and had some fun with us and some of them even had children in the location.[93]

[88] IBIIR Monthly Report, Election Special, April 1994 p. 5.
[89] Karl Maier, 'Zulu anger builds against SA army', *The Independent*, 9 April 1994.
[90] *Sowetan*, 17 January 1994.
[91] *Star*, 16 January 1994.
[92] Bill Keller, 'South African Troops Find New Role: Peacemaker', *New York Times*, 22 February 1994.
[93] Interview, G2, male SDU member, Thokoza, 16 July 2008.

Several SDU members reported that soldiers supported them in the fight against Inkatha:

> Definitely, the soldiers used to sympathise with us. I'll give you an example of what happened. We would have a situation where we were going to attack the hostel, we would gather in the township in our own section and then we'd get into a section that was nearer to the hostel. The soldiers would come and tell us where those IFP people were, the soldiers would come with their armoured vehicles and tell us what the IFP people were doing, where they were and what we must do.[94]

In some cases, respondents reported fighting between the SADF and the ISD:

> SADF was on our side. I remember the day when the Zulus were from Pretoria they had the rally there, and when they were coming back with the train, they were protected by the Stability Unit, and the Zulus started shooting the township people and the SADF shot back and it was now Stability Unit fighting SADF, and mind you SADF is stronger than Stability Unit, so the support we got from SADF was good.[95]

Another SDU member adds, 'I can say that soldiers came to our rescue because the police, especially the Stability Unit, were really killing us ... The soldiers were able to fight the Stability Unit and they would talk to us, we had a good relationship with soldiers.'[96] Many township respondents corroborated the accounts of hostel dwellers who claimed they witnessed ISD–SADF clashes. Invariably, in these stories, the ISD backs Inkatha while the SADF assists township residents or SDUs:

> The SADF was actually good, it protected us, and I remember there was a time when SADF fought with the Stability Unit, the IFP was from a march and the Stability was in the train with the IFP supporters to protect them. As usual when they come back they would kill people but that day there was SADF and they shot back and some of the people that died there were white police.[97]

Peace Accord official David Storey also heard about ISD–SADF clashes from his monitors: 'There were actually incidents where army guys were firing on police who were assisting Inkatha.'[98]

Our interviews indicated a strong appreciation for the SADF among ANC-aligned township residents. Some were partisan: 'The SADF ... were brought to stop the violence but the way they did that you could see they were on our side. They had no mercy towards the Zulus, it was

[94] Interview, G3, male SDU member, Thokoza, 16 July 2008.
[95] Interview, Z57, male SDU member, Katlehong, 2006.
[96] Interview, Z95, male SDU member, Katlehong, 2006.
[97] Interview, Z63, male resident, Katlehong, 2006.
[98] Interview, David Storey, Johannesburg, 26 May 2006.

really good to have them.'[99] Others applauded the effectiveness and neutrality of the SADF: 'I must say that SADF was much better than the police ... because when they were around the violence would stop and they were not scared of anyone. They could go to the hostel and also come here in the township without being intimidated.'[100] A Phola Park SDU commander credited the SADF with saving residents from an Inkatha onslaught: 'On this day we were helped by the SADF ... had the SADF not come, I think we would have been killed and our houses, or shacks, would have been burnt down, because they were shooting at random, they were attacking, we had absolutely nowhere to run'.[101] An SDU member contrasted the SADF with the ISD: 'Soldiers were better because we could explain to them what was happening, unlike the Stability Unit that would just shoot. The soldiers would listen to us and I can say that they were neutral and wanted to ensure that there was peace in the community.'[102]

The SADF's relatively positive relationship with ANC-aligned township residents could in part be ascribed to the pragmatism of SADF leaders who recognised the inevitability of an ANC government and began working with the ANC to secure their own institutional interests in a post-apartheid military. As Ellis points out, 'It is known that after mid-1992 senior SADF commanders, including the Chief of Staff (Intelligence), had a series of discreet bilateral meetings with the leaders of the ANC and its armed wing Umkhonto we Sizwe.'[103] Negotiations between SADF and ANC leadership on the composition of a post-transition military were going well, and the SADF had nothing to gain by ruthless crackdowns on ANC supporters. Thus, the commander of Operation PROTECTO, which made the SADF the primary force responsible for violence reduction in the East Rand townships in early 1994, describes an evolved approach to peacekeeping that reflected changing political realities: 'The area was stabilized by means of an absolute minimum use of force. I, as group commander, spent most of my time facilitating negotiations between rival parties, political groupings, community leaders and local government structures.'[104]

The 32 Battalion, primarily composed of Angolans who had fought in the Angolan and Namibian conflicts, provided the foremost exception to the SADF's improved rapport with township residents. These veterans were brought to South Africa when the SADF pulled out of Namibia in 1989. They had years of combat experience, no ties to the

[99] Interview, Z62, male resident, Katlehong, 2006.
[100] Interview, Z82, male SDU member, Katlehong, 2006.
[101] TRC Amnesty Hearing, Bhekindile Davis Ndwangu.
[102] Interview, Z101, female SDU member, Thokoza, 24 June 2008.
[103] Ellis, 'Third Force', p. 292.
[104] Colonel C.P du Toit, 'Peacekeeping in East Rand Townships' in Mark Shaw and Jackie Cilliers (eds), *South Africa and Peacekeeping in Africa*, vol. 1 (Institute for Security Studies, Pretoria, 1995), p. 77, http://www.issafrica.org/pubs/Books/BlurbPk1.html

ANC or identification with the anti-apartheid struggle and shared no linguistic or ethnic affinities with township residents. Almost immediately after being deployed in the townships, they gained a reputation for using excessive force. ISD members remarked on this aspect of 32 Battalion:

> The SADF was scared of us. They wouldn't come near us. The only SADF guys we got along with was the 32 Battalion and the 32 Battalion became a little bit too brutal for us at the end of the day. They were hardened soldiers from a bush war and it was a stupid thing to put them into an urban warfare situation. But they were good guys, we could talk to them. They had a good sense of humour and everything but when they were under attack they were brutal, and it was like 'whoa, stop!'[105]

A 32 veteran, who authored a history of the Battalion, judged that it was a mistake to utilise 'soldiers taught to measure their success by kill ratio' in a peacekeeping capacity. This was especially the case as they would be confronting South Africans 'who rejected any semblance of apartheid authority, let alone black troops of foreign origin supporting the last vestiges of the white regime'.[106] The ANC excoriated the government's decision to use 32 Battalion in the townships. The 32 Battalion clashed with SDUs almost immediately after it was stationed in Thokoza and Katlehong in early 1991. A soldier was killed in Thokoza in May 1991, and 'By this time the ANC's self-defence units regarded 32 Battalion as no less an enemy than Inkatha, and the feeling was largely mutual.'[107] The Battalion had received negative publicity from the very beginning of its deployment in South Africa, but the aftermath of a firefight in Phola Park sparked a massive backlash. On 8 April, 1992, while investigating a shooting at Phola Park, a platoon from 32 Battalion was fired upon and one of its members was wounded. A gun battle with SDUs ensued and, when the SDU fighters withdrew, the platoon called in reinforcements to search nearby shacks. Two Phola Park residents had been killed in the shoot-out and more residents were injured by soldiers in the sweep through the area that lasted several hours. The fallout was immediate as the media carried the story of 32 Battalion abuses, including charges of rape, and advocacy groups focused on the plight of Phola Park victims. The IBIIR claimed that more than a hundred people had been injured during the raid and 'a board researcher accompanied [fifty-eight] Phola Park residents to the Thokoza Police Station to lay charges against members of 32 Battalion'.[108] The Goldstone Commission investigated 32 Battalion's

---

[105] Interview, ISD1, Unit 6, 2015.
[106] Piet Nortje, *32 Battalion: The Inside Story of South Africa's Elite Fighting Unit* (Zebra Press, Cape Town, 2003), pp. 255–6.
[107] Nortje, *32 Battalion*, p. 265.
[108] IBIIR Monthly Report, April 1992, p. 20.

actions in Phola Park and, while it made no definitive findings with regard to the alleged rapes and the specifics of the assaults that took place, it concluded that 'the entry into Phola Park was unjustified, and that in certain unspecified incidents members of 32 Battalion acted in a manner completely inconsistent with the function of a peacekeeping force and in fact became perpetrators of violence'.[109] The report recommended 32 Battalion's withdrawal from township duties, and it was disbanded shortly thereafter.

National Peacekeeping Force

Thokoza became the site of a peacekeeping experiment in the weeks before the April 1994 elections. Urged by many civil society voices, the ANC and the government began negotiating for the creation of an integrated peacekeeping force to maintain public order in the lead-up to elections. This was largely a response to the allegations that had been levied against state security forces throughout the transition period, but it also served as a test case for the integration of the various military and police groups that was sure to come after the elections. Parliament approved the formation of the NPKF in September 1993 to be overseen by the Transitional Executive Council's Sub-Council on Defence. It was apparent from the earliest stages that this force would be very different from the SADF. As the *Weekly Mail* reported, 'It is understood that the TEC is pressing for a black officer to be put in charge, and that it wants the bulk of the soldiers to be drawn from township backgrounds.'[110] As it turned out, the TEC appointed Brigadier Gabriel Ramushwana, the head of state of the Venda homeland and an ANC candidate in the forthcoming elections, to command the NPKF.[111] For a number of reasons, not least the pressures of time, the grand designs for the NPKF in terms of its size and mandate were never realised, but a few battalions were mustered to receive cursory training. From the outset, the NPKF was plagued with logistical problems, insubordination, poor relations between its constituent groups and, critically, a lack of legitimacy in the eyes of the IFP. The NPKF was supposed to have been made up of personnel from all the standing military and police groups in the country but the IFP refused to take part and a majority of NPKF soldiers were drawn from MK, the Transkei Defence Force and black members of the SADF. Various homeland

[109] *Goldstone Commission Interim Report to the Commission of Inquiry Regarding the Prevention of Public Violence and Intimidation from the Committee established to inquire into the involvement of 32 Battalion at Phola Park*, 3 June, 1992, http://www.historicalpapers.wits.ac.za/inventories/inv_pdfo/AK2702/AK2702-A12-001-jpeg.pdf
[110] *Weekly Mail*, 4 February 1994.
[111] Douglas Anglin, 'The Life and Death of South Africa's National Peacekeeping Force', *Journal of Modern African Studies* 33, 1 (1995), p. 33.

armies and police forces, along with a handful of SAP, but not the ISD, made up the remainder.[112]

The SADF was withdrawn from Thokoza and Katlehong in mid-April and several hundred NPKF troops assumed responsibility for keeping order in the still volatile East Rand townships. The IFP objected vigorously and referred to the NPKF as an ANC army. The stage was set for a renewed outbreak of violence. Predictably, most of the conflict took place between the hostels and the NPKF. The peacekeepers proved ill prepared for this scale of fighting.[113] Journalists Joao Silva and Greg Marinovich (who was shot and wounded that day) described the scene as an NPKF patrol came under fire from Thokoza's Mshayazafe Hostel: 'The soldiers were scared – this is more than they had bargained for when they signed on as peace-keepers. Some were so reluctant that a stocky black officer was kicking them to get them moving.'[114] Initially, some NPKF personnel also confronted and disarmed SDUs, but this led to dissension in the ranks on 18 April when MK members demanded the release of the arrested youths and held their SADF-seconded battalion commander hostage until their demand was met. These MK veterans wanted no part of operations against SDUs and pushed for more forceful actions against the hostels.[115] And, for the most part, they got what they wanted. IFP respondents recount the hostility of the NPKF: 'The peace keeping force, those were Holomisa's [Transkei head of government] soldiers. They killed us so much.'[116] SDU members report that the soldiers worked closely with them against the hostel residents, providing them with ammunition and covering fire.[117] Commenting on the massive SDU assault on Mshayazafe Hostel on 18 and 19 April, Katlehong SDU member Mbongeni Mabuza testified that his unit was called by their comrades in Thokoza to assist with the attack and, when they arrived at the hostel, they found their fellow SDUs fighting alongside the NPKF. When Mabuza ran out of ammunition for his AK47, he pointed out targets in the hostel to an NPKF soldier. The soldier then handed his rifle to Mabuza who used it for the remainder of the fight and then kept it for himself.[118] Instead of keeping the peace, the NPKF presided over

---

[112] For details of the composition of the NPKF along with the logistical and training challenges it faced, see Human Sciences Research Council and the Institute for Defence Policy, *The National Peacekeeping Force, Violence on the East Rand and Public Perceptions of the NPKF in Katorus*, Pretoria, June 1994.

[113] Anglin, 'Life and Death', p. 43.

[114] Marinovich and Silva, *Bang Bang Club*, p. 202.

[115] Anglin, 'Life and Death', p. 44. The beating and arrest of SDU members is described in Marinovich and Silva, *Bang Bang Club*, p. 195.

[116] Interview, Z10, male resident, Buyafuthi Hostel, 4 July 2006.

[117] Missing Voices Project, Interview no. 1 with Victor Mngomezulu, SDU Commander, Phenduka section.

[118] Truth and Reconciliation Commission Amnesty Hearing, Jeremia Mbongeni Mabuza, AM7633/97, 8 December, 1998, Palm Ridge, http://www.justice.gov.za/trc/amntrans%5C1998/9811231210_pr_981208th.htm

an escalation of violence that was a public relations nightmare. By the evening of 19 April, it was apparent that the force was not up to the job it had been assigned. The death toll had risen to thirty-four, with many more injured, and the NPKF requested assistance from the SADF.[119] The battles with hostel residents, the partial mutiny and IFP demands for the return of the SADF (which it now preferred to the NPKF), led to the end of the ill-fated experiment on 20 April when the TEC sent the SADF back into the townships and confined the NPKF to barracks for the week prior to the election.

Conclusion

Some township SAP officers supplied ammunition to SDUs, helped them to procure guns and provided them with intelligence. Some SADF patrols, especially those composed primarily of black soldiers, were also sympathetic to ANC supporters and hostile to the IFP. The NPKF, although operational for a very short time and only deployed in a limited area, clearly backed the ANC. However, many at the highest levels of the security forces were virulently anti-ANC and those who supported the IFP were far more powerful and directly interventionist than any who favoured the ANC. No security force ally on the ANC side was capable of supplying militants with truckloads of heavy weapons, as Vlakplaas did to the IFP, nor did any have the resources of the DMI, which worked hand in hand with the IFP. ANC militants were not without resources, as some benefitted from close relationships with the Transkei Defence Force and MK had weapons caches in the country, but the support the ANC received from state security forces was negligible compared to that received by the IFP.

When considering the impact of state security forces on transition violence, we also must consider how the process of political negotiations influenced security force involvement. The NP's grudging acceptance by late 1992 – that it needed to work with the ANC to achieve a political solution – undermined covert operators within the ranks of the security forces and limited the scope of their operations. Recognising the imminence of an ANC victory at the polls also encouraged the security force hierarchy to adopt a more conciliatory approach towards the government in waiting.

Because of the long history of security force repression in South Africa, the well- publicised instances of continuing malfeasances in the transition period and the fact that these personnel were still in the service of a white minority government, it has proved tempting to commentators to condemn all police and soldiers as holdovers of a destructive, reac-

---

[119] IBIIR Monthly Report, Election Special, April 1994, p. 6; *Star*, 20 April 1994.

tionary state machinery. Certainly, many black South Africans had come to expect the worst of the security forces and were quick to believe any allegations levelled at the police or military. However, many members of the SAP and SADF were not invested in politicised violence for any side and performed their duties without political bias. For example, in their investigation of a 1991 mass shooting in Thokoza, the Goldstone Commission expressed 'great concern' at the persistent rumours of security force involvement. The report exonerated the police and army from any wrongdoing and commended them for their actions in preventing further violence.[120] As Ellis notes, 'Ordinary police officers who risked their lives in war-zones on the East Rand and elsewhere, without themselves being party to any covert activity, naturally enough resented being labelled as instigators of violence by opponents of the government.'[121] Even critics of the ISD acknowledged that patrols often prevented violence by coming between ANC and IFP militants and by dispersing attackers once fighting had begun.[122] Police also initiated and sometimes brokered local peace agreements between ANC and IFP antagonists.[123] For all the observations about security forces aiding one side or the other, a pervasive sentiment that emerged from our interviews was a profound insecurity related to police, military and peacekeepers. Township and hostel residents greatly feared security force violence, and it was often the unpredictability that heightened anxiety. Although the ISD was seen as pro-IFP, hostel residents in Katlehong complained that when their IFP compatriots in township streets adjacent to the hostels were under attack from the SDUs, the ISD blocked the hostel entrances to prevent them from assisting their associates.[124] And, whereas the IFP consistently complained about SADF hostility, ANC-supporting township residents and SDUs also claimed abuses at the hands of the soldiers.[125] A Katlehong hostel resident captures the uncertainty that permeated potential encounters with the security forces:

[120] Sithole Report, p. 26.
[121] Ellis, 'Third Force', p. 286.
[122] Beyond the claims of ISD members themselves, monitors working with the Peace Accord, who were no friends of the ISD, spoke of its role in preventing violence and numerous press reports confirmed the role of ISD patrols in keeping militants apart. Combatants from both sides also mentioned having to break off attacks when the ISD arrived.
[123] Minnaar, 'Hostels and Violent Conflict', p. 13.
[124] Reed, *Beloved Country*, p. 88.
[125] See, for example, IBIIR Monthly Report, February/March 1994, p. 45, in which the Board received sixteen complaints of alleged torture by members of the SADF based in Thokoza. A Thokoza SDU member who reported that relationships with the SADF were generally good added that this was not always the case: 'There were some certain units that had no bond with us, they would beat us, and we even started to shoot them. I remember one day I was with a certain friend, we were staying next to the camp. They will go to a nearby tavern and beat us there. One day my friend said, "I will never be beaten by these people again. I will shoot them." And he managed to shoot them.' Interview, G2 male SDU member, Thokoza, 16 July 2008.

The role of police at that time was a bit confusing because they were mixed; there were those who supported us and those who were against us. So, when they came here you could not know why they were coming. Those that were on our side, when they come they would not take weapons that we used to protect ourselves, they would also come when there was a fight to check if everything was okay. But those who were against us they would come and take our weapons so that we cannot defend ourselves, you could see that they were supporting the other group, so their role was not clear.[126]

The political preferences of some state security forces were an important element of transition violence and the rule of law was abrogated when different security forces became players in the violence. While some police and military units worked diligently to suppress conflict, their efforts were undermined by a history of repressive policing, 'third force' activities and a government that failed to prioritise peace in the townships. This was the NP government's final contribution to the violence that consumed black townships. While some security forces abetted the violence, the state's negligence guaranteed its persistence. All parties to the conflict share responsibility, but it is impossible to imagine that, had white areas been in flames, the government and security force response would not have been more comprehensive and effective.

[126] Interview, Z8, male resident, Buyafuthi Hostel, 24 June 2006.

Part 2
Katlehong and Thokoza

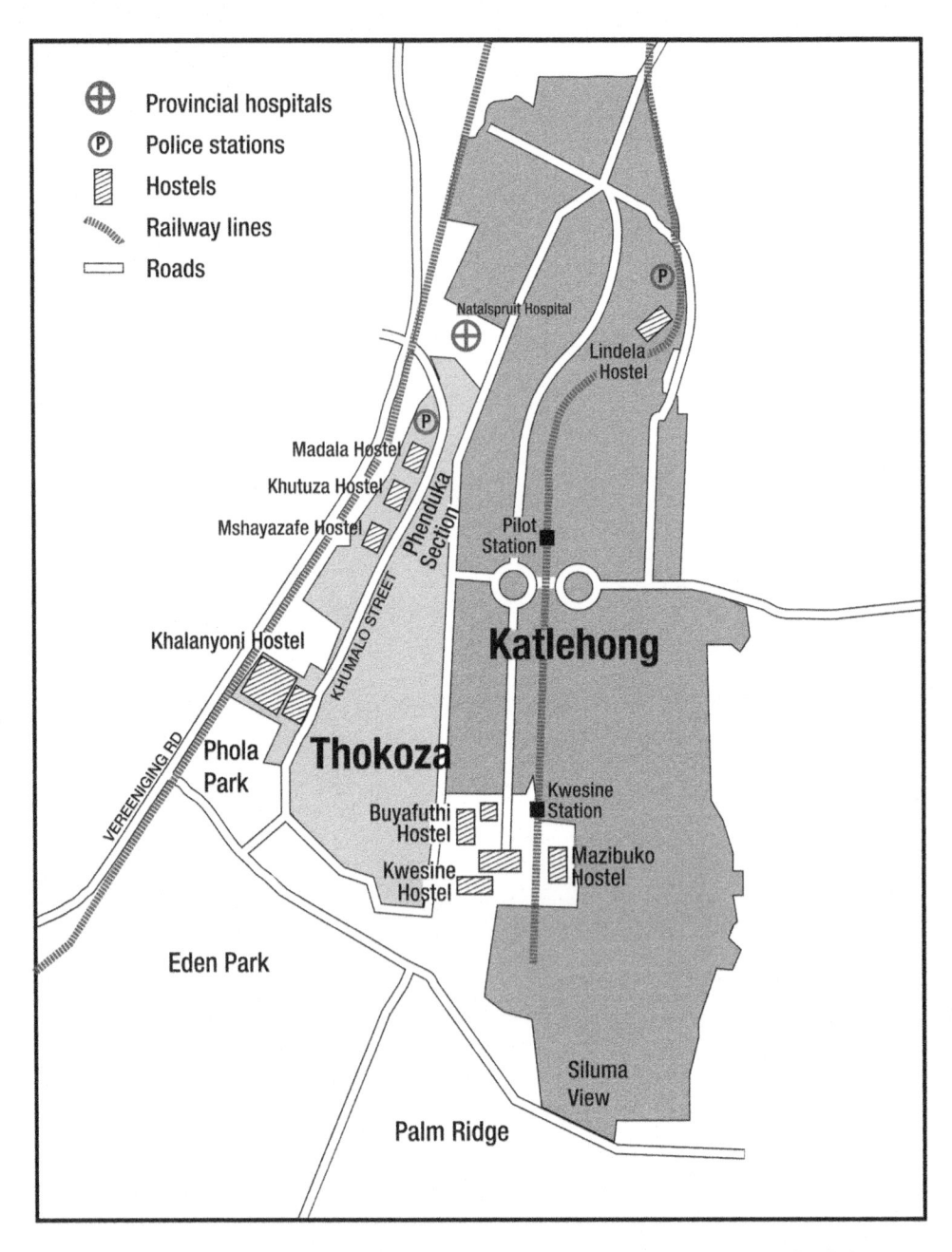

Map 3 The townships of Katlehong and Thokoza where so much of the fighting took place

5 A Tale of Two Townships

> The social and moral fabric of the Thokoza/Katlehong community has been shattered. Death is an everyday occurrence that seldom shocks. The sound of gunfire can be heard day and night. At the height of the violence in July and August 1993, there were frequent reports of corpses lying untended in the street, sometimes for as long as four or five days. This ongoing violence has led to a complete breakdown of civil society.[1]

Many areas on the Rand experienced politicised conflict, but nowhere as intensely as the streets, squatter camps, and hostels of Thokoza and Katlehong. These became battlegrounds for the better part of four years. Thousands of residents mobilised for combat and communal violence directly affected hundreds of thousands more.[2] ISD Unit 6 maintained a permanent presence, while other ISD and SADF forces were posted on a temporary basis. The violence assumed different forms including massive street battles, hostel raids into the surrounding areas, attacks on hostels, assassinations, massacres and skirmishes with security forces. Casualties ran into the thousands and militants' campaigns to secure territory and expel suspected enemy supporters created enormous insecurity, resulted in substantial material damage and displaced much of the population.

The prelude to the formal ANC–IFP conflict was provided first by the early 1990 Katlehong taxi violence that pitted migrant Zulu men against township youth and, secondly, by the Zulu–Xhosa fighting that consumed Phola Park and Khalanyoni Hostel. With the IFP concentrating its recruiting efforts in hostels and the ANC positioning itself as the champion of township communities, these clashes festered and swelled into an all-out war between ANC and IFP supporters.

---

[1] IBIIR/Peace Action, *Before we were good friends*, p. 7.
[2] Based on records kept for the Ekurhuleni Demilitarisation Project, estimates supplied by an ex-combatants organisation in Thokoza representing former SDUs, as well as anecdotal evidence from those involved with SDUs, the number of active SDU members in Katlehong and Thokoza between 1990–94 never exceeded a thousand. I am not aware of any SPU records but, given the much smaller base of IFP support, they were almost certainly fewer in number than the SDUs. In addition, many hostel and township residents who were not attached to these fighting units took up arms on occasion.

At the centre of this war stood six IFP-dominated hostels. The ANC–IFP conflict across the Rand was waged between the inhabitants of IFP-controlled hostels and neighbouring township residents. Parts of Soweto, Sebokeng, Vosloorus, Alexandra and many other townships experienced this pattern of violence. However, only Katlehong and Thokoza featured such a density of IFP hostels in a relatively small area and this concentration of power enabled the IFP to contest these townships throughout the transition period. In Thokoza, a complex comprising three side-by-side hostels – Mshayazafe, Khutuza and Madala – all front Khumalo Street. Several kilometres away in neighbouring Katlehong, Buyafuthi, Kwesine and Mazibuko Hostels are clustered within a few hundred metres of each other. Two more isolated hostels that housed Zulu migrants were destroyed in the first weeks of the conflict, Khalanyoni in Thokoza and Lindela in Katlehong. Although a block of Mazibuko Hostel was burnt down during a 1993 attack and repeated assaults were launched against the other hostels, the IFP managed to hold the remaining six hostels throughout the fighting. IFP supporters also laid claim to some of the streets in the immediate vicinity of the hostels and these areas were bitterly contested. In addition, informal settlements served as combat zones, with Crossroads and Zonkizizwe in Katlehong becoming IFP strongholds while Mandela Park and Holomisa Park in Katlehong and Phola Park in Thokoza were ANC preserves.

All-out war: mid-1990 to late 1993

Immediately before the violence erupted, the hostels in Thokoza and Katlehong probably housed twenty thousand to thirty thousand men, along with far fewer women and very few children.[3] From 1990–94, the hostel population fluctuated. Many hostel residents, especially non-Zulus, left when the violence began, and others departed as the conflict intensified. However, the hostels also absorbed Zulu refugees, including women and children who were periodically chased out of the townships because of their suspected affiliation with the IFP. Fighters who arrived from KZN further bolstered the hostel population. In 1990 the combined population of Thokoza and Katlehong was well over five hundred thousand.[4] This population was multi-ethnic and included a core of long-standing residents whose families had been settled in the townships for decades. Zulu migrants from

---

[3] At the beginning of the fighting, Reed places the population of Thokoza's three Khumalo Street hostels at thirteen thousand. There were three similarly sized hostels – Buyafuthi, Kwesine and Mazibuko – in Katlehong. See Reed, *Beloved Country*, p. 39.
[4] Bonner and Nieftagodien, *Kathorus*, pp. 54, 88.

KZN and Xhosa migrants from Transkei/Ciskei made up the bulk of squatter camp residents.

The Phola Park–Khalanyoni conflict ignited a conflagration between Xhosa and Zulu migrants that gradually drew in township residents. In the initial fighting, Xhosa residents of Khalanyoni fled to Phola Park leaving Zulus in sole possession of the hostel until its destruction. The displaced Xhosa mounted revenge attacks on Khalanyoni but also on other Zulu-dominated hostels and squatter camps. A Xhosa refugee from Khalanyoni, who stated that he had been forced to flee the hostel and abandon all his belongings, grouped together with other Xhosa migrants to plan revenge attacks on the Zulus. They met in a predominantly Xhosa hostel in the nearby town of Germiston:

> We then started retaliating at Crossroads. We killed people there. We then proceeded to the Lindela Hostel and attacked it. We surrounded the Lindela Hostel. It was during the night. Our sign to each other was to fold up a trouser on one leg and to leave the other. We killed many people in that hostel.

After attempts to attack Madala and Kwesine Hostels were thwarted by security forces, this group 'came back to finish the Khalanyoni Hostel and destroyed it to the ground'.[5] Zulu testimony aligns with this account. A Lindela resident reported,

> Khalanyoni was the first one that was attacked and Lindela followed. I was staying at Lindela because my wife was staying at Mavimbela section [in Katlehong] and we were closer to each other. Those that attacked the hostel caught us off guard. We were not expecting violence. So, we ran away ... and the hostel was destroyed in one day and all our belongings remained there.[6]

Once Khalanyoni and Lindela were demolished, surviving Zulus left the townships altogether or retreated to other hostels and squatter camps. In these initial months of fighting before SDUs became operational, attacks from the hostels took a fearsome toll on the surrounding townships. Large war parties descended on township sections and indiscriminately slaughtered residents. In addition to the ongoing conflicts between the Khumalo Street hostels and Phola Park, local squatter camps became embroiled in the fighting. In August 1990, Zulu militants emerged victorious after a series of clashes in Crossroads camp and, in November, the violence moved to Zonkizizwe. The fighting here was all the more tragic because it involved refugees from

---

[5] Bonner and Nieftagodien, *Kathorus*, p. 135.
[6] Interview, Z13, male resident, Madala Hostel, 10 July 2006. *City Press*, 19 August 1990, reported nine Zulu dead in the Lindela attack.

both sides who had already been forced out of their places of residence. Some Zulus from Lindela and Khalanyoni settled in Zonkizizwe as did Xhosas from Phola Park.[7] The IFP established control over Zonkizizwe following a final confrontation in which Zulu residents backed by hostel dwellers from Katlehong killed eighteen ANC supporters. Media sources speculated that the Zonkizizwe attacks marked a change in the IFP's approach to the East Rand conflict:

> The fighting at Zonkezizwe was unlike any other Inkatha attack on squatter camps on the Reef. The week-long battle which ended with Sunday's bloody massacre, could best be described as territorial with the opposing forces each determined to hold their positions. In August and September violence on the other hand, Inkatha's well-armed 'rooi doeke' [red headbands] always retreated back to their township hostels after attacking squatter settlements. This change in strategy could lie in a new thrust by Inkatha to establish territorially defined political strongholds, thus breaking out of its isolated pockets of support in the hostels, which are almost always encircled by hostile township residents.[8]

The Zonkizizwe violence had a knock-on effect in Phola Park where an estimated three thousand Xhosa refugees settled. The IBIIR recorded an early December surge in violence in Phola Park, noting that, prior to the influx of people fleeing from Zonkizizwe, 'Phola Park had been relatively quiet'.[9] Reed provides a more colourful description:

> In November [1990] refugees began to arrive in Phola Park by the dozen, carrying their belongings in plastic bags and supermarket trolleys. They were running away from Zonkezizwe ... where ... forty-five people had died. The IFP was in control of Zonkezizwe. The fugitives were bitter. They wanted revenge. A decisive onslaught on the Thokoza hostels was planned.[10]

December witnessed a series of attacks and counter-attacks between Phola Park and the Khumalo Street hostels with hundreds of participants and heavy casualties on both sides. The conflict was only suspended when 'the South African Defence Force threw a ring of steel around [Phola Park]. A soldier stood guard every [thirty] metres and an armoured vehicle every [one hundred] metres.'[11]

The December Phola Park hostel fighting also drew in substantial numbers of Thokoza township residents, particularly from the

[7] IBIIR Monthly Report, November 1990, pp. 3–4.
[8] *Sunday Star*, 25 November, 1990.
[9] IBIIR Monthly Report, December 1990/January 1991, p. 1.
[10] Reed, *Beloved Country*, p. 53.
[11] Reed, *Beloved Country*, p. 57.

sections fronting the main Khumalo Street thoroughfare, along which attackers from both sides travelled. Phola Park militants demanded ANC solidarity against the hostels, while hostel fighters levied taxes and pressured township residents for support. It became increasingly difficult to stay neutral and, while some township Zulus sided with the IFP, most township residents, including Zulus, identified as ANC supporters and began forming SDUs to protect their communities. According to a Mosotho SDU member, Zulu hostel dwellers expanded the conflict when they began targeting township residents: 'The violence between the Zulus and the Xhosas quickly moved to the township because the Zulus would just shoot the township people as they would say the township people hide the Xhosas. When they started killing the township people the Zulus became our enemies.'[12]

The December 1990 violence seems to have temporarily exhausted all parties and this fatigue, in combination with a heightened security force presence, led to a relatively peaceful next several months. The exception was an April 1991 skirmish between the neighbouring squatter settlements of Mandela Park and Holomisa Park. Mandela Park harboured residents of different ethnicities, while Holomisa Park was overwhelmingly Xhosa. Mandela Park was better serviced in terms of water and sanitation than Holomisa Park and jealousy over resources seems to have acquired an ethnic inflection. Portable toilets that had been stolen from Mandela Park by Holomisa residents were reclaimed by a Mandela Park group said to have included a number of Zulus. Most Holomisa denizens had settled there after being evicted from Zonkizizwe and Crossroads by IFP supporters, and a militant Holomisa faction insisted that Zulus should not be allowed in Mandela Park. A Xhosa resident of Mandela Park reported that the Holomisa faction 'told us we were harbouring our own enemies who might turn against us and them, therefore we should get rid of them before they do this. But we have been living happily together here and no one has ever threatened anyone.'[13] Fifteen people died and more than a hundred shacks were burnt down in a series of attacks by Holomisa residents, and Zulus were forced out of Mandela Park. The prominence of ethnic nationalism was on display when MK Chief of Staff Chris Hani attempted to broker a settlement between the two camps. 'Holomisa Park residents arriving at Wednesday's peace rally to be addressed by Hani made no secret of their feelings. They arrived bearing an ANC flag and singing Xhosa songs: My home is Umtata. My home is in Pondoland.'[14] This marked the final demarcation of

---

[12] Interview, Z97, male SDU member, Thokoza, 21 June 2008.
[13] *Weekly Mail*, 12–18 April 1991, Mondli Makhanya, 'The toilets that started the trouble'.
[14] *Weekly Mail*, 12–18 April 1991, Mondli Makhanya, 'The toilets that started the trouble'.

informal settlement territory in Thokoza and Katlehong between IFP and ANC supporters.

The conflict entered a new phase in 1991 with pitched battles becoming less common. Instead, 'a war of attrition began in which the factions tried to wear each other down by terrorizing "civilians" and assassinating leaders'.[15] These hostilities were still punctuated by occasional massacres that triggered cycles of revenge. In September 1991, an attack on IFP marchers in Thokoza served this purpose. The Thokoza Hostel Dwellers' Association announced that it was holding a peace rally at Thokoza Stadium on 8 September and invited all township residents to attend. Hostel residents spread the message that their only quarrel was with Phola Park and they did not wish to fight with township people. As we saw in Chapter 2, Phola Park militants applied heavy pressure to get township residents to join them in the fight against the IFP hostels and, according to Reed, they were determined to preserve this alliance:

> The Phola Park section commanders saw right through the hostel's strategy. It was a cunning political manoeuvre. The aim was to weaken Phola Park by driving a wedge between the township and the shanty town. Something had to be done, the section commanders agreed. They made a plan. Operators would be deployed at the four corners of the stadium, and inside the stadium. Once the stadium had filled with hostel-dwellers, the assembled masses would be scythed with AK-47s.[16]

The Goldstone Commission confirmed that the shooting was part of a planned ambush by Phola Park SDU commanders, in which teams of SDU operators were tasked with the wholesale slaughter of IFP supporters. Sixteen were killed and thirteen injured in the primary shooting by three SDU members and another two IFP supporters were killed immediately after in a secondary attack by Phola Park residents in which 'the hostel dwellers were assaulted with spears, pangas, assegais and axes'.[17] If it had not been for the impulsiveness of SDU member Michael Phama, the casualties would have been much higher. Phama could not restrain himself from opening fire with his AK47 as the marchers approached the stadium, and he was immediately joined by the other two members of his team. As deadly as it was, the premature shooting pre-empted the planned ambush. A Phola Park resident reported that militants condemned Phama's indiscipline: 'He disappointed everyone by shooting first. So, people were angry with him.'[18]

---

[15] Reed, *Beloved Country*, p. 68.
[16] Reed, *Beloved Country*, p. 72.
[17] Sithole Report, p. 11.
[18] Reed, *Beloved Country*, p. 72.

The repercussions were not long in coming. Thokoza resident and popular ANC activist, Sam Ntuli, was assassinated on 29 September, 1991. Two Khumalo gang members applying for amnesty claimed local IFP officials organised the execution, but no one was ever charged with Ntuli's murder.[19] ANC supporters from Holomisa Park were mown down as they returned from the Ntuli funeral on 7 October. Much like the previous month's stadium killings, this was a premeditated event. The mourners walked through a taxi rank and assaulted drivers and passengers who were not complying with a stayaway called in observance of the funeral. Just as they cleared the rank,

> there was a vicious and sustained attack (using AK-47s) on the funeral-goers who were proceeding across the open area adjacent to the Natalspruit Hospital. This attack was perpetrated by a number of individuals clearly working in co-operation with one another from different points around the open area ... [eighteen] people were killed during the course of this attack.[20]

The Goldstone Commission speculated that this ambush was in retaliation for the stadium shootings, but no definitive link was established. As to the identity and political affiliation of the attackers, the Commission only noted that the one person directly implicated was a hostel resident.

The National Peace Accord devoted much of its energies in Gauteng to the troubled East Rand townships. The local peace committees, including the Thokoza committee which was formed in October 1991, were comprised of members from all stakeholders as were the peace monitors who sought to negotiate solutions to on-the-ground disputes, accompanied marches and rallies and generally worked to defuse tensions. Peace Accord official David Storey explained,

> When I went out in a vehicle I had an Inkatha person and an ANC person with me. If it was an ANC march the ANC person would get out and I would get out and we would deal with it. The Inkatha guy would stay in the car but the Inkatha guy would be able to report back that it was dealt with, that the ANC was playing ball on this issue and vice versa if we drove into a hostel. It was the Inkatha guy who got us into the hostel.[21]

Despite a considerable presence on the East Rand, many observers questioned the Peace Accord's effectiveness. According to Davin Bremner, an independent observer who sat in on Thokoza Local

---

[19] TRC Amnesty Hearing, Themba Stephen Zimu; TRC Amnesty Hearing, Thulani Terrence Tsotsetse (Mlaba), AM4400/96, Ngema Tavern Shooting, 9 December 1999, Johannesburg, http://sabctrc.saha.org.za/documents/amntrans/palm_ridge/53973.htm
[20] Sithole Report, pp. 21–2.
[21] Interview, David Storey, Johannesburg, 26 May 2006.

Peace Committee (LPC) meetings from its inception, 'the Thokoza LPC became increasingly irrelevant to preventing the bloodshed in Thokoza ... There were constant allegations of biased monitoring, weapons smuggling by peace monitors, and other destabilizing failures.' He lamented that, in the final reckoning, 'the LPC was unable to meet or respond to violence, threats, or rumours'.[22] A Katlehong SDU commander concurred, 'I knew that there was a Peace Committee that was based near the hospital, that was making attempts for peace at the township, but they were just as good as not being there, because people were killed day in and day out in their presence.'[23] The fact that monitoring teams contained both IFP and ANC members was both a strength and weakness. Dual representation lent these structures legitimacy, but it also led to charges that militants participated to gain an advantage. IFP leader Gertrude Mzizi, who sat on the Thokoza LPC, complained that 'We could see that many things are done deliberately. And in the whole monitoring [ANC monitors] are not monitoring they are surveying; this house belongs to IFP, this house belongs to IFP members, this house belongs to IFP member.'[24] From the side of ANC-supporting township residents, the IBIIR reported that the lack of confidence in the Thokoza LPC stemmed in large part from the fact that Mzizi, who was sometimes labelled as a 'warlord', served as the IFP representative. She 'is seen as a key to the violence. Local residents believe that she has been involved in the planning of attacks on residents.'[25] Certainly militants were prominent on the various peace committees. Robert McBride represented the ANC at numerous meetings and used monitors to smuggle weapons. Storey acknowledged that, 'McBride came to meetings for intelligence. He made no bones about what he was there for.'[26]

Despite its limitations, the Peace Accord seems to have had some impact on averting clashes, particularly during staged rallies and marches.[27] When they got wind of potential confrontations, Peace Accord officials liaised with the SADF and ISD and the presence of the security forces sometimes dissuaded militants from attacking.

[22] Davin Bremner, 'South African Experiences with Identity and Community Conflicts', *Journal of Peace Research,* 38, 3 (2001), p. 398.
[23] TRC Amnesty Hearing, Samuel Mafolane Hlophe, AM5878/97, 23 November 1999, http://www.doj.gov.za/trc/amntrans/1999/99112325_jhb_991123jb.htm
[24] *The Heart of Hope: South Africa's Transition from Apartheid to Democracy, O'Malley Interviews 1985–2005,* 'Interview with Gertrude and Abraham Mzizi', August 4 1993, https://www.nelsonmandela.org/omalley/index.php/site/q/03lv00017/04lv00344/05lv00730/06lv00758.htm
[25] IBIIR Thokoza, 'Briefing on the Violence in Thokoza'.
[26] Interview, David Storey, Johannesburg, 26 May 2006.
[27] For a specific example, see Chapter 1 of Peter Harris' book for an account of the Peace Accord's work to secure peace during an IFP march in Thokoza. Harris was the head of the Witwatersrand-Vaal Region of the NPA (Storey was his deputy). *Birth: The Conspiracy to Stop the '94 Election* (Struik Publishers, Cape Town, 2010).

A monitor working the radio at the Peace Secretariat's Joint Operations Control Centre in Katlehong informed a journalist in 1993 that, 'Group conflicts are less now. We can prevent those. Now it's individuals kidnapped and killed. The face of the violence changes. Families avenge their dead, their burned houses. Criminals exploit the chaos. Society has fallen apart.'[28] For some militants, Peace Accord structures presented one possible option for achieving their goals. An SDU member who worked for the Peace Accord explained to Storey, 'I want to protect my family and in the day you open up the option to do that peacefully. In the night when you're not around anymore, I only have one other choice and that's the SDU.' Storey reflected,

> I don't think they would have allowed us to do what we did if they could have won, but leadership on both sides and especially the guys at the local level knew they couldn't win. This was a war of attrition so there was an incentive to say, maybe we should actually try this thing.[29]

Even McBride, who was generally critical of the Accord, admitted, 'The fact that it made us talk to each other limited what would have been a worse situation. The fact that we got to know each other and we held each other accountable in those meetings'.[30]

The conflict in Thokoza and Katlehong did indeed settle into a war of attrition. A relentless conflict that featured smaller engagements, attacks on individuals and campaigns of intimidation was interposed with occasional mass attacks or territorial offensives right up until the April 1994 elections. In addition to the ANC–IFP conflict, SDUs frequently skirmished with the security forces. Phola Park's reputation as an armed camp was well established by this time and, after being pinned down in Phola Park with one officer shot and wounded, ISD sergeant Nick Howarth advised his superiors, 'We should stay well away from Phola Park unless it was absolutely essential to go in there. It always resulted in the death – or at least serious injury – of policemen or civilians.'[31] The hostels served as IFP redoubts and, although they were well defended, still came under sporadic assault. A particularly bold attack involved the hijacking of a police Casspir. Sometime in 1991, Thokoza SDU members used the ruse of a woman in distress to lure a police patrol away from their vehicle. The SDU killed at least one officer, wounded others, stole their weapons and hijacked the Casspir. A Mozambican SDU member, who evidently had experience with armoured vehicles, served as the driver and the SDU proceeded up Khumalo Street

---

[28] Reed, *Beloved Country*, p. 102.
[29] Interview, David Storey, Johannesburg, 26 May 2006.
[30] Interview, Robert McBride, Johannesburg, 21 June 2006.
[31] Howarth, *War in Peace*, p. 166.

towards the IFP hostels. Just outside the gates of Khutuza Hostel, the SDU members, pretending they were police, used a megaphone to call out to the hostel residents telling them to assemble at the gates. When the residents grouped together the SDU opened fire. SDU member Aubrey Radebe recalled, 'We started shooting at them. And then we had some few hand grenades and some few petrol bombs with us, we started throwing'.[32] Following the attack, the SDU drove the Casspir back down Khumalo Street towards Phola Park before dumping it and making their getaway.

In addition to the hostels, there were occasional flare-ups of violence in the squatter camps, including massacres at the IFP-controlled settlements Crossroads and Zonkiziwe. On 3 April, 1992, hundreds of armed men attacked Crossroads, killing nineteen residents, including two children, and burning dozens of shacks. Survivors identified the attackers as former residents who had settled in nearby Holomisa Park after they had been forced out of the camp. They reported that the attackers had been threatening revenge for some time.[33] Three days later Zonkizizwe came under attack by a large raiding party that killed four, wounded many more and destroyed considerable property. Evidence indicated that the attackers came from Phola Park. The Goldstone Commission situated the violence within the framework of the ANC–IFP conflict and concluded, 'It is almost certain that the attacks involved at least an element of revenge by former residents who had been driven out of the settlements in the course of earlier feuds.'[34]

A final squatter camp attack took place in May 1993 following a shooting between ANC marchers and the residents of Mshayazafe Hostel. Peace Accord procedures were well established by this time, but it appears that the march organisers failed to co-ordinate with Peace Accord officials. Consequently, the security forces neither assigned additional personnel to accompany the march, nor were there sufficient monitors or marshals present. This may or may not have been deliberate. On 22 May a large group of armed ANC supporters proceeded up Khumalo Street and, as they approached Mshayazafe Hostel, some of the leaders called for a halt approximately one hundred metres from the hostel entrance. At this point the contingent from Phola Park 'immediately accused the leadership of cowardice and surged forward'. Insults were exchanged between hostel dwellers and marchers, firing commenced from both sides and thirteen marchers

---

[32] Missing Voices Project, Interview no. 12 with Aubrey 'Mgidi' Radebe. See also, Truth and Reconciliation Commission Amnesty Committee, SDU Amnesty Decisions, Aubrey Stimbeko Radebe, AC/99/0186, 11 February 1999, http://sabctrc.saha.org.za/hearing.php?id=58864&t.
[33] IBIIR Monthly Report, April 1992, p. 22; *Los Angeles Times*, 5 April 1992.
[34] Sithole Report, p. 33.

were shot. The IBIIR speculated that elements within both groups may have welcomed the conflict given the tensions that preceded the march: 'During the week leading up to the march, residents of Phola Park and IFP hostel dwellers clashed outside the Rand Supreme Court where Phola Park resident Michael Phama is standing trial for the massacre of IFP marchers in Thokoza on September 8 1991.'[35] As so often happened, this conflict led to a renewed surge in violence that began later that same day, when residents of Mandela Park attacked Crossroads:

> The attack was clearly one of revenge for the shooting of ANC marchers. In the ensuing attack, several women and children were killed and houses set alight. Following this attack, Crossroads was reinforced by hostel dwellers staying at the Kwesine and Buyafuthi Hostels in Katlehong. This joint force then attacked the residents of Mavimbela section leaving chaos in their wake.[36]

The conflict became increasingly ferocious in 1993, pulling in all the township sections close to the hostels. With squatter camps and hostels solidly in one camp or the other, township streets became front lines, with the IFP seeking to maintain and extend buffer zones adjacent to the hostels and the SDUs fighting to reduce IFP-controlled territory and further isolate the hostels. In 1993, Phenduka section, directly across Khumalo Street from Thokoza's massive hostel complex, was torn apart in this deadly contest. IFP militants concentrated their forces on Phenduka because of proximity, but also because it was a majority Zulu section in which they attempted to enforce ethnic solidarity.

The campaign to colonise Phenduka intensified in January with hostel leaders pressuring township residents to attend IFP meetings in the hostel, to join the party, to enrol in the SPUs if they were young males, and to contribute funds for weapons. These demands prompted an exodus by male youth who refused to fight for the IFP. Victor Mngomezulu, who went on to become an SDU commander, left Phenduka for exactly this reason:

> So most of the boys in that area were supposed to join the IFP. And during that time ... they tried to recruit us. Firstly, they approached us but secondly, by force ... Early 1993, it's where they showed that now if you are not a member of the IFP or you are not attending anything that concerns IFP, then you have to be killed. And we witnessed some dangerous things happening.[37]

---

[35] IBIIR Monthly Report, May 1993, p. 33.
[36] IBIIR Monthly Report, May 1993, p. 1.
[37] Missing Voices Project, Interview no. 1 with Victor Mngomezulu, SDU Commander, Phenduka section.

Any remaining residents whose loyalties were suspect were harassed and extorted. This was particularly the case with the families of males who had abandoned the area – some of whom, like Mngomezulu, had joined SDUs to fight against the hostels. Over the next few months as it became clear the IFP was unable to command the allegiance of most Phenduka residents, hostel leaders began to evict all those who refused to align with the IFP. In his application to the TRC, IFP enforcer Thulani Tsotsetse described the process:

> There will be people who were not necessarily supporting the IFP thoughts and activities, but dwelling within the area of IFP, so that we would harass them and force them to do things we want them to do or to act in line with the rest and sometimes I would have heard that a certain person is not wanted in the area. I would go together with other people in my company and go and inform such a person that tomorrow or the next day he must not be seen at all, he must just vacate the area, because he is not working hand in hand with us and is not acting in line with our actions.

When asked who made such decisions, Tsotsetse replied, 'such things will be discussed at our meetings when we will be furnished with the information that certain people will have to leave the area and if they don't leave the area, they will have to be eliminated or killed, because they were problematic in the area of IFP.'[38] In addition to visits by IFP militants, many residents received written notices telling them to vacate their homes within a certain time period. Hostel residents and IFP stalwarts who had been living in backyard shacks moved into the empty homes:

> Reasons given for eviction varied – some were accused of selling ANC cards, families running away, non-attendance at meetings, failure to join the IFP, refusal to pay money etc. However, time and again statements revealed that the real reason for the eviction was that the houses had been allocated to IFP members/supporters.[39]

It was estimated that at least two hundred families in Phenduka had been forced from their homes by September 1993.[40] These evictions were accompanied by widespread looting, as fleeing residents left behind many household goods.

The IFP's sustained incursion into Phenduka did not go unchallenged and the conflict spread to neighbouring sections as the SDUs worked to roll back the IFP gains. This included evicting suspected IFP sympathisers in nearby areas and from the periphery of Phenduka that was still under SDU control, burning houses and shacks that had

---

[38] TRC Amnesty Hearing, Thulani Terrence Tsotsetse (Mlaba).
[39] IBIIR/Peace Action, *Before we were good friends*, p. 14.
[40] *Weekly Mail*, 10 September 1993.

been taken over by IFP supporters and assassinating township residents suspected of co-operating with the IFP. SDU member Mbongeni Mabuza described an expedition into Phenduka:

> we started burning their houses, we started with the first row. The other thing that I want to explain is this, where I used to stay is a bit far from the hostel. The people who were staying in the houses that were next to the hostel, just opposite the hostel, they ran away, they left their houses and went to a place where I was staying ... Those were the people who were helping us in identifying the IFP members. If they said this house belongs to an IFP member, then we would set that house alight.[41]

SDU commanders also parcelled out the houses of those they had evicted to loyal supporters – often, people who had fled the initial IFP onslaught in Phenduka. Distributing houses 'that had been left behind by fleeing Inkatha members' was one of the primary jobs of Jabulani Ngwenya, the Secretary of Thokoza's Lusaka-B SDU.[42] Other areas of Thokoza and Katlehong bordering the Katlehong hostels underwent similar processes of ethnic/political cleansing. Township residents abandoned homes closest to the hostels, primarily because of attacks that were launched from the IFP fortresses, and even 'sections a considerable distance away from the hostels were ... purged of Zulus and alleged IFP members/supporters'.[43]

Thokoza and Katlehong were carved into ANC (and to a much lesser extent PAC) and IFP territories. Abandoned areas, referred to as 'dead zones' or 'no-go zones,' marked the boundaries between ANC and IFP regions in both Thokoza and Katlehong. Here the SPUs and SDUs used burnt-out houses as bases from which to keep watch and snipe at the enemy. Reed provides an impression of these contested borderlands:

> The north end of Schoeman Street, close to Natalspruit Hospital, is relatively safe during the daytime... Drive another [fifty] metres towards the hostels and you cross an invisible line. Suddenly, Katlehong is dead. The houses on either side of the road appear deserted. The silence is unsettling. Nothing and nobody moves. Further on, every second or third house displays smashed windows fringed with scorch marks. Here and there the flames have buckled the roof, or spread to the garage. For [two and a half] kilometres each and every smart four- or five-roomed house lies desolate and empty.[44]

---

[41] TRC Amnesty Hearing, Jeremia Mbongeni Mabuza, 8 December 1998, AM7633/97 Palm Ridge, http://www.justice.gov.za/trc/amntrans%5C1998/9811231210_pr_981208th.htm
[42] TRC Amnesty Hearing, Jabulani Aaron Ngwenya, 1 December 1998, AM7300/97, Palm Ridge, http://sabctrc.saha.org.za/documents/amntrans/palm_ridge/53024.htm
[43] IBIIR/Peace Action, *Before we were good friends*, p. 16.
[44] Reed, *Beloved Country*, p. 80.

In his amnesty application for murder, SDU Commander Sidney Nkosi outlined how territorial perceptions could be a matter of life and death. The name of the person killed by Nkosi appeared on a hit list of suspected IFP supporters. Their guilt was determined in large part by the fact that they remained in IFP-controlled Phenduka. In Nkosi's words,

> We were forced by the situation because there was a certain date that was set by the SDU's [sic] that on such and such a date if the people were not, all the people were not at Slovo section or Tambo section [Phenduka areas that remained under SDU/ANC control], the people who would be left at the Penduka [sic] section would be regarded as Inkatha members.[45]

The boundaries shifted with the fighting and it was crucial for residents to keep up to date. Both sides regularly targeted non-combatants and to be caught in 'enemy' territory was to risk being executed. Once an area was identified as belonging to the enemy, SDU Commander Victor Mngomezulu revealed, 'When we go there, we find you there, we will kill you. We don't care if we grow up together or what but if you are on the other side, that simply means you are IFP.'[46] Avoiding misidentification was crucial, as a resident living close to a hostel explained: 'If you are trying to protect yourself you have to put something like an IFP card or a red [headband]. And in your yard your tree you have to [do the same] ... so that they can see it's an IFP yard'.[47] The following exchange from an SDU member's amnesty hearing illustrates the centrality of politicised space:

> MR MABUZA: When you move from Katlehong to Thokoza, you would see if that was Inkatha terrain, because the power stations were painted. If you are working in an ANC terrain, you would see the colours on the power stations. If you were a youngster, like myself, even if you get lost on walking on the IFP terrain, you would see their colours on the power stations.
>
> CHAIRPERSON: Do you mean that people would paint the colours of the IFP flag, on some of the structures, the buildings and things and the ANC people would do likewise in their strongholds?
>
> MR MABUZA: Yes, the reason was to make people to be aware where to go if you are an ANC member, you must know where to walk, and then they would see the power stations painted. If you happen to get lost, and you

---

[45] TRC Amnesty Hearing, Sidney Vincent Nkosi, 2 February 1999, Johannesburg, http://sabctrc.saha.org.za/hearing.php?id=53171&t
[46] Missing Voices Project, Interview no. 1 with Victor Mngomezulu, SDU Commander, Phenduka section.
[47] Vanessa Barolsky, *Transitioning out of Violence: Snapshots from Kathorus* (Centre for the Study of Violence and Reconciliation, Johannesburg, 2005), p. 50, http://www.csvr.org.za/wits/papers/papvtp11.pdf

land at an IFP territory, you would see the buildings were painted in IFP colours.

CHAIRPERSON: Just for my own clarity ... Are you saying that they used those colours exactly to indicate which is ANC area, and which is IFP area?

MR MABUZA: Yes, they were using those colours. But no one who is staying in Katlehong, who doesn't know the ANC colour or IFP colour. You were forced to know it during those days because the situation was very bad. The people who did not know the colours, would get injured, but the people who knew, I knew very well that if I am going to Thokoza, visiting someone, I know where to go and what route to take.[48]

In accordance with this militarisation of space, both sides renamed township sections to reflect their allegiances and the fact that Thokoza and Katlehong were on a war footing. IFP hostel dwellers referred to colonised territory in Thokoza as 'Ulundi', the Zulu capital in their KZN homeland, while SDUs christened their sections after ANC leaders and prominent international combat zones. Thus, for example, Vergenoeg near Phola Park became 'Beirut', Phenduka was divided into '[Joe] Slovo' and '[Oliver] Tambo' sections and Mavimbela in Katlehong was renamed 'Sarajevo'.

Taxi routes and taxi violence also featured in the territorial nature of the conflict. The Thokoza Taxi Association (TTA) chairman Piet Mbele was a leading figure in taxi-related violence before he was gunned down in May 1993.[49] A 1992 *Weekly Mail* story profiled Mbele, who was alleged to have been an IFP supporter with close ties to the police:

> Over the past few months he has apparently recruited hostel dwellers and his 'friends and cousins' as taxi drivers, keeping legitimate drivers on the waiting list and those on existing routes out of work. Many drivers and taxi owners in the TTA have been harassed and intimidated to pay exorbitant fines for refusing to pay their weekly rate of R13,50 – money they withheld because they believe it was being squandered on arms to fuel the war and protect Mbele. Several drivers have died and scores of taxis have been gutted since members began their boycott.[50]

More than a year later the IBIIR claimed that taxi violence had taken dozens of lives in Thokoza and Katlehong. Because of the violence that had erupted in Phenduka from early 1993, many township residents refused to use taxis that travelled along Khumalo Street past the hostels. Instead, they used an alternate route that gained access to

---

[48] TRC Amnesty Hearing, Jeremia Mbongeni Mabuza.
[49] IBIIR Monthly Report, May 1993, p. 35.
[50] *Weekly Mail*, 12–18 June 1992, Philippa Garson, 'Caught in the middle of the elephants' war'.

Thokoza through Phola Park. This reduced the income of IFP-aligned drivers who plied the Khumalo route and they resorted to violence to force drivers and customers to abandon the Phola Park alternative.[51]

The association of ANC-affiliated taxis with certain routes and IFP taxis with others facilitated militant attacks. This was especially problematic for hostel residents who had to travel through the townships to get to work and purchase supplies. SDUs made a practice of ambushing IFP taxis. SDU member Simphiwe Ndlovu applied for amnesty for shooting up a taxi returning from an IFP rally. When asked how he was able to determine that the taxi in question carried IFP members, he replied, 'The taxis in the township were now using different routes. ANC or taxis belonging to ANC areas were using Polla [sic] Park and those areas and therefore it was well-known that any taxi that was taking the Khumalo road should be an IFP taxi.'[52] The chief commander of Thokoza SDUs used to sleep on the roadside with his fellow SDU members to ambush IFP taxis on the early morning commute.[53] Hostel taxi drivers ran this gauntlet daily to make a living and took armed escorts to counter the threat of SDU attacks:

> Taking people to work was our bread so we could not stop working, but it was very tense. Our taxis would meet with bullets. We tried all routes we could think of and we would use that route for a month and after that they discover it and they would sleep on the route and be there to attack in the morning.[54]

The final phase

From late 1993 SDUs from both townships cooperated in a concerted attempt to isolate and overwhelm the hostels. It was widely believed that there could be no peace as long as the hostels provided safe haven for IFP militants and, by this time, the SDUs were better armed, trained and co-ordinated. A Katlehong SDU member is convinced that SDU efforts brought an end to the war:

> The hostel people could not fight anymore, they had to give in. You know when the violence started there were peace negotiations, but the hostel people were untouchable, they did not want to hear a thing and that is when we realised that we needed to fight back, and we fought hard and they realised that they had no way out but to surrender. I can really say that

---

[51] IBIIR Monthly Report, October/November 1993, pp. 14–15.
[52] TRC Amnesty Hearing, Simphiwe Ndlovu, AM7074/97, 25 November 1998, Palm Ridge http://www.justice.gov.za/trc/amntrans/1998/9811231210_pr_981125th.htm
[53] Missing Voices Project, Interview no. 29 with Bongani Caswell Nkosi, Chief Commander, Thokoza SDUs.
[54] Interview, Z20, male resident, Madala Hostel, 18 July 2006.

the violence ended because we fought hard. At the end, they did not have food and they could not go to work. They just could not fight anymore and the people that were supporting them were fading away because they were exposed in so many ways.[55]

In the Thokoza sections close to Phola Park, a renewed campaign was launched to support the purchase of heavy weapons and ammunition. 'The decision to raise funds, which was unanimously supported, was taken at a residents' meeting ... "The hostels must go, once and for all and at all costs," is the message that is on the lips of most residents.'[56] It was difficult to besiege the Thokoza hostels as they were located on a main thoroughfare at the northern edge of Thokoza with easy egress out of the township. The SDUs launched occasional assaults but the complex was well defended so they concentrated their efforts on reversing the IFP's encroachment in Phenduka and containing IFP supporters within the hostels. The Katlehong hostels were surrounded by township homes on three sides and the only roads led through these neighbourhoods. SDUs cut off taxi routes by barricading the streets leading to the hostels and because the three hostels were separated by a few hundred metres of open ground, a single hostel was more easily surrounded and attacked. In 1993 Katlehong SDUs, assisted by compatriots from Thokoza, launched an assault on Mazibuko Hostel with the intent of burning it to the ground. A Thokoza SDU member who was seconded for the attack explained:

> We planned that we were going to gain access into the hostel at night and set everything alight, and yes indeed, one evening we gained entrance or entry into the hostel with comrades from different sections, and we met a few people at the hostel and exchanged gunshots right at the hostel premises.

On this sortie, the SDUs were forced to retreat but not before they burnt down and looted a section of the hostel. 'Some of our people took ownership of these things, they took whatever they could lay their hands on.'[57]

With the taxis cut off, the train that went directly to Kwesine Hostel was Katlehong hostel dwellers' sole remaining access to the world beyond the war-torn township. By late 1993 these hostels were in dire circumstances. Reed captured the plight of the hostel residents:

> Kwesine and the two adjacent hostels [Buyafuthi and Mazibuko] are being slowly throttled by the township comrades. There is a complete blockade in force, in which neither goods nor people can enter the hostel. Taxi drivers

---

[55] Interview, Z82, male SDU member, Katlehong, 2006.
[56] *Sunday Star*, August 8 1993.
[57] TRC Amnesty Hearing, Thomazile Eric Mhlauli.

who worked the hostel routes have gone bankrupt and have had their vehicles repossessed, increasing the market share of township taxi owners. Any hostel-dwellers caught outside the hostel are automatically put to death by the comrades, usually by burning them alive.[58]

SDUs fired on the hostels regularly, including RPG attacks when these heavy weapons were available, but the most effective tactic was the blockade. McBride directed the SDU campaign:

> We put the hostels under siege, especially Kwesine and Buyafuthi, where they couldn't go in, they couldn't go out. We shot their water tanks out, we sabotaged their sewage system, so they couldn't wash, they couldn't shit, they couldn't go out. But they had the Kwesine railway line that went almost into the hostel and they would shoot from the train and they had access out, so we blew that line up so they couldn't go in and they couldn't go out anymore.[59]

Fighting raged along the Kwesine line and although the SDUs, sometimes with the assistance of community members, damaged the tracks and even derailed trains, the railway authorities kept repairing the line. So, along with sabotaging the line, the SDUs blasted away at the trains travelling between Pilot Station and Kwesine as they knew only IFP supporters would be aboard.[60] For their part, hostel dwellers commandeered entire carriages and fired into the township from the moving train. SDU member Mbongeni Mabuza was involved in several train attacks:

> At the first time, we burned one railway line. When the train comes, the driver saw that the rail has been damaged. And Inkatha members were left in Pilot station and there come members of Stability and they're transporting these Inkatha members to the hostel ... Then they called the soldiers to guard their rail and they repaired the rail. The train started to work. And we called another meeting, we started by the grinding we failed and then my comrade proposed the cutting torch, we cut the rail and we put it as undamaged. And the train comes, we shoot at the train, the Inkatha members were coming from rally, they've been shot in Shell House that day, they came from rally and the train derailed. And the two coaches were derailed and we shoot all the passengers in that coaches.[61]

A resident of Mazibuko Hostel remembers the terror of having to abandon the train and, along with his fellow commuters, make his way through enemy territory:

[58] Reed, *Beloved Country*, p. 86.
[59] Interview, Robert McBride, Johannesburg, 21 June 2006.
[60] TRC Amnesty Hearing, Jeremia Mbongeni Mabuza.
[61] Missing Voices Project, Interview no. 21 with Jeremiah Mbongeni Mabuza 'Boikie', SDU Katlehong.

The day that the train line was cut off we had to walk from the township to the hostel. You know we were in the middle of the township and we all knew in our hearts that anything could happen, but we did not say a thing. We were many but still we knew that the township people were more than us, they could overpower us if they attacked.[62]

Despite the stranglehold the SDUs put on the hostels and the deplorable living conditions to which hostel dwellers were reduced, the six hostels survived the conflict under IFP control. In the week prior to the elections, when the NPKF assumed peacekeeping duties, a combination of SDUs from both townships launched a massive frontal attack on Mshayazafe Hostel in a last-ditch attempt to eradicate the Khumalo Street hostels before the elections. An SDU member from Slovo section remembers: 'I was involved in the attack on Mshayazafe Hostel ... we mobilised the people to go and destroy the hostel because we wanted to make sure that the IFP is completely erased in the township.'[63] This was undoubtedly the largest military engagement in the entire Rand conflict as dozens of SDU members with AK47s, along with a handful who wielded rocket propelled grenades and petrol bombs, did their best to destroy Mshayazafe. An operator from Beirut section in Thokoza vividly remembers the second day of the attack:

> It was early, maybe half past four in the morning when we provoked the fight. Then there were these peacekeeping force members and ... about seven or eight o'clock they deserted their post. We encouraged them that they must just leave. We did launch our attacks ... We provoked the fight at half past four or five and it became furious at about half past seven or eight o'clock and we had a fight until three o'clock in the afternoon. The people who came to stop that fight were soldiers, I still remember they came from that side and going to the hostels, that's when the violence stopped. During that incident I saw so, so many AK47s and that's when I saw RPG7s. I heard that thing *boom* and then a second time *boom* and then we were advised that we must advance again and in fact we took one block of Mshayazafe Hostel and now the fight was between these two blocks, the middle block and the third block. We wanted to advance and take Khutuza and even Madala Hostel but we were disturbed by the soldiers. Many people died but we went on and on until half past three when the soldiers came and then we came back to the location. During that day so many people died, and we were involved in killing some of the people there.[64]

The hostel defendants were securely dug in and well-armed. The fighting on the second day was particularly fierce and a journalist who had covered conflicts all over the world, including Bosnia and Somalia, commented that there were more bullets flying through the air than he

[62] Interview, Z41, male resident, Mazibuko Hostel, 2006.
[63] Interview, Z103, male SDU member, Thokoza, 23 November 2008.
[64] Interview, G2, male SDU member, Thokoza, 16 July 2006.

Plate 5 Thokoza SDU member during an assault on Mshayazafe Hostel, 1994 (© Kevin Carter, Getty Images)

had ever seen before.[65] SDU attackers who had occupied a section of Mshayazafe and set part of the roof ablaze, only abandoned the assault when the SADF appeared on the scene.[66] This incident marked the last major conflict prior to the elections, after which the level of violence dropped precipitously. With a political settlement in place, neither the ANC nor the IFP supported continued hostilities and combatants were urged to put down (and eventually turn in) their weapons. The ANC–IFP war on the Rand was over and an uneasy peace began, albeit marred by isolated killings, occasional SDU clashes and violent crime. The residents of Thokoza and Katlehong had endured four years of brutal conflict. Many participated in violence; all felt its effects. The final two chapters highlight the experiences of these people.

---

[65] Marinovich and Silva, *Bang Bang Club*, p. 219.
[66] See Marinovich and Silva, *Bang Bang Club* for a description of the battle. For testimony from an SDU member who participated in the attack see, TRC Amnesty Hearing, Sipho Japtha Maduna, AM5475/97, Johannesburg, 16 February 1999, http://sabctrc.saha.org.za/hearing.php?id=53191&t=AM5475%2F97&tab=hearings

6 Combatant Stories

Apart from a small minority of MK veterans and perhaps a few Inkatha SPU fighters who had received training from the apartheid security forces in Caprivi, non-state combatants in Thokoza and Katlehong had no previous military training or experience. Some had prior exposure to violence as student activists or through criminal activities but, for the most part, SDU members and IFP fighters were civilians drawn into the conflict because of the violence that consumed their communities. In the initial stages of the violence, prior to the formation of specialised fighting units, large groups of township residents, primarily male, participated in defensive patrols. However, once SDUs were in place they assumed responsibility for defending their communities and taking the war to IFP supporters. Hostels and IFP squatter camps had men slotted into fighting units, but all males were expected to defend their homes and occasionally to participate in mass attacks on ANC areas. Hostel dwellers also carried weapons when commuting to work in case of confrontations with SDUs. Thus, there was a mixture of full-time and part-time non-state combatants in these townships. For all but a few months of the transition period, ISD Unit 6 supplied the primary security force presence in Katlehong and Thokoza.

SDU experiences

Former SDUs from the township of Thokoza on the East Rand (Gauteng) are categorised separately from other MK/SDU respondents for their very particular combat experiences. They participated in some of the most intense violent conflict that took place within South Africa's boundaries. The violence that engulfed Thokoza in the early 1990s was akin to that of high-intensity warfare.[1]

Many of the SDUs viewed their involvement less as a matter of choice than as a fight for their survival and that of their families. The intensity of the violence in Thokoza and Katlehong compelled many SDUs

[1] Gear, 'Wishing Us Away', p. 6.

to join the fight. Sasha Gear noted the difference between the Thokoza SDUs and other SDUs and MK veterans interviewed for her study of ex-combatants: 'Thokoza SDUs took up arms primarily in response to the rapidly deteriorating security situation and not for any political ideals, as was the case for many other MK/SDU respondents.'[2] For some it was as simple as safeguarding relatives from IFP attacks: 'I volunteered. I had no choice because I had to protect my family ... People were dying like flies, we could not sit and watch. As a man I had to stand up and do something.'[3] For others, joining the SDU was a response to the initial involvement of adults. Nkosinathi Makhondo was sixteen years old when his father was called out to patrol the streets, armed only with an axe. After witnessing his father's struggles and considering the possible consequences for the family, Makhondo volunteered to spare his father from the ordeal:

> So our fathers, they are old, most of them. So they run away, others they get killed you see ... when I was looking at my father ... my father, always he's getting tired every day. So I started to see that *ai*, this life, it's hard, and if I can lose my father, we won't be eating at home.[4]

Young Zulu men living close to the hostels came under enormous strain as hostel militants pressured them to fight alongside their Zulu brethren. Proximity to the hostels made these men and their families vulnerable to intimidation. Some complied, others moved away and still others joined SDUs to combat the hostel dwellers. Wanda Mabaso, a young Zulu resident of Phenduka, resisted IFP recruitment pressure and instead became an SDU commander. As a result, his family home was attacked, four relatives were killed and IFP supporters took over the house. Mabaso explained to the TRC the distinction between township and migrant Zulus:

> There are many people who are amaZulu who did not join the IFP. They actually wanted us to join the IFP because we were boys and we were the youth. They thought it would be easy for us to get hold of AK-47's to defend the IFP. My being an umZulu ... I would say we are divided into two. We have amaZulu A and amaZulu B. There are those who come from Natal who are referred to amaZulu A, and we from the township are referred to as amaZulu who are not in line with them ... We are amaZulu B because we speak a different isiZulu. It is different from that of a person who comes from Durban, Umlazi or Natal.[5]

[2] Gear, 'Wishing Us Away', p. 15.
[3] Interview, Z93, male SDU member, Katlehong, 2006.
[4] Missing Voices Project, Interview no. 27 with Nkosinathi Jimmy Makhondo, SDU Ext. 2.
[5] TRC Amnesty Hearing, Victor Wanda Muchacho Mabaso, 2 February 1999, Johannesburg http://www.justice.gov.za/trc/amntrans%5C1999/99020118_jhb_990202jh.htm. The 'Zulu A' and 'Zulu B' designation also appeared in interviews with township residents.

Those who were 'amaZulu B' found themselves in a precarious position, under suspicion in the townships unless they were fervently ANC and targeted by IFP fighters as traitors if they refused to join SPUs. These youths had little choice but to support the IFP, flee the area or join an SDU:

> [Hostel militants] started going house to house. They were killing all boys, it did not matter how old they were, and they would just come and kill them. So, we did not have a choice but to go out and fight, the first street from the hostel was the one that they started with and we could see that if we don't take an action they were going to kill us all because they were saying boys were their future enemies.[6]

Many judged that fighting with an SDU provided the best possibility for reclaiming their homes and securing their families' future. In the words of a Phenduka SDU who had been forced to leave the area, 'If you want to go back home you must attack.'[7]

Revenge figured prominently in many enlistment decisions. A young woman from Thokoza's Sisulu section explained that, once the violence began, her family moved to Vereeniging. However, when she learnt that one of her friends had been shot by the 'Zulus', she returned to Thokoza to join an SDU. 'For me being part of the SDU was good because we were able to pay that revenge and we would burn them so that they can feel the pain that we were feeling when they were killing our people.'[8]

The majority of SDUs described situations in which they responded to IFP aggression. A few reported other motives. The pressure applied by Phola Park militants to join them in the struggle was one such factor: 'I heard the Phola Park people when they told us to fight. They were not laughing, in fact they were very harsh, and we could see that they meant it when they said they would kill us if we don't help them.'[9] Another factor was the status and excitement offered by serving as a 'soldier': 'I volunteered. I was fascinated by this idea of carrying a gun ... I was the youngest member in our group. I could carry a gun, and I was very happy.'[10] A final factor was peer and romantic relationships. Several men related that they joined the SDU because their friends did, and one young woman became active in the SDU because her boyfriend was a member. When he was killed, she left the SDU.[11]

[6] Interview, Z98, male SDU member, Thokoza, 21 June 2008.
[7] Missing Voices Project, Interview no. 19 with Mlungisi Duke Tshabalala, SDU Thokoza.
[8] Interview, Z99, female SDU member, Thokoza, 24 June 2008.
[9] Interview, Z96, male SDU member, Thokoza, 21 June 2008.
[10] Interview, Z92, male SDU member, Katlehong, 2006.
[11] Interview, Z101, female SDU member, Thokoza, 24 June 2008.

The day-to-day activities of SDUs differed depending on their proximity to front line areas. Units that bordered the hostels had to be on constant alert for IFP incursions and were often engaged in combat:

> There were sections that were more at risk like the Sisulu section and Slovo section [in Thokoza] because they were next to the hostel. We made sure that we were strong in those sections. We defended ourselves in every aspect we could. We had guns and we would hit the targets and the police were also our targets because they were working with the hostel people.[12]

Without question, these SDUs were also more apt to come into conflict with the security forces. Front line SDUs devoted the bulk of their time to staffing bases – usually abandoned houses situated on the edge of 'no-go zones' – from which they could monitor IFP movements. In addition to keeping watch for possible attacks, they confronted and sometimes executed suspected IFP people caught in their sections and launched attacks on hostels and IFP-held areas in the townships. Those further removed from the hostels saw less fighting and, instead, ostensibly focused on crime reduction along with occasionally lending support to more hard-pressed sections. We can, for example, contrast a description of SDU life from Sisulu section, which fronted Khumalo Street in Thokoza, with that of Phooko section on Katlehong's north-eastern border, which was insulated from the front lines by several other sections. In Sisulu,

> We would sleep two hours a day because we had to watch twenty-four hours a day. We could not afford to risk anything because we were attacked continuously, so our job was to fight. We had shifts so when some people were sleeping some would be watching and it depended on the situation. If the violence was intense we did not even have those shifts because everyone had to be involved. So, there was nothing that we were doing besides watching and fighting.[13]

In Phooko, 'There was no threat around here. Sometimes we move here to go there and assist other sections, because there was no threat here.'[14]

Effective vigilance required scheduling and organisation and most SDUs in combat areas were tightly regulated. 'In each base, we had a schedule book that will explain who is on duty and not. Like with me, I was still at school, so the book will show that I am not in during the day and I will be on duty in the evening.'[15] Along with watching and fighting, even front line SDUs had other activities and responsibilities as detailed by a section commander.

[12] Interview, Z104, male SDU commander, Thokoza, 23 November 2008.
[13] Interview, Z98, male SDU member, Thokoza, 21 June 2008.
[14] Missing Voices Project, Interview no. 10 with Sephiwe Leslie Mokoena, SDU Phooko section.
[15] Interview, Z96, male SDU member, Thokoza, 21 June 2008.

Our day involved many things depending on the intensity of the violence. If violence was less, our day to day activities would be to make sure that when the violence starts we would be ready. There was training every morning, so we could keep fit. Then the groups would go to their spot because we had two groups in Slovo section. My job as a commander would be checking if everything was in order and I needed to report the status of our unit to the chief commander daily. So, it was quite a busy schedule, because then the chief commander would give us other responsibilities that would add on the activities I have included. But if the violence was tense, our day-to-day activities changed altogether as we needed to be in the post 24/7, and during those times we did not even have time to strategise, we would just respond to the violence and defend ourselves in the best way we could.[16]

These respondents were fixated on the danger posed by the 'Zulus', and their preoccupation with the fight against hostel dwellers reflects the scale and ferocity of this conflict. Where the threat was less immediate, SDUs had more time for other tasks – typically related to community security that focused on residents rather than IFP outsiders. Siluma View in Katlehong was close enough to the hostels for the IFP to be a factor, but the conflict there was not as all-consuming as in a handful of other sections. Thus, 'We did many things, our main goal was to protect the community, so that included watching things that seemed to be causing problems, like the sheebens, youngsters that were causing havoc and the sell-outs issue.'[17] Policing communities sometimes caused divisions and, without the immediate threat of an IFP enemy to unite them, militants in these sections were more prone to internecine violence such as the SDU–ANCYL feud in Moleleki Extension 2 that resulted in a mass execution.

Although the SDU experience in Katlehong and Thokoza was diverse, a few common themes emerge from respondents' testimony. The reciprocal arrangement with their home communities was critical for the operation of most SDUs. To secure their own protection, residents provided financial support for the SDUs. This money was used principally for arms and ammunition and sometimes for food. People also cooked for the SDUs, stored weapons and assisted them in evading the police. SDU members were generally proud of their role in safeguarding their communities:

> The relationship was good because the community would assist us when we needed their help. We would hide in people's houses and they would never tell the police and even the weapons, they were kept at people's houses. The community appreciated what we were doing because we brought about peace in the area as they could not sleep before. We had spots where we could sit and watch, so the attackers could not enter the township easily

[16] Interview, Z104, male SDU commander, Thokoza, 23 November 2008.
[17] Interview, Z90, male SDU member, Katlehong, 2006.

and therefore the community could sleep. We would escort people who were going to work because even the transport was attacked. We wanted to make sure that in the township life was okay. We sacrificed our lives for that.[18]

Trauma was manifested in different ways – sometimes it was attached to actions that SDU members took or witnessed, sometimes it was their own victimisation or that of comrades and loved ones. These stories highlight the fact that they were living in a state of difference – these were not normal times. Many remained at home with their families (although others did not), attended school and church, held down jobs and were in romantic relationships despite living in war zones and engaging in combat in their home areas. Their involvement in violence, as perpetrators, victims and witnesses took a toll and many reported family hardships and violence in their intimate relationships.[19] An SDU commander related,

> My family was not happy because they could see that I was faced with death every day. ... The situation was bad, the police would always go to my place and search the place, so their lives were also affected directly. They would wake them up at night and *klap* [hit] them wanting the guns. As you know how people are, some would tell the police that now X is a commander and the guns are with him and the police would go to my place looking for those guns. So, at home there was no peace because the police would always be there, to the extent that I could no longer stay at home.[20]

SDU members reported being traumatised at the hands of the IFP and the security forces. At a special TRC hearing devoted to children's experiences, a TRC investigator and former SDU member related the story of Jimmy Nkondo, who joined a Katlehong SDU at the age of thirteen. Jimmy lived directly across from the Buyafuthi Hostel and joined to protect his family home. As he grew more experienced, Jimmy graduated from throwing petrol bombs to carrying an AK47. In November 1993, some members of his unit were arrested and then induced by the police to identify their remaining SDU comrades. Nkondo was subsequently spotted by the police carrying his AK47 and was shot, arrested and tortured over an extended period. His family heard that he had been arrested and made inquiries as to where he was being held. They made no progress for days until, 'attorneys intervened and found Jimmy chained to a wall in a cell in Germiston'. He was convicted of attempted murder and possession of an AK47 for which he received a

---

[18] Interview, Z97, male SDU member, Thokoza, 21 June 2008.
[19] For discussions of domestic violence, see the interviews from the Missing Voices Project.
[20] Interview, Z100, male SDU commander, Thokoza, 24 June 2008.

twelve-year sentence. At the time of the TRC hearing, Nkondo was out on bail pending an appeal.[21]

SDUs greatly feared being taken into custody because of the experiences of those like Jimmy and a Thokoza SDU member who explained his ordeal. He and several of his fellow SDU members were picked up by the police because one of his unit had been arrested and then supplied the names and descriptions of his comrades. Presumably because they were unable to charge the SDU members with a crime, the police took the youngsters to a field where they had stacked bodies gathered on patrol. The SDU members were forced to march around the field carrying the corpses while the police berated them for being responsible for all the killings in the township. They were eventually released without being charged.[22]

Sidney Nkosi, a Thokoza SDU, relates an event that illustrates the totality of a conflict in which mercy was neither extended nor expected. He was shot in Phenduka section during an attack on IFP-occupied homes. The attack was repulsed and Nkosi and his comrades were forced to retreat. Because he had been shot in the leg, Nkosi was unable to keep up and, as they fled through the township, he asked a friend to hide him in an outside toilet and come back for him later. He was resolved not to let IFP militants capture him:

> I was still having this gun. I told myself this gun has only six bullets further, I recall I said, if they open the door, I'll use this and then the one bullet I'll shoot myself because I don't want them to find me alive, they will burn me as we usually burn them.[23]

Most SDUs had seen comrades killed and injured in different ways and they carried these fears with them:

> I was scared of police; those people were cruel. It would be better if they would just kill you, but no, they would not do that, instead they would take you to the hostel and obviously you were going to be killed, but the killing would not be the merciful one, where you are just shot. There is torture first, because at that time, we were enemies. That is what I was scared of, to be taken to the hostel.[24]

To help allay these fears SDU members used traditional medicines that were believed to impart bravery and provide protection from bullets. 'If you were using *intelezi*, two things that is there on that *umuti*. One,

---

[21] TRC Special Hearings, Children's Hearing, George Ndlozi, 12 June 1997, http://sabctrc.saha.org.za/hearing.php?id=56292&t.
[22] Interview, Z102, male SDU member, Thokoza, 23 November 2008.
[23] Missing Voices Project, Interview no. 6 with Sidney Vincent Nkosi, SDU Thokoza Gardens.
[24] Interview, Z91, male SDU member, Katlehong, 2006.

you are strong. Two, nothing will come to you. They can shoot, but they cannot touch you. It was the two things.'[25] Alcohol and drugs were also used to blunt the trauma and cope with fear:

> We were defending the community, so we could not leave, what we did instead we drank a lot. That became the only way to escape violence, we even smoked dagga because it was tough. I started then to drink heavily, because sometimes I did not want to see what was happening and alcohol helped in doing that.[26]

These experiences and fears led to a particular conceptualisation of the enemy. The security forces were sometimes attacked but the worst excesses were reserved for suspected IFP supporters, as well as *izimpimpi*. Lerato Nteo, a Thokoza SDU member, told the TRC: 'I had this deep hatred, I was consumed by this hatred for Inkatha.'[27] Thokoza Commander Bongani Nkosi elaborated, 'As soon as you recognised that this person or identify the person as an IFP, you have to attack the person. Whoever will come around, wearing an IFP T-shirt, I will kill him, I wouldn't leave such a person. I would have killed such a person.'[28] A conversation between a Peace Accord official and an SDU member indicates the depth of hatred that had developed. The official was questioning the SDU member about a rumour that the ANC had put together a special squad of MK veterans armed with heavy weapons to be deployed in Thokoza. The operator rejected the claim as fanciful, and when asked how he could be so sure he responded, 'If we had weapons like you say. If we had armed people with training like you say, we would go inside those hostels and we would kill every single one of those motherfucking Zulus, every one, and then the problem would be over.'[29]

In some cases, this hatred was a direct result of losses suffered by SDU members. In addition to an estimated thirty SDU comrades who were killed during the conflict, Victor Mngomezulu lost several close family members to an IFP attack. He explained that, 'I fight to make the revenge for my family. And to do that, it's like I was not having a heart, I was heartless … I attacked the IFP. I thought if I will kill more IFP, my heart – I will heal. But it never happened.'[30] Neither side respected the concept of non-combatants. 'Burning these people, it was our strategy actually', reported Sidney Nkosi.

[25] Missing Voices Project, Interview no. 29 with Bongani Caswell Nkosi, Chief Commander Thokoza SDUs.
[26] Interview, Z93, male SDU member, Katlehong, 2006.
[27] TRC Amnesty Hearing, Colin Lerato Nteo, AM7278/97, 4 December 1998, Palm Ridge, http://sabctrc.saha.org.za/documents/amntrans/palm_ridge/53039.htm
[28] TRC Amnesty Hearing, Bongani Nkosi, AM7268/97, 9 February 1999, Johannesburg, http://sabctrc.saha.org.za/documents/amntrans/johannesburg/53186.htm
[29] Interview, David Storey, Johannesburg, 26 May 2006.
[30] Missing Voices Project, Interview no. 1 with Victor Mngomezulu, SDU Commander, Phenduka section.

It was our strategy to burn them to make [them] feel more pain, you see, because they were killing young children, innocent children. So our strategy is to burn them ... IFP men. But if you find women, you had no choice because we told ourselves, these women they going to cook for IFP members. After they are full, they are going to kill us ... so we shoot both of them.[31]

In a TRC hearing, an advocate for the IFP victims of the Thokoza Stadium massacre challenged Michael Phama, the SDU member from Phola Park who initiated the shooting: 'You were not defending yourself or your community when you on that day went and massacred the people.' Phama responded,

That is the same with them when they go to Polla [sic] Park, they were not selective, they would kill everything in front of their eyes. That is why we couldn't go there and tell ourselves that we were going to be selective in shooting. We were supposed to do what they did to us.[32]

In this environment, atrocities were commonplace. Robert McBride described the fate of a suspected IFP double agent uncovered by the Phola Park SDU:

It was really a fucking brutal issue, she was killed really brutally. These guys had killed her and burnt her ... I mean in these circumstances now we have the luxury of condemning this kind of stuff, but she had confessed and they had tape recorded her confession so when Inkatha came to me and said they wanted the body of this woman, I said, 'No, I'll go and negotiate for you,' and I got the shock of my life because they didn't want to give me the woman. And I said, 'I want the woman's body' and they were all sheepish and funny and I said, 'Go and get the body and bring it here, where did you dump the body?' Because they admitted – they played the tape recording and they said we killed her. And they used language like she was a snake and we chopped her head off and stuff like that. And they didn't want to tell me, so eventually the guys who were with me got rough with one of the SDU guys and, he then said, 'No, she's in the bin.' And then when I went to the bin, basically there was just like meat as if it was a butchers. So, the person had been dismembered and that was the woman.[33]

Along with strangers, violence was also committed against people well known to the perpetrators. This was especially the case in contested sections such as Phenduka, where neighbours took up arms against each other and even families were sometimes divided between the

---

[31] Missing Voices Project, Interview no. 6 with Sidney Vincent Nkosi, SDU Thokoza Gardens.
[32] TRC Amnesty Hearing, Michael Phama, Day 2.
[33] Interview, Robert McBride, Johannesburg, 21 June 2006.

ANC and IFP. Bongani Nkosi applied for amnesty for burning out his neighbours in Phenduka, who were suspected IFP supporters:

> I was staying at 18 and the Thabete family was staying at 21. We were planning how to destroy that household. There were lots of shacks in that yard, and the Zulu's [sic] were there. As this was my favourite job, shooting was my favourite job, and I decided to do the job myself, I went there shooting and when they were still taking the covers, we got the opportunity to set the shacks alight and they did not come back again, they ran away since then. We told ourselves that we had defeated them ... We stoned the house, we used hammers to demolish the house until nothing was left.[34]

When queried at the hearing as to how he would determine who was a legitimate target, Nkosi explained that any person identified as IFP was considered an enemy and this included all those living in an IFP-controlled area, including family members: 'Even our relatives, even you might find that your relatives were on the other side, and during the time of the fighting, we didn't have to select, we have to kill anyone who was on the other side.'[35]

SDU member Sidney Nkosi described killing a childhood friend, Jabulane Dube, who had been identified as an IFP informer. Nkosi had grown up with Dube and because of this familiarity, he served as a decoy. He met Dube in a tavern and told him he wanted to speak to him outside. Once they exited the tavern, Dube was apprehended by waiting SDU members who took him to a field and executed him on Nkosi's orders. At the TRC hearing, Nkosi maintained that, given the circumstances, he had no choice in the matter, but he appealed to Dube's family who were in attendance: 'I would like to ask for forgiveness more especially his mother, the one I grew up in front of and his sisters, the whole family.'[36]

Some of the most horrific incidents involved the victimisation of migrant Zulus – often outsiders – who were caught in the townships. A Thokoza operator explained that many of these killings were opportunistic when youngsters acted on their own initiative without any formal direction:

> The commanders in the townships would not give an instruction that we should kill a young Zulu child, they wouldn't do that, but I had an experience that I will not forget. I was doing standard nine or maybe matric, I can't remember very well. We met this family, a father, a mother and a young boy, they were just asking us directions, 'guys we want a place like this', and they were asking for a Zulu section but they were here in our township, so these guys said 'no, you must just go this way'. And they actually told them

---

[34] TRC Amnesty Hearing, Bongani Nkosi.
[35] TRC Amnesty Hearing, Bongani Nkosi.
[36] TRC Amnesty Hearing, Sidney Vincent Nkosi.

to go in the opposite direction from the Zulu section and so they found themselves in the township. What happened was they started with this young child, they poured petrol over him, burnt him and shot him. They were just schoolchildren you know. They wouldn't have instructions from a commander to do such things, but some guys went above whatever we were told to do and these were young children just like me, schoolchildren just like myself.[37]

Clearly many operators struggle with these memories:

I mean there were bad things we did and as I have said sometimes you did not want to take part but because of the pressure from our fellow comrades you had no choice but to carry out the act. I remember when two guys were killed by the graveside, that was one of the most gruesome sights I have ever seen. They died a painful death. These two guys were from Natal. You could see by the way they dressed and their language. They had a suitcase each, there was a passage and we were standing on guard there as they walked past. They were stopped and asked where they were going. According to them, they were going to Kwesine [Hostel] and they were promised work there. They were taken to the graveyard where they were told that today they are going to be killed. We tied one to a tree and the other one was asked how he wanted to die. Either by gun or to be set alight. He refused to choose. The one tied to the tree was then shot in his knees. That is when they realised we meant business and they pled for their lives, but the comrades were determined to kill them. They were both shot, first through their eyes; they were then set alight still alive.[38]

SDUs differed from both SPUs and the ISD in terms of the composition of their members. Although young men made up the bulk of combatants in all these formations, the SDUs tended to take on younger members and a greater proportion of females. The migrant status of most IFP militants limited the possibilities for young boys to become involved as SPU members, whereas the fighting took place on the home turf of township youth. The ANC's attempts to set a minimum age for SDU combatants was rejected by the SDUs. Some women in the hostels participated in violence, but it seems that the SPUs were exclusively male. Of the two hundred or so members of ISD Unit 6, there were only a few women who were brought in to search female suspects. By contrast female SDU members, while a minority, were by no means uncommon.[39]

The decision to include female members as combatants issued with AK47s was made on a section by section basis. Some only allowed

[37] Interview, G1, male SDU member, Thokoza, 11 June 2004.
[38] Interview, T9, male SDU member, Thokoza, 27 May 2006.
[39] For a discussion of female activists' involvement in violence in the 1980s, see Emily Bridger, 'Soweto's Female Comrades: Gender, Youth and Violence in South Africa's Township Uprisings', *Journal of Southern African Studies*, 44, 4 (2018).

women to serve in a support capacity: 'No, we did not have girls. Women were only helping us cooking, but in patrolling, they were not involved. Our job was very difficult; we were facing bullets, so we could not allow women to be part of that.'[40] Females were also valued as spies, messengers and weapons conveyors because they could travel more easily into enemy territory than young males and they were less likely to be searched by police: 'They would watch for us and tell us what was happening outside, and they would be sent to transport guns because the police did not harass women as much as they harassed us. They had different jobs than ours, but they were very active.'[41] In several SDUs, however, women were full-fledged combatants. In Thokoza's Sisulu section, which was in the thick of the fighting, a male operator stated,

> We did everything together and they were also defending themselves, so they were just like us. We did not have this thing of saying these are women therefore they cannot do this or that. We were all equal, when they joined the SDU they knew what they were getting themselves into so there was no special treatment for them.[42]

Many SDU respondents who served in units that included both sexes echoed this sentiment: 'The girls did whatever thing we did, we did not have time to nurse them. We just assumed that the fact that they were there meant that they could do everything we could do.'[43] Female combatant status may have been dictated by need in some sections. If there was a shortage of members or if casualties were high, then women were more apt to be accepted as combatants. Women began as cooks, according to a female member from Slovo section, but as time went on, 'We started doing what boys were doing as they would say we were all soldiers, so we got a crash course on how to use the guns. We were told about different guns and we also started carrying guns.'[44]

In addition to the fears and trauma they shared with male combatants, female SDU members had to contend with sexual violence, from their comrades as well as from the enemy:

> We were all comrades but there were those guys who would want to take chances. One guy tried to rape me, but I fought back and reported him, and they disciplined him. I was sleeping alone in one of those bases and he came and said I must not scream, trying to undress me. I did not scream, but I fought so much with him and he ran away. When I reported him, our

[40] Interview, Z93, male SDU member, Katlehong, 2006.
[41] Interview, Z97, male SDU member, Thokoza, 21 June 2008.
[42] Interview, Z98, male SDU member, Thokoza, 21 June 2008.
[43] Interview, Z104, male SDU member, Thokoza, 23 November 2008.
[44] Interview, Z101, female SDU member, Thokoza, 24 June 2008.

commander was very angry at him and he got one hundred lashes and he could not even walk for a week. He never came near me ever since.[45]

Their smaller numbers in relation to male SDUs compounded feelings of vulnerability:

> Where we were staying for a girl it was not safe. We would sleep with so many boys, even though my boyfriend was there, but he was not always there so at times I would sleep with nine boys in one house. You understand that if I was afraid I would die of fear because there was no other place to sleep. So, I just had to kill all my emotions and just live and expect the worst.[46]

Boys under the age of eighteen made up a significant portion of the SDUs – anecdotal evidence suggests more than half. Many of these boys were left on their own to protect family homes that had been abandoned. Sally Sealey, who worked closely with Thokoza and Katlehong SDUs during the fighting, remarked on this phenomenon:

> The big question for me is that in places like Phenduka, why did the parents move out and leave the children there? Why did they do that? How can you leave your thirteen- and fourteen-year-old there with instructions to defend the house? What does that say about the parents? And I used to find that really difficult because in Phenduka you had households led by children. [SDU commander] Muchacho was just a boy at that time, he was about fifteen.[47]

Entire sections of some neighbourhoods were largely absent of people except for these youngsters, who banded together to guard against IFP incursions. A Katlehong SDU member who was seventeen when the violence began recounted, 'There were not many community members at that time, many had run away and I remember that I had keys for twenty houses.'[48] A young SDU member from Thokoza characterised his section as an 'all-boys town after the old people ran away: the area was conducted by boys'.[49] Some young SDU members managed to stay in school, but others sacrificed their education to become operators.

Boys as young as ten were part of the SDUs, although the youngest cohort were typically tasked with carrying messages, cleaning weapons and keeping watch for the police or IFP. When a Thokoza SDU commander was asked in a TRC hearing why he used pre-teen children for warfare, he responded, 'To answer this question I would say

---

[45] Interview, Z99, female SDU member, Thokoza, 24 June 2008.
[46] Interview, Z101, female SDU member, Thokoza, 24 June 2008.
[47] Interview, Sally Sealey, London, July 2006.
[48] Interview, Z90, male SDU member, Katlehong, 2006.
[49] Gear, 'Wishing Us Away', p.25.

that there was no young, there was no old, we all had to go and fight.'[50] Although many younger boys participated in the SDUs, it seems that most were only entrusted with AK47s when they reached the age of fifteen or sixteen. Siluma View in Katlehong had two SDUs differentiated by age, one for adults and the other for youngsters, and according to some older members, the younger contingent was sometimes difficult to control:

> The youth are the ones who dealt with many things because they were excited, they had guns, they wanted to use them. We had strict rules on the usage of guns, but you know young people, they would always find reasons to use them, they were the one who would initiate some of the things.[51]

In another Katlehong section, SDU members ranged in age from fifteen to fifty and, as an adult member explains, some degree of friction was evident:

> Young boys had to grow up quickly because they had to fight. But there were challenges with that because young boys thought we were now the same age, and they could speak anyhow with an elder, but we really tried to manage the situation, teaching younger boys that we were still their elders even though we were fighting together. But it was difficult to manage that because we all carried guns, we were all 'men'.[52]

A younger member believes that the adults sometimes exploited the youth's inexperience and enthusiasm to get them to perform specific acts of violence:

> The elders would shift their responsibility to us like when there was a problem they would say, 'take care of this problem'. For an example when someone has been caught that he was selling us out, after looking into a matter the elders would say, 'yes, this person is guilty, you take care of him.' And as young people we would do what we can do best, we would kill. And you see that they were using us in a way because their hands are clean. But we never thought of it in that way, we just thought we were doing our job, taking orders from our elders.[53]

IFP militants

In the absence of testimony from SPU members, we can rely only on the experiences and perspectives of male hostel dwellers who

[50] TRC Amnesty Hearing, Mosa Danton Msimango, AM7370/97, Pretoria, 23 November 1998, http://sabctrc.saha.org.za/hearing.php?id=52995&t
[51] Interview, Z91, male SDU member, Katlehong, 2006.
[52] Interview, Z93, male SDU member, Katlehong, 2006.
[53] Interview, Z90, male SDU member, Katlehong, 2006.

engaged in violence. These men saw themselves as under siege both as Zulus and hostel residents, and sometimes lashed out indiscriminately. A resident of Soweto's Merafe Hostel who was interviewed during the conflict explained that during attacks on township residents, 'We just destroy everything that moves and has life, even dogs or cats suffer the same fate.'[54] The most infamous example of justifying an atrocity was supplied at a TRC Amnesty hearing by IFP member, Victor Mthembu, a participant in the Boipatong massacre. Following his explanation that the attack on Boipatong was in retaliation for violence directed at IFP members by ANC-supporting residents, Mthembu was asked why children, including a nine-month-old baby, were killed. Much to the dismay of the audience, he responded, 'What you should understand is … a snake gives birth to another snake.'[55] A Katlehong SPU who did speak to researchers confirmed that his unit did not distinguish between combatants and non-combatants and instead targeted any person associated with the enemy. Claiming that ANC fighters killed women and children, he stated that IFP fighters began to do the same. He recalled a specific incident in which he and fellow SPU members broke into a house during an attack and killed the mother, the father and two children.[56] Both sides demonised the other for engaging in atrocities. Both sides were guilty.

For Zulu men, the protection of migrant Zulus – especially women and children – who had been forced out of the township was cited as a powerful motivation for resorting to arms:

> In isiZulu we say if you want to make a man angry, beat his wife then you will see that man getting angry. So, when the township people were attacking our women they wanted to make us angry and sure they made us full of anger when they had started beating, killing and chasing women in the township.[57]

ANC proposals to demolish the hostels were frequently cited as a provocation for violence. The preservation of these hostels was critical for migrant Zulus who worked urban jobs to support rural families:

> We knew that we were on our own. So, we had only two options: to fight with all we had or flee and lose our rooms in the hostel and our jobs. Some people chose that and they fled, but some of us chose to fight because we were thinking about the future of our children. If we all flee, all these hostels would have been demolished because those were the intentions of

---

[54] Xeketwane, 'Hostels and the Political Violence', p. 176.
[55] TRC Amnesty Hearing, Victor Mthandeni Mthembu, AM1707/96, Sebokeng, 13 July 1998. http://sabctrc.saha.org.za/hearing.php?id=52721&t
[56] Foster, Haupt and de Beer, *Theatre of Violence*, p. 256.
[57] Interview, Z54, male resident, Kwesine Hostel, 2006.

the township people so that they can build their houses. Should we have allowed that where would our children be now? As you see they are full here, they have come to look for employment as you know that in the rural areas there are no jobs, so we would all stay at home and die of hunger. So now I can say that we won because we still have the hostel.[58]

Just as with the 1990 taxi conflict in Katlehong, respondents believed that violence was directed against migrant Zulus:

> Before I came here [Kwesine Hostel], I was staying at Khalanyoni, it was a hostel for everyone. But then the Xhosas attacked ... After we ran away, they destroyed the hostel completely and built their own houses with those bricks. ... We had to fight very hard to sustain ourselves and if we did not fight you wouldn't find us here. In fact, there wouldn't be anyone who is speaking Zulu in this area because they were trying to finish us.[59]

The destruction of Khalanyoni and Lindela Hostels reinforced the notion that ANC-supporting residents wished to rid the townships of migrant Zulus. A Mazibuko Hostel resident declared,

> The township people did not want us here. They wanted to destroy all the hostels here so that they can build houses, so we were fighting to protect the hostels so that they do not get demolished. They tried, Lindela and Khalanyoni were destroyed and block d [Mazibuko] was also destroyed. If we did not fight you wouldn't be here interviewing us. We fought that is why you still see these buildings.[60]

Defeats at Khalanyoni and Lindela also served as a cautionary tale to hostel residents:

> We were fighting like in a war, you know you strategise and you plan, there were *indunas* that used to group people and say these are going to fight at this time, like when we go to work some will remain behind so that when they attack, there are people to fight unlike in Lindela and Khalanyoni where they were caught off guard. So here there was no chance to be off guard, we needed to be awake all the time.[61]

Hostel residents reported that, as the hostels became militarised, they were compelled to fight and a sense of fatalism is evident in their accounts:

> I did not want to fight, that is not in my personality. I am not someone who likes to fight but I found myself carrying weapons because I had to. Who

[58] Interview, Z54, male resident, Kwesine Hostel, 2006.
[59] Interview, Z31, male resident, Kwesine Hostel, 20 October 2006.
[60] Interview, Z46, male resident, Mazibuko Hostel, 2006.
[61] Interview, Z46, male resident, Mazibuko Hostel, 2006.

was supposed to fight for me? I am man, I had to fight for my life, but it was something very terrible.[62]

It soon became apparent that the only options were leaving or fighting: 'The only choice to avoid violence was to go home, which would not make sense because there were no white people at home so one cannot work at home.'[63]

Revenge killings featured on all sides of the conflict. When asked about the response to a night-time attack by Phola Park militants on Thokoza's Madala Hostel, a Madala resident proclaimed, 'We decided to retaliate, to get revenge, because one Zulu person deserves a hundred people.'[64] For many hostel dwellers, especially in the initial stages of the conflict when Khalanyoni and Lindela were destroyed and Zulu-dominated hostels were purged of Xhosa, this was a war of intimates. From a Mshayazafe resident:

> We fought with the Xhosas, people we used to stay with. It was physical fighting because we took anything, knives, axes, anything that you can use to beat a person, and we used it to beat them to death. It was not like the normal fights that you see where people fight because they had a disagreement, but they do not want to kill each other. During the violence we were killing people because the Xhosas had killed our people. We used to divide ourselves into groups so that we can protect ourselves. We formed *amabutho*, so that we could plan how to protect ourselves.[65]

Being under siege was a terrible ordeal for hostel dwellers. Not only were they at risk when they travelled to work, they were on constant alert for an attack on the hostels. Such assaults were frequently launched at night:

> We used to sleep with our clothes on. You would hear a loud noise saying, 'Get ready!' You would hear gunshots at the gate. You would see Xhosas appearing, shooting and a loud cry, 'Get ready!' We would guard the gate and make sure that no one entered ... Sometimes they would be shooting from the township. We would sit until the following day without any sleep, sometimes until the police arrived. They would then run away, it was that kind of problem. We stayed with our clothes on, because should they say, 'Get ready!' you would have no time to look for a shoe that you don't know where you put it. Other people would be out and you wouldn't like to be left alone in the room. You wouldn't like them to find you alone while others had run away, while you were looking for a shoe. You wouldn't like to be delayed by pants that did not fit you well and that you would struggle to

---

[62] Interview, Z8, male resident, Buyafuthi Hostel, 24 June 2006.
[63] Interview, Z46, male resident, Mazibuko Hostel, 2006.
[64] *Heart of Hope*, 'Interview with Thokoza Hostel Residents'.
[65] Interview, Z4, male resident, Mshayazafe Hostel, 14 June 2006.

wear. You would sleep with everything on, so that when they said, 'Get ready!' you would take your stick and go. If you had a spear you would take it.[66]

Just as SDUs were terrified of being abducted and taken to the hostels, IFP fighters greatly feared being captured and tortured:

> When I left my room for work, I always wondered if I would be able to come back in one piece. Xhosas kidnapped people and took them to Mandela Park to kill them. They would also castrate them. You would hear that some people were kidnapped at Mandela Park and no one could go there to rescue them.[67]

For a Buyafuthi resident, the fear of commuting was so profound that he opted to surrender his job and stay within the confines of the hostel:

> Many of our brothers died while they were going to work. That is why I ended up losing my job because I stayed here. I was too scared to risk my life and go to work and we were also encouraged to stay here and protect the hostel because sometimes the hostel would be attacked during the day because they knew many people are working. So, when you decide to stay and not go to work it was welcomed by the *indunas* because that was regarded as a sacrifice on your part to choose to protect the hostel. They did not know that some of us we were choosing that because we were scared to go outside.[68]

SPUs appear to have been exclusively male, but IFP women did take part in the violence. Photographer Joao Silva captured an image on Khumalo Street of a group of Inkatha women with sticks beating a suspected ANC woman who lay helpless on the ground.[69] A male hostel dweller reported that women 'fought a bit. They fought with other women saying, "your men are killing our men", that kind of thing, "your Xhosa men are killing our men"'.[70] One woman in Buyafuthi Hostel was renowned for her proficiency with a firearm:

> I remember there was this woman that used to stay upstairs here. She shot I think about six people dead and she knew how to use the gun and did not miss. That day she saved us because they were coming to attack us, and we did not have guns in our room and she had one and she shot, those people ran away. Some women were stronger than men, they were so fearless.[71]

---

[66] Interview, JH1, male resident, Mshayazafe Hostel, 10 July 2004.
[67] Interview, JH1, male resident, Mshayazafe Hostel, 10 July 2004.
[68] Interview, Z10, male resident, Buyafuthi Hostel, 4 July 2006.
[69] Marinovich and Silva, *Bang Bang Club*. Photograph located between pages 80–81.
[70] Interview, JH1, male resident, Mshayazafe Hostel, 10 July 2004.
[71] Interview, Z11, male resident, Buyafuthi Hostel 4 July 2006.

Women hid and transported weapons 'because they were not searched, there were no women soldiers so no one could search women'.[72] They also encouraged male fighters. 'When people come to attack we would go out to push it away and women will also come to ululate so that we get power and they will also try and help those that would get injured because many people would be shot, so women would be there for that.'[73]

ISD veterans

ISD veterans interviewed for this study approached the conflict from an entirely different perspective from township combatants because they did not fight on their home ground, their family members were not in jeopardy and they were white men operating in black townships.[74] They were not at risk of being overrun and deprived of their homes. And, because they did not live in the warzone, there was a respite when they went home to their families and friends in white areas.

ISD veterans joined the police for a variety of reasons with some citing a stint in the SAP as a preferable alternative to military service. 'I joined because my call up papers were for 1st battalion and I never wanted to be a foot soldier, so I thought I'd join the police force.'[75] One veteran noted the financial benefits: 'I was conscripted in my matric year, it was 1986. Got my call up papers and one of my uncles suggested that I go to the police force. It was four years conscription instead of two years in the SADF, but the pay was better so off I went.'[76] For a few who had a family history of police service, the SAP was a natural career path, but none chose the ISD; rather they were assigned to their units, usually immediately after graduation from police college. Veterans described a range of political attitudes and levels of awareness. Some commented that there were a few hard-line racists in their unit and that negative attitudes towards the ANC were present. When asked what the ISD was fighting for in the townships, one veteran responded,

> To keep South Africa the way it was. To keep control. We didn't want to be overrun by an unknown enemy. They were unknown to us, the ANC. It was

[72] Interview, Z11, male resident, Buyafuthi Hostel 4 July 2006.
[73] Interview, Z46, male resident, Mazibuko Hostel, 2006.
[74] There were black regular members of Unit 6, but they were a small minority. Other black men served as special constables. These men received cursory training and, although they were often pressed into combat roles, Nick Howarth's description of 'specials' clearly sets them apart from 'regular' members of the ISD: 'They had only achieved standard six at school and were initially recruited for gardening duties, washing state vehicles and the like, but they got rather more than they bargained for when they were posted to our unit.' *War in Peace*, p. 109.
[75] Interview, ISD3, Unit 19, 2017.
[76] Interview, ISD5, Unit 6, 2017.

161

the fear of the unknown. What will happen if they controlled us, if they became the new power, and I was afraid of that.[77]

More common though were professions of ignorance and disinterest. 'We were too young for that shit, man and you don't understand it anyways ... I mean I didn't even know who Nelson Mandela was when he came out of prison.'[78] For many, youth was an important factor in their lack of political engagement. 'I didn't understand the politics of the situation that was going on as I was coming right out of school, but I knew what I had to do as a cop. For us, we just went where there was trouble and dealt with the shit.'[79]

The nature of township duty on the East Rand was often a shock for the newly initiated:

> We were young and now we were in the townships – this one's been shot, this one's been hit, this one's head's open, this one's been hacked, and you put them in the Casspir and, boom, off you go. Either drop them at the morgue or drop them at the hospital and off you go. Not things that we were taught, not things that we were used to, not things that some oke came to us and said, 'Listen you're going to go into this situation now and remember this can happen, this can go wrong, this is what you can encounter.' No, you just go and, boom, deal with it.[80]

> When the ANC–IFP shit started we noticed a difference. There was a definite change. Up until that time it was pretty boring. We were playing around hanging out the riot bus doors, because we were just basically kids. Up until that point it was pretty quiet and then suddenly things changed. Overnight.[81]

ISD patrols were keenly aware of the animosity directed at them by a significant portion of the township population. Nick Howarth's reaction to a group of Phola Park residents is instructive. The refugees traipsing past his Casspir had been burnt out of their shacks the previous night during an IFP attack. 'They had just lost their homes, which made me feel compassionate towards them. On the other hand, they were the same people who made no secret about how much they hated us. We were under no illusion that given half a chance they would try to kill us.'[82]

As the conflict intensified so did the enmity between the ISD and many residents, particularly those aligned with the ANC:

[77] Interview, ISD5, Unit 6, 2017.
[78] Interview, ISD6, Unit 6, 2017.
[79] Interview, ISD7, Unit 6, 2017.
[80] Interview, ISD2, Unit 6, 2015.
[81] Interview, ISD5, Unit 6, 2017.
[82] Howarth, *War in Peace*, p. 112.

We were very much aggressive and our aggression grew as time went on, especially towards the ANC. It got bad, the animosity grew stronger towards us; you could see it the way they looked at us and our responses towards them wasn't professional in a lot of cases. It was unnecessary, hand signals and things like that. We sort of goaded one another. We'd say things. It got bad. I blame it on aggression. Definitely there was a lot of tension between the township residents and ourselves. A lot of them didn't want us there and they made it known. You could just see it. Even the kids you know would do this – [gun firing gesture with hand] – towards us. Like they were shooting at us with a gun. And you could see their mouths going as we moved past and you knew they weren't saying anything nice. Yeah, we became hated, definitely. If we'd been out there alone none of us would have lived more than an hour.[83]

Another veteran recounted how ISD patrols constantly took abuse in the townships. They were sworn at, taunted, gestured at obscenely and pelted with rocks. As a result, his section tended to welcome actions that justified a violent response because, by that point, 'we were happy to give them a fucking hiding'.[84] By contrast, 'an opportunity to work in "white areas" was always welcomed … There was a feeling of safety and acceptance when we were among our own kind.'[85]

Despite all the challenges of operating in a dangerous environment, many remarked that the job was consuming and intoxicating:

It was the adrenaline, it was the adrenaline … You get into this situation and you make friends and you form this brotherhood and these guys are your life. Everything revolves around your group, more so than your own family at home and it's like a betrayal if you leave. And that's a part of it. The other part was that it was exciting. You know for a young man, it's exciting, it was like a game, it was like a blooming TV game and then when the bullets start getting closer it changes from a TV game to reality. … I just went there to do my national service and then you just get sucked in to this whole thing. You get blinkers on and you can't see your way out.[86]

One Unit 6 veteran recalled his squad's reaction when their Casspir was shot at or petrol-bombed: 'We laughed. The adrenaline's flowing and we were loving it. We were youngsters, nineteen, twenty, twenty-one, twenty-two. We lived for it. We loved it. I don't know how. It became normal.'[87] The allure of action was such that patrols sometimes deliberately incited violence. 'When we were bored we knew there were places where if we went in we would draw fire, like Phola

[83] Interview, ISD5, Unit 6, 2017.
[84] Interview, ISD7, Unit 6, 2017.
[85] Howarth, *War in Peace*, p. 181.
[86] Interview, ISD1, Unit 6, 2015.
[87] Interview, ISD5, Unit 6, 2017.

Park and an area that we called Bosnia, just off Khumalo Street. We knew if we drove down there shots would be fired no matter what.'[88]

As the conflict dragged on, however, veterans began to feel the strain. It was impossible to escape the carnage and patrols were often chaotic:

> In our Casspirs, patrol the streets and if something happens you've got to deal with it ... We were just ready for action. If somebody started shooting at us, we would deal with it. We didn't care who they were, and it was an absolute mess, it was a mind fuck. Nobody knew what was going on 90 per cent of the time because it was just a case of you've got to be on this street or there's something happening over there and then you make your way there and that's it. 'Okay, now what's going on, oh, these guys shot at those guys' and there were bodies lying everywhere ... Really all I remember doing is picking up bodies, getting shot at and shooting back. It was a mess, an absolute mess.[89]

Collecting corpses became a routine part of patrols. When asked about the greatest challenges facing ISD members, one veteran replied,

> Bodies. Picking up the bodies because there was no mortuary van. I've got photos of us carrying them and you sit with them. You throw them in a passage in the vehicle and you physically sit with your feet on top of them. Some were shot but many of them were chopped to bits.[90]

At times, the scale of the violence was such that mortuaries were full and, after carrying bodies in their Casspirs throughout their shifts, sometimes even napping among them, the ISD had to stack corpses at their bases. Towards the end of the transition period ISD patrols were issued with special trailers to transport the dead. This offered some relief:

> Initially it seemed like a good idea because it would keep the stinking mess out of our vehicles. The trailers had [eighteen] trays and on a bad day we would often have two bodies per tray. After the first three days trailers also became a stinking mess. Pieces of bone, skin, hair, feces, urine, blood and other bodily fluids sloshed around the bottom of each tray. We rarely had time to clean them.[91]

Over the course of the conflict, clashes with SDUs became ubiquitous. Veterans recall being worn down by the relentless nature of these confrontations:

> It sounds very disrespectful but when it became too much for us, we'd go to the cemeteries literally to go and sleep on those tombstones or just to eat

---

[88] Interview, ISD3, Unit 19, 2017.
[89] Interview, ISD5, Unit 6, 2017.
[90] Interview, ISD6, Unit 6, 2017.
[91] Howarth, *War in Peace*, p. 231.

and drink something or whatever because we knew we were not going to get disturbed there, because they're very superstitious and we'd just take a break and recap, 'Okay, everybody still got ammo' and whatever. This was like a temporary withdrawal place because you know the moment you stick your vehicle out there you're going to get shot at, you're going to get a hand grenade, you're going to get a petrol bomb. This is how it is.[92]

White ISD personnel lived outside the townships, but they were required to work as needed during periods of heavy fighting. 'When the shit hit the fan, you just worked. You would work twenty-four hours a day. You would sleep in the Casspir, wake up, try and find some food and then patrol again.'[93] As one veteran commented, 'you'd keep working because you can't just go home when the place was burning down'.[94] This grind inevitably took a toll:

> There were periods where it would go for three or four months when you'd be working three days, four days and then you'd be off for not even a day ... I was personally not coping well and nor were the rest of the guys in my section. We were fed up with being pushed to the limit.[95]

The ability of ISD patrols to police war-torn townships depended on an aura of ruthlessness and invincibility. Although heavily armed and provided with the protection of armoured vehicles, they effectively operated as outsiders in enemy territory and were almost always outnumbered in hostile situations. They could not afford to appear vulnerable and confrontations triggered a forceful response. In March 1991, a squad from Unit 6 engaged a large group of ANC supporters in Daveyton township. The police claimed that the crowd launched an unprovoked attack. The ANC contended that the police opened fire first. However it began, in the ensuing melee thirteen crowd members and an ISD sergeant were killed and two other officers and more than two dozen township residents were wounded. A veteran who was present during the incident relates events at the hospital where the gravely wounded sergeant had been transported:

> On arrival there's nothing they can do for him, he's dead. Now I'm at the hospital, I'm upset, I'm tired, I'm dirty, I'm full of blood and now these ambulances start coming in one by one with all these guys [ANC wounded], two and two together and the next moment the colonel comes and he says 'no' and we go and get these guys and we flippin' lock them up. As they get out we lock them and we're doing that kind of stuff. ... And that was kind of the attitude we had. Don't take us on cause we will

[92] Interview, ISD2, Unit 6, 2015.
[93] Interview, ISD6, Unit 6, 2017.
[94] Interview, ISD1, Unit 6, 2015.
[95] Howarth, *War in Peace*, p. 71.

definitely hunt you down and get you ... If you want to engage us, you got trouble.[96]

Another veteran put things more graphically, 'If we drew AK fire, we would retaliate with our R5s and maybe deliver a dose of AAAs or SSGs or even SGs with shotguns. It was up to them to make the call. We had no problem blowing away some guy if he was spraying us with AK fire.'[97]

Despite having grenades thrown at them and being stoned, shot at and petrol-bombed with regularity, ISD casualties were relatively light. There were numerous injuries of varying severity, but Unit 6 had only one officer killed during the transition period. Officers were vulnerable when they debussed and patrolled on foot, especially at night. Unit 19 lost two members and had another two badly injured in Phola Park. The SDUs were more familiar with the warren of shacks and, in the darkness, SDU operators had the advantage over their ISD foes. A Unit 19 section was stationed on the border of the settlement when they heard shots fired. They divided into three groups and went in on foot to investigate:

Less than five minutes after we started moving forward slowly all hell broke loose on the right flank and there was a lot of firing going on. So, my group from the bottom flank moved through to the main group and the main group said it's not them, it's on top and that road that comes out onto the soccer field, we had to cross that road and the shooting was still going on. I was trying to get hold of the guy that was that side, but no answer, no answer, so I crossed the road, two or three other guys came with me and we could hear a lot of running between the shacks. We got to X. He'd taken some shotgun shots in his right leg and he was lying between two shacks. We went to check the positions of the other guys, we go to the first one and he was shot in the heart, didn't make it. The other guy took an AK round in his right arm and his elbow was severed and he had to lose his arm. And the other guy we couldn't find and we started looking for him immediately. Now it's pitch dark, it's just after midnight and I started hearing a lot of noise coming from the cemetery side where the hostel was broken down, from that side. So, I started moving up in that direction; it was pitch dark, there was no moon out that night. And I could see some silhouettes running but you can't just fire at anything so I start to call out and there's still running and then I could hear moaning going on the ground and when I got there he'd been shot both knees, both elbows and he'd been chopped with a panga in the chest. He was still alive and we tried to get him out but as we drove him out he didn't make it out of Phola Park, he went.[98]

[96] Interview, ISD2, Unit 6, 2015.
[97] Howarth, *War in Peace*, p. 167.
[98] Interview, ISD3, Unit 19, 2017.

In this sort of environment, the ISD performed more of a military than a traditional policing role. In some instances, ISD officers would not even bother to report fatal shootings:

> You would see a guy chopped up in front of you and if I see that I shoot and we'd leave them there, just leave them, because you can't get out. Sometimes there was thousands of people around fighting and if you get out of the vehicle you're gonna get knocked. So, you shoot them and leave them there. Later you'll come back and with all the other bodies you'll pick them up. And you won't even declare it. That's another thing, you won't declare it. It just gets mixed up with the rest.[99]

At times, the scale of the violence overwhelmed the ISD officers and a sense of futility is evident. When asked how ISD patrols handled large altercations, a veteran responded,

> We'd get the Casspirs in between them and they knew what we were trying to do, and it seemed to work. It worked temporarily but the moment we withdrew all hell would break loose. It wasn't effective and if you think about it, it really didn't do anything. We just kept it calm for a few hours, but the moment we weren't there they were going to climb into one another and that was how it was every single day. The moment we were gone bodies were going to be lying everywhere.[100]

Unit 6 veterans were helpless to stop a massive confrontation on Khumalo Street:

> Probably the most violent thing I saw in the townships it was late December 1990 or maybe early '91 in Thokoza on Khumalo Street. There must have been two or three thousand Zulus who had gotten out of the hostel and they'd gone into Thokoza and they were just massacring people in a massive way. It made Boipatong look mild. Boipatong was the first one that was really publicised but that was mild compared to some of the things that went on earlier but were never spoken about in the media. Anyway, we got there and there were bodies all over the street. It was horrible, and my point is that there were two vehicles and there were about six guys in each vehicle so how are you going to try and handle this? I mean the guys were on the way but even with everybody in our unit there we still wouldn't have been able to handle it. There was just too much going on. They were all over the show just running riot.[101]

One of the foremost frustrations felt by ISD veterans is what they considered to be biased reporting by the media. Much of this they attributed to the efficacy of the ANC 'propaganda machine'. Certainly,

---

[99] Interview, ISD6, Unit 6, 2017.
[100] Interview, ISD5, Unit 6, 2017.
[101] Interview, ISD1, Unit 6, 2015.

the changing political climate brought a degree of media and NGO oversight to security force actions that was largely absent in earlier years. And, with some of the activities of Vlakplaas and other covert units coming to light, the security forces were subjected to intensive scrutiny. As a front line combat unit, the ISD was particularly vulnerable to allegations of misconduct. A Unit 6 medic recalls with disgust an incident for which he was 'crucified by the press':

> We were driving down Khumalo Street and the Zulus have just gone past on their way to Phola Park and we were responding there to try and stop them. And on their way they were killing people. And we stopped at one house that was burning and there were two guys lying there. The one guy was kind of still breathing and the other guy was dead. So, as we debussed photographs were taken there I think by the *Weekly Mail* and the *Citizen* and the *Guardian* and who knows what else. I jumped out with my kit to look at them and the guy who was dead was dead, there's nothing you could do for him. The other guy was gargling but what they didn't know, and what I was never asked but later on during the inquiry I had to explain it, it's called triage basically. Triage is not only mass casualties, triage is also situation bound. Everything in the medical field is SABC – safety first, then airway, then breathing and then circulation. Having assessed him, he's got multiple trauma wounds, hacked, the whole katoot. He's having difficulty breathing, he had a very faint pulse. There was nothing … it would have taken me X amount of minutes, ten or fifteen minutes to get him stabilised, then the next point was to get him into the vehicle to take him out of there. By that time, I could have put up as many lines as I possibly can; he had what we call hypovolemic shock. He was bleeding all over the place. And at that specific time they started shooting at us. Our guys are returning fire and I'm thinking this guy's about to go. To now put my life in danger plus the rest of my crew trying to protect me for somebody that I could possibly maybe not save because in triage there is black, red, yellow, green. He was a red priority, one bordering on black. He might not live through this so why put fourteen other guys at risk. We then left him and carried on down the road. We called it in and did whatever and there's transcripts and on our way down we got to the Zulus and they were turning back. On their way back they came by these two and added insult to injury and hacked off the one's arms and feet and his groin and everything else and once again the newspaper was there and it's 'Police left people to die'. Big nonsense. On the red carpet, the Minister of Police was Vlok at that stage – 'what happened?' – got the transcripts of the radio. After that we had to attend a press conference where all these guys were peppering us with questions and that kind of stuff.[102]

One veteran went so far as to label the media as the ISD's greatest challenge. He maintained that the media typically ignored violence perpetrated by township residents and focused instead on the count-

---

[102] Interview, ISD2, Unit 6, 2015.

er-violence of the ISD. This included journalists who rode along with the ISD and then distorted events that had occurred during patrol:

> The press was our biggest problem and it was my biggest fear ... you didn't trust them. You didn't know what they were going to say ... We saw the press at that stage as the enemy ... I'm not saying we were right all the time, we were wrong in many cases, but the story should be told down the middle.[103]

Several men related specific incidents in which the media either misinterpreted or misrepresented events on the ground:

> I saw a clip that had one of our Casspirs driving next to a massive group of Inkatha guys who were running down Khumalo Street in Thokoza and the news was saying that we were escorting Zulus, but that's not what we were doing. It was one vehicle with six guys and thousands of Inkatha and we were just trying to keep them under control. That happened a lot ... At Zonkizizwe [IFP dominated squatter camp in Katlehong] we went and picked up some Inkatha guys because we were trying to have some kind of mediation between ANC and Inkatha and we had tables set out and cool drinks and those types of things. Another vehicle went to fetch the ANC delegates and we went to get the Inkatha side and I loaded the Inkatha guys in and the newspapers took a photo of the Inkatha guys getting into my vehicle. So, the next day it's like 'look they're loading these guys in' and that would fuel things ... I remember these guys from Phola Park who were burying someone who had been killed by Inkatha and they were marching down Khumalo Street and we got wind of it so we had about thirty guys in the road armed to the teeth because they wanted to come past the hostel and that wasn't going to work, so we made a line and they got to the line and they were very aggressive. They wanted to basically go and take on the hostel guys. But we turned them around and the media reported that we were disrupting a funeral.[104]

The ISD's role in transporting people opened units up to accusations of partiality. 'We collected people, did fingerprinting on them, did screening, everything and if you picked the people up you had to go drop them off again ... There were days when there were negotiations and we'd have to support people with transport and a lot of those stories were twisted as well.'[105] Unit 6's commanding officer bitterly recounted press coverage of negotiations he conducted between representatives from ANC and IFP groups in Katlehong engaged in an armed stand-off. His men ferried representatives from both groups to the negotiations, but film footage of the incident was edited to delete images of the ANC people travelling with the ISD. This edited footage was featured in

[103] Interview, ISD3, Unit 19, 2017.
[104] Interview, ISD1, Unit 6, 2015.
[105] Interview, ISD3, Unit 19, 2017.

news broadcasts and newspapers reported that the ISD was working with Inkatha. Unit 6 effectively countered these charges because they had documented the entire proceedings with their own camera, but there was still political fallout:

> Adriaan Vlok [Minister of Law and Order] called me the next day and said, 'What's the story here. Why are you only taking Inkatha?' And I said, 'No, that's bullshit', and we made a photo album and I took it through to headquarters in Pretoria. Adriaan Vlok was there, Gill Marcus [ANC Department of Information and Publicity] was there and a couple of other people. She was the spokesperson for the ANC. And we showed them the photos which showed the part that they edited out with the ANC ... But the damage was done.[106]

The optics of some situations were such that it is easy to understand why observers often believed the ISD favoured Inkatha. A veteran described an incident in which SDUs were advancing on a hostel while firing their weapons. The hostel dwellers were shooting back and, in an effort to prevent the situation from escalating, the ISD patrol used their Casspirs to block the hostel entrances. Once they pulled up in front of the hostels, they started taking fire from the SDUs. Naturally, the police turned towards their attackers to return fire and, as they did so, a few of the hostel fighters darted out of the hostel and used the Casspirs as cover to shoot at the SDUs. The ISD veteran insisted that parking in front of the hostels was the most effective way of keeping the combatants apart and there was no intention of assisting the IFP contingent. Perhaps so, but this situation again illustrates the ISD's differential relationship with the two warring parties. It would have been unthinkable for the police to turn their backs on SDUs in the middle of a firefight and to allow SDU fighters to shelter behind ISD vehicles while sniping at IFP militants. Not surprisingly in such situations, the press and violence monitors questioned ISD neutrality. Much of the resentment directed at the media is due to ISD veterans' conviction that they sacrificed for their country and the communities they believed they served. They are convinced that their actions saved many lives and that, as bad as things were in Thokoza and Katlehong, they would have been much worse without the presence of the ISD: 'If it wasn't for the Unit, I promise you the East Rand would have burned. The whole East Rand would have been a no-go area.'[107] For these men, their stigmatisation as racist killers is a bitter pill to swallow.

While all the men interviewed denied any knowledge of unprovoked killings or rendering assistance to the IFP, they did not shy away from admissions of physical abuse and intimidation of suspects. As

---

[106] Interview, Hein Kilian, Unit 6 Commanding Officer, 2017.
[107] Interview, Hein Kilian, Unit 6 Commanding Officer, 2017.

related by veterans, SDU attacks almost invariably occurred at night and took the form of shots fired or grenades and petrol bombs hurled under the cover of darkness. The difficulty of arresting assailants in these circumstances led to feelings of immense frustration:

> With the SDUs it was very difficult because we never knew who they were. They wore civilian clothes and would stand around on the street corners and as your vehicle comes by and then you know [snaps his fingers] a hand grenade or a petrol bomb. And they never keep it on them, it'll be hidden in the grass or around some rocks … In that situation it was very, very hard to do the policing because, like I said, they didn't have the weapons on them, the weapons were hidden around them so you could get out and you know it's him but there's nothing you could do about it.[108]

A Unit 6 veteran explained that the pressures of the job caused many ISD officers to have a short fuse:

> If you're under this constant pressure and constant magnifying glass from opposite sides, from the press, from your own police people, from your own family and everybody else to do the right thing, whatever that might have been at that stage, you become intolerant. And if you say to a guy 'do this' and he does it, naturally you go 'okay'. You'll still be suspect but at least now I can carry on. When you start to get confrontation back or resistance, you go 'no, no, no, you're rubbing up the wrong party'.[109]

On those occasions when they managed to catch SDU members who they believed had been shooting at them, ISD patrols often administered a beating before booking the suspect in at a police station. Unit 6's commanding officer readily admitted that this was standard practice when his men had been shot at. In the words of a Unit 6 veteran, 'If I caught someone firing at me who wanted me dead, if I hunted him down and caught him the chances are I'm going to give him a good hiding.' He added that his section would sometimes round up suspected SDU members and threaten to drop them at the hostels unless they revealed the whereabouts of their weapons.[110] Unit 19 sometimes dealt with suspects in a similar fashion: 'I suppose there was a bit of jungle justice. The guys would be flared up and then you would follow through with an arrest. The problem would be that the local police station sometimes wouldn't take him because of external injuries or something.'[111]

Their experiences in the townships, the scale of death and destruction they witnessed and the combat they engaged in affected their

[108] Interview, ISD1, Unit 6, 2015.
[109] Interview, ISD2, Unit 6, 2015.
[110] Interview, ISD1, Unit 6, 2015.
[111] Interview, ISD5, Unit 6, 2017.

personal lives. A sense of being alienated from mainstream white society is pervasive in ISD veterans' accounts. 'The guy on the street – you know the whites in this country were totally oblivious to this, they didn't have a clue ... they didn't know what was happening a few kilometres from their homes while they were asleep in their beds'.[112] This estrangement extended to family members. 'You come home and you can't talk to them. You can't tell them what happened. You just can't.'[113] One offered a frank portrayal of his response to the pressures of the job:

> I would get as drunk as possible as quick as possible and my poor wife ... I'd go off my nut sometimes, pull a gun and shoot it off and everyone would disappear from the house. It was nuts, it was really crazy. It was really, really hard to fit in with society. And my mom and dad didn't know me. No one knew me. I really turned into something I never thought I would turn into. My eyes were dark and my soul was dark. It was really a very bad time.[114]

Conclusion

> [T]he average young guerrilla fighter is neither an angel nor a demon. He, because with a few exceptions this is a man's world, is more of a 'man-child' than anything else. He is fragile, damaged, and hurt. Yes, he undoubtedly commits horrific acts of human rights violation; he is a bandit, but also by all means a political actor, and sometimes he is regarded both by his peers and in his home community as a freedom fighter or a defender of certain rights, values and identities.[115]

The above passage speaks directly to the experiences and perspectives of Thokoza and Katlehong combatants. Most were young males, many committed horrific acts and almost all saw themselves as defenders of some sort. SDU members defended their neighbourhoods, but also indiscriminately ambushed and slaughtered migrant Zulus and sometimes victimised their home communities. These youngsters lost family members and friends and were traumatised by the violence they suffered, witnessed and committed. Hostel residents provided sanctuary to non-combatant Zulus and fought to preserve their urban bases, but also went on killing sprees in the townships. They were frequently the objects of ethnic hatred and were reduced to a desperate state during hostel sieges. ISD veterans risked their lives to protect

---

[112] Interview, ISD1, Unit 6, 2015.
[113] Interview, ISD3, Unit 19, 2017.
[114] Interview, ISD1, Unit 6, 2015.
[115] Morten Bøås, 'Marginalized Youth' in Bøås and Kevin Dunn (eds) *African Guerrillas: Raging Against the Machine* (Lynne Reinner Publishers, Boulder, 2007), p. 39.

Combatant Stories

township residents, but at the same time used deadly force against them and sometimes abused suspects. These police officers encountered countless atrocities, were condemned as racists and, as front line combatants in a township war, often felt estranged from white society.

The line between perpetrators and victims was a shifting, murky and precarious divide. Virtually all the combatants described in this book straddled that line. As their accounts make clear, doing so exposed them to acute physical danger; the psychic and moral costs are incalculable.

7 Living in a War Zone

We lived like animals, always scared.[1]

This is a story of communal trauma. Residents of Katlehong and Thokoza contended with four years of violent conflicts and, although some areas were more directly affected than others and the intensity of the conflict varied, the ANC–IFP fighting and all the associated violence persisted for the duration of the transition period. Its impacts were felt in many ways by different groups of residents, but a consistent theme appearing in survivor narratives is the inescapability of violence: 'If you lived in the townships, you were automatically involved. It was better for those who had money, they simply found new places to stay.'[2] The accounts of those who remained provide an impression of what people endured and how life changed during the conflict.

Duma Nkosi, the chairperson of Thokoza's ANC branch, relates an incident that indicates the scale of the carnage. Police regularly collected corpses and transported them to mortuaries. Nkosi explained that the local ANC kept a record of such bodies in the hope of notifying relatives:

> There were lots of people, we buried people which we couldn't get to be claimed by family ... There were five hundred graves without names. We had a record because we took fingerprints but if ever someone has been burnt it will just be a piece of a charred body, human remains, but the point is you won't know who the person is. Even now we actually have the grave numbers ... There were terrible albums where we tried to even take photos of people who were butchered and killed ... so that we can try to encourage people to identify their relatives.

A father whose son had been shot and killed and whose body had been taken away by police approached Nkosi for assistance in locating his son's remains. After several inquiries, they were directed to one of the local mortuaries:

---

[1] Interview, T4, male resident, Thokoza, 15 December 2005.
[2] Interview, T1, male resident, Thokoza, 5 July 2005.

Plate 6 Thokoza residents walk to work through burning barricades on Khumalo Street, 1990 (© Greg Marinovich)

> There were piles of bodies. They said, 'When did the person die?' I said, 'No, he was shot today.' I was with the family and someone behind the counter said, 'I saw a body of a young man who was looking like you. I put him somewhere at the back.' So, we went to identify the body, you know if you have seen the movies of the German massacres of the Jews, it was just stacked bodies. They said, 'These ones are from last week. If someone disappeared last week you have to look here. If it's a week before, it's here.' But when you go look there are bodies on top of each other and you will have to remove a corpse, check, remove a corpse, check and then put them back again. People never went, so those were the bodies we buried without names, it was actually just numbers. But there will be a corner where people who were necklaced or burnt were thrown so it will be a heap of charred bodies.[3]

All respondents reported their fears of being victimised at the hands of militants and the security forces. For most township residents, IFP-supporting hostel dwellers and their allies in the townships represented the greatest danger, whereas for migrant Zulus it was primarily township youth, particularly the SDUs. People from either side of the divide had common security concerns, but township and hostel residents also experienced challenges and voiced fears that reflected their different living circumstances and vulnerabilities.

[3] Interview, Duma Nkosi, Ekurhuleni, 27 June 2008.

Migrant Zulus: Violence became the only life I knew

Those associated with the IFP, overwhelmingly migrant Zulus, had no real respite from the violence because the hostels, squatter camps and nearby streets controlled by the IFP were all on the front lines. As Bonner and Ndima observed, township militants 'did everything in their power to extinguish the presence of Zulu migrants'.[4] A woman who took refuge in Kwesine Hostel after being chased out of the township recalled, 'When I think of that violence I remember the smoke, there was always smoke. They used to burn everything, even people. The trucks that used to deliver food were called targets and would be burnt, some stores were burnt, our shacks were burnt, fire was the greatest weapon.'[5] Without exception, these respondents reported that they were targeted on an ethnic basis and that township militants wished to purge the area of migrant Zulus: 'A Zulu person was hated! They didn't want Zulus at all. When they saw a Zulu person, they would stop him and ask him. If you could not speak Sesotho, you would be attacked, killed, and burnt there and then.'[6] Many were convinced that their political affiliation, if indeed they had any, was secondary:

> To be an IFP supporter is not written in the face, so if we have to be honest we don't know who was IFP and not and we could not tell, hence we just emphasised the fact that we were killed because we were Zulus. There was nothing you could do to hide that you are Zulu but you could hide that you are IFP so that did not matter. What mattered was the fact that you were Zulu.[7]

Migrant Zulus stood out from their more urbanised counterparts because of the 'deep' isiZulu they spoke, and because many had distinctive facial scarring and cut earlobes. Respondents often attributed their politicisation to ethnic persecution, as only the IFP offered support to migrant Zulus:

> We all became IFP supporters during that time, even though before political organisations were not an important thing. During the violence it became very important to become a member of an organisation to get protection. We as hostel dwellers became IFP members and people like Themba Khoza would come and help us and he would go to those people in higher position and tell them about our sufferings. We would get trucks that bring food because of such people, so it became important to become a member of a political party.[8]

---

[4] Bonner and Ndima, 'Roots of Violence', p. 377.
[5] Interview, Z49, female resident, Kwesine Hostel, 2006.
[6] Interview, JH2, male resident, Buyafuthi Hostel, 18 July 2004.
[7] Interview, Z38, male resident, Mazibuko Hostel, 24 October 2006.
[8] Interview, Z45, male resident, Mazibuko Hostel, July 2006.

Living in a War Zone

As a relatively small minority in townships that housed more than half a million residents, migrant Zulus became increasingly isolated as the conflict dragged on. They were contained in their ethnic/political enclaves and entered the townships at their peril. A profound insecurity pervades respondents' accounts of the conflict. The destruction of Khalanyoni and Lindela was the first stage of migrant Zulu displacement and, for many forced to abandon these hostels, it fuelled a rage that sustained the conflict:

> We lost our humanity; you know when you have lost so many things you lose yourself. At Khalanyoni I left everything, I just left with the clothes that I was wearing. You don't know how that affects you until it happens. The anger you develop turns into hatred and when you hate with that passion you are no longer a person. And that is what the violence did to people.[9]

In concert with the skirmishing that finalised the composition of local squatter camps, campaigns against migrant Zulus residing in the townships prompted a wave of dislocations. A man who fled to Mazibuko Hostel recalls,

> Where I was renting a room, the owner of the house was a very nice woman and she came to me and said, 'I have been told that they are going to burn my house because I have a Zulu tenant.' And she continued and said, 'I don't know what to do because you are a good tenant and I have not seen you doing anything wrong.' I just felt that I should not put her life at risk and rumours were spreading that in the township they want to kill all the Zulus, even their women because they give birth to rats. So, I left the room and came to the hostel.[10]

Township residents noted the plight of these people in different ways. Some sympathised: 'It was very difficult, for the Zulus that were from KZN, many of them left the township, and went to the hostel, and they sent their children back home. ... They used to kill the Zulus that were from KZN.'[11] Others approved: 'Township people started to burn the houses where IFP people stayed and chased them away, to go and stay with their brothers in the hostel. We could not afford to stay with those snakes because snakes all bite the same.'[12] A woman who escaped to Mazibuko Hostel after being attacked describes the fallout from this event:

> One night in 1991 while we were sleeping we heard a big noise as if it's a gunshot, but it wasn't, it was a petrol bomb. They were burning our

---

[9] Interview, Z47, male resident, Mazibuko Hostel, 2006.
[10] Interview, Z22, male resident, Kwesine Hostel, 19 July 2006.
[11] Interview, Z56, female resident, Katlehong, 2006.
[12] Interview, Z66, female resident, Katlehong, 25 May 2007.

house and we had to wake in the night and run away, we ran away to here ... I think I stayed only a week here at the hostel and as soon as I got a chance I went back home to Nquthu [KZN]. But that was painful to lose everything that you have worked hard for just like that. It took a day to lose my house with everything we had worked hard for. When I left this place my husband remained behind and he still had his taxi. Three months after I had left our taxi was burnt too and now we had no source of income. That devastated my husband and he went straight to alcohol ... We stayed at home, but it was difficult because there was no money coming in and the children were still small. I had to do something, so I came back again in 1993 ... I came straight here because I couldn't go back to the township as our house was burnt. That is how I started staying here in the hostel. ... I was lucky because I got a job at Alberton as a domestic worker and my job was a stay in, so I could not be affected that much. And when the violence was strong I wouldn't come, I would stay there. But I would hear when I come that things were bad, and some people died. Many people left the hostel.[13]

Women with male relations or partners residing in IFP dominated hostels were acutely vulnerable. Many had their homes burnt, some were killed and survivors had little option but to leave the township entirely or take refuge in the hostels. The hostels were built as single-sex dormitories and several women commented on the humiliation of sharing communal toilets and bathing facilities with men:

We as women were affected differently from men because we had to leave everything and come and stay in a place that is designed for men. When you stay here you can see that women were not in the heads of the architects when they were designing hostels. The bathroom, the toilets, everything and living in such a place makes you feel as if you don't love yourself enough.[14]

They also reported that their dependence on male hostel dwellers exposed them to sexual violence and exploitation. Male residents acknowledged that the influx of women posed challenges: 'Women were affected immensely because they suffered the violence from the township and they were not protected 100 per cent here ... Remember we did not use to [sic] have women here; it was a place for men.'[15] Several men claimed that measures were put in place to assist women. 'We tried to make this place conducive and to protect them. There was one *induna* who was responsible for women's issues. If a woman was abused in any way she would go and report her case to that *induna* and the *induna* will deal with that.'[16] Although all women coped with

[13] Interview, Z39, female resident, Mazibuko Hostel, 25 October 2006.
[14] Interview, Z43, female resident, Mazibuko Hostel, 2006.
[15] Interview, Z9, male resident, Buyafuthi Hostel, 4 July 2006.
[16] Interview, Z11, male resident, Buyafuthi Hostel, 4 July 2006.

challenging circumstances in the hostels, the plight of non-Zulus forced to flee the townships because they were involved with Zulu men was especially stark. A woman who settled in Buyafuthi Hostel after being run out of Katlehong for 'sleeping with Inkatha' describes the additional difficulties such women faced:

> When I arrived here in the hostel it was not easy ... because I was not a Zulu. I was a Xhosa, so I got a lot of abuse as a result. I could not leave the room, I could not even go to a spaza shop inside the hostel because I was not Zulu. Violence affected me so much because I did not belong anywhere ... My personality had to change because if I was soft the women here in the hostel would play with me because I was not Zulu, so I had to learn to defend myself.[17]

For those Zulus who remained in or fled to the hostels, their identity was sealed. 'If you stay in the hostel, you have to be IFP. Maybe not a Zulu, but not Xhosa. It was a point where ethnicity becomes profound.'[18] A woman who sought sanctuary in Katlehong's Kwesine Hostel explained,

> When you were in the hostel that was joining IFP. You need not fill any forms, just by being there you are IFP. ... To stay in hostel meant that you are IFP and there is nothing you could do about that and ANC people would kill you when you come from the hostel. The hostel was your [IFP] card.'[19]

Ethnic cleansing was followed by a blockade of the hostels which created great hardship. Journalist Daniel Reed observed that Kwesine Hostel 'looks like the bombed-out remains of a prisoner-of-war camp or a battery chicken farm'.[20] An early 1994 NGO report outlined the situation in Kwesine:

> Food and medical supplies could only enter under armed escort ... The hostel is overcrowded and is ill-equipped to cope with the hundreds of people who have sought refuge there. Single rooms now house up to eight people. As many as [fifty] families share two hot plates to prepare meals. One sink is used for washing clothes, dishes and bathing. Conditions are squalid and completely unhygienic. Such overcrowding has put a serious strain on the inhabitants' health. Children are the most vulnerable.[21]

Conditions became so desperate that, towards the end of the conflict, 'when hostel residents were "holed up and starved", a group of them

---

[17] Interview, Z16, female resident, Buyafuthi Hostel, 12 July 2006.
[18] Interview, Duma Nkosi, Ekurhuleni, 27 June 2008.
[19] Interview, Z18, female resident, Kwesine Hostel, 18 July 2006.
[20] Reed, *Beloved Country*, p. 85.
[21] IBIIR/Peace Action, *Before we were good friends*, p. 35.

dissected a dead body in search of a liver to eat'.[22] By late 1993 many hostel residents were dependent on the Red Cross for basic supplies:

> There were times where we could not even get food because all roads that come here were closed and the trucks that do deliveries were attacked. They were called targets, so we could not get food. We were saved by the Red Cross that came and brought food. There was this guy who was an IFP leader here at the hostel, his name was Sibiya. He is the one who called the Red Cross, he was very helpful.[23]

In addition to this isolation, hostel residents had to contend with occasional attacks by the SDUs. A Mazibuko resident recalls a sustained assault:

> There is a week that I cannot forget. I stayed the whole week without going to work. If I did not lose my job then I will never lose it again. In that week we could not even go out to buy food. It was black outside because of smoke, the gun shots, the screams, people singing. We would not sleep. We slept in shifts and if we did not do that this hostel would not be here. We had another block that was completely destroyed ... I have never seen anything like that in my life. I don't know how many people died in that week alone. I never thought I would leave this hostel alive.[24]

Zulu migrants came to the Rand because of the paucity of wage earning opportunities in their home areas. The hostels served as affordable accommodation that allowed them to support rural homesteads and families, and many of those who remained despite the violence framed the issue in terms of economic survival:

> The township people did not want us to stay here; they wanted us to go back where we come from. But we could not leave this place because if we left our children would die of hunger as we came here because there are no jobs where we come from. We did not come here for anything else because it is not a luxury to stay here.[25]

Some clung to hostel life, praying that the violence would end and they could keep their jobs:

> At some point we could not even go to shops and buy food, and the shop that we had was burnt so it was difficult to go and buy food even if you had money. ... You know that when you go back home you will never find employment, so we stayed with the hope that the violence will stop but it

[22] Bonner and Ndima, 'Roots of Violence', p. 378.
[23] Interview, Z23, male resident, Kwesine Hostel, 19 July 2006.
[24] Interview, Z40, male resident, Mazibuko Hostel, 25 October 2006.
[25] Interview, Z45, male resident, Mazibuko Hostel, July 2006.

dragged on for five years. At the end, violence became the only life I knew here in Johannesburg.[26]

A hostel-based taxi driver explained that continuing to drive through the conflict was an attempt to preserve his right to an occupation:

> I was working because I needed to survive but it was more than that. If we did not continue working they would rule us out and when the violence ended we would not be able to come and rank again, so in other words we were securing our jobs because I cannot say we were making that much money as very few were working, and the routes that we were taking were very long to avoid violence.[27]

Travelling through the township was the single most dangerous aspect of the conflict for hostel residents:

> Going to work was the worst thing because the hostel, the buildings, could provide protection. But when you are going to work, even when you are using the train at some point you needed to get out and there you are visible and people like us with these scars on our faces we could not deny that we are Zulus. Leaving the hostel was like committing suicide.[28]

Almost every hostel respondent had a harrowing tale of running the transport gauntlet:

> The day I thought I am leaving this world was when I was from work and the railway line got cut off. We saw the children standing and they were singing ... We could not go towards the children because when they get you, they will burn you. We were three and we decided to take another route to avoid them, but they saw us, and we started running and they shot uKhumalo. Fortunately, he did not fall there. He was able to run for a short time and when he was losing strength we could pick him up. When we arrived at the hostel he had bled so much, and they called the police and he was taken to hospital and he did not make it. I was really hurt by his death, and I realised how close I was to death. It could have been me that was shot that day.[29]

The greatest fear for those associated with the IFP was to be burned by the comrades. Many respondents were haunted by the necklacings they had observed, and these images came to represent the most brutal aspect of the violence. Two accounts by hostel residents illustrate the depth and power of this grisly spectacle:

---

[26] Interview, Z7, male resident, Buyafuthi Hostel, 24 June 2006.
[27] Interview, Z20, male resident, Madala Hostel, 18 July 2006.
[28] Interview, Z37, male resident, Mazibuko Hostel, 24 October 2006.
[29] Interview, Z22, male resident, Kwesine Hostel, 19 July 2006.

I was scared to be necklaced. I used to pray that when I died I must not die like that because that is the most painful death I have seen. When the violence was still starting they caught this woman from Natal who was visiting her relatives. I don't know how they got her, but they burnt her in front of our eyes. You see these shacks? They were not there, it was just an open space. They came singing and when we all went out they had this woman and set her alight and she burned and when she was trying to run away they beat her with stones. She cried for a long time, maybe it was not that long but to me it was long. We watched her helplessly and that cry stayed with me, I still remember that. That is when I realised that some people can be like animals. That was the cruellest thing I have ever seen, although it became normal.[30]

A woman who had taken refuge in Buyafuthi Hostel related an incident in which comrades burnt a 'target' they had captured directly across the road from the hostel:

I think I had two days here at the hostel when we heard people screaming and making noise saying 'come, come' and we went out and we saw a child burning. I think he was around twelve. He was very young, and they said it was a Zulu child and they wanted to show us what they do with *inzule* [derogatory term for Zulus]. That was so painful to watch, and I don't know what kind of people could do such things and be able to sleep at night. The cry of that child stayed with me for a long time, even now I can still hear it. I think about his mother and how would I feel if they burnt my child.[31]

Township residents: Our children made this their war

So-called 'township Zulus' – long-standing residents with no clear ties to the hostels or the IFP – were viewed differently from migrants, but still were under pressure to prove their loyalties and were sometimes targeted by mistake or because of heightened xenophobic sentiment. Thokoza's ANC Chairperson, Duma Nkosi, worked hard to convince residents that Zulu speakers in the township should not automatically be considered the enemy. He lamented that this was often an uphill battle and innocent isiZulu-speakers sometimes bore the wrath of outraged township residents: 'We had shop stewards and leaders of COSATU killed in Katlehong because they were Zulu speaking. Because the distinction was not there because they may not be coming from a branch of the ANC where people were known.'[32] Even well-established township Zulus were watched closely: 'If you were Zulu in the township you had to really show that you are an ANC and be

---

[30] Interview, Z52, male resident, Mazibuko Hostel, 2006.
[31] Interview, Z15, female resident, Buyafuthi Hostel, 10 July 2006.
[32] Interview, Duma Nkosi, Ekurhuleni, 27 June 2008.

very active or else you would become a suspect.'[33] ANC-supporting Zulus were a particular sore point for the IFP. Duma Nkosi, who is of Swazi and Zulu descent, recalled a Peace Committee meeting with *indunas* from the Thokoza hostels at which he was condemned for being a sell-out. Some of these men had been friends with Nkosi's father, who had been a hostel resident before moving to the township. They rebuked Nkosi, telling him, 'You have eaten the saliva of the Xhosa. You are poison among us.'[34]

The presence of a substantial Zulu township population, along with the fact that some Zulus took up arms against the IFP, led some township residents to have a more flexible attitude toward ethnicity. For these people the fight against the IFP was often viewed as an extension of the liberation struggle, and political allegiances trumped ethnicity. An SDU member remarked,

> When the Zulus started killing people they said they were killing the Xhosas, and that brought the element of ethnicity, but in the township we could not do that because we had all the ethnic groups. Like, I am Xhosa, but I was working with the Zulus because they were my comrades. We never entertained that, we focused on the real enemy, the people that were attacking us.[35]

The wife of an SDU commander concurred, 'It was reported that Zulus were fighting Xhosa but that was never the case. We know better, we were here. My husband is Zulu and he was fighting the Zulus in the hostel. That logic does not hold at all.' [36]

Although township residents were not besieged in the same way as hostel residents, many still reported on the ubiquity of the violence. 'Zulus attacked us everywhere, you go to the trains to avoid the violence in the taxis, and they were there. You drove your own car, they killed you. It was bad. They killed babies who knew nothing.'[37] Residents located close to the hostels were most exposed and, although attacks could come at any time, people anticipated cyclical aspects of the violence:

> Sometimes they would catch a Zulu person on the street and they would be saying we got *umdlwembe* [derogatory term for a wild, uncivilised person] and kill the person, and then at night we won't sleep because the Zulu people will be seeking revenge and that will drag on maybe for two weeks.[38]

---

[33] Interview, Z66, female resident, Katlehong, 25 May 2007.
[34] Interview, Duma Nkosi, Ekurhuleni, 27 June 2008.
[35] Interview, Z95, male SDU member, Katlehong, 2006.
[36] Interview, Z80, female resident, Katlehong, 9 June 2007.
[37] Interview, T1, male resident, Thokoza, 5 July, 2005.
[38] Interview, Z84, female resident, Katlehong, 2006.

Such insecurity induced a constant state of anxiety:

> We used to dress our children ready for running away, and even when it was two in the morning we would be fully ready and dressed with enough clothes on for us and our children. This was done so that when they attack us we were then ready to run away. We always carried our important documents like marriage certificate, birth certificate and others with us tight around our body.[39]

In the same way that migrant Zulus dreaded the necklace, township residents feared the atrocities attributed to IFP militants. Accounts of people being abducted and transported to the hostels to be tortured, raped and murdered were common currency:

> Zulus attacked us while we were on our way to work one morning. The taxi we were travelling on was taken to Buyafuthi Hostel. They asked us our names and surnames. I survived because you can see I am light in complexion and I lied and said that I was a Coloured. When they asked for our ID I said I left it at home and spoke in Afrikaans. It was I and another woman, she had a small baby who was left to go, and the rest were killed. I can't forget that day.[40]

Often, IFP-aligned taxi drivers functioned as the malign element in these narratives, as they were said to lure unsuspecting township residents into their vehicles for delivery to the hostels. In one variation, victims' body parts were used to enhance the fighting ability of IFP militants:

> I was scared of being abducted by the IFP because there were stories about abductions. We would hear that the Zulus were taking people to make traditional medicines for fighting and those people were killed in a painful way because they would cut their parts while they were alive because the traditional healers wanted to use them while they were still hot and after they will kill that person.[41]

Several respondents related being terrified for their children, as IFP marauders were said to spare no one:

> Even a child of one year they will take him by the legs and smash him into a wall. That's what makes me afraid of the Zulus even now – how can a person do something like that to kill a one year old. For me a normal human being cannot do that.[42]

---

[39] Interview, D1, female resident, Thokoza, 2 June 2006.
[40] Interview, T6, male resident, Thokoza, 27 April 2006.
[41] Interview, Z78, male resident, Katlehong, 9 June 2007.
[42] Interview, G1, male SDU member, Thokoza, 11 June 2004.

Large scale raids out of the hostels resulted in mayhem, including sexual violence. On a July night in 1993, residents from Kwesine Hostel launched an attack into the surrounding townships. A group of men broke into Catherine M.'s house:

> They came in and beat me hard, they raped me – they meant business. I begged them not to kill me. I even told them if they stopped hurting me I would let them take all the furniture – but it seems they were going to take that anyway. They took everything, from the most important and most expensive sofa, to my hangers. They even took clothes. Then they shot me in the leg.[43]

Many were sickened by the bloodshed and desperately wished for the conflict to end:

> I worked in the hospital and treated the injured, so I saw really bad things and I used to ask myself what kind of people are we, when we did all that to each other? I used to treat people who were badly injured, you would think that it was animals that did that. I remember one patient we were treating. It was a baby hacked with a panga or an axe. It was just bad. Those people had let their hearts die.[44]

For others, however, their losses and widely circulated stories of IFP barbarity contributed to an environment in which any violence directed at the 'enemy' was sanctioned. 'You can tell that people really lost themselves when they could even necklace a person', explained a woman from Katlehong. 'To be honest with you I used to support children when they were doing that because I was convinced that IFP supporters were dogs.'[45] A man from Thokoza expressed similar sentiments: 'You know when they were burning people we celebrated. I remember there was a car that was caught with people from Natal, all those people were killed and then burnt. The community was celebrating that, and everyone was saying they deserved to die because they are killing us.'[46] Along with revelling in anti-IFP violence, residents sometimes initiated defensive actions. After Khalanyoni Hostel had been burnt down and the Zulu residents had fled, IFP militants used the ruins to snipe at Phola Park. A group of Phola Park female residents then took it upon themselves to completely dismantle the remains.

---

[43] Judy Seidman and NomaRussia Bonasa, '*Tsogang Basadi:* Finding women's voice from South Africa's political conflict', http://www.judyseidman.com/tsogang%20basadi%20paper.html
[44] Interview, T4, male resident, Thokoza, 15 December 2005.
[45] Interview, Z69, female resident, Katlehong, 26 May 2007.
[46] Interview, Z72, male resident, Thokoza, 1 June 2007.

The hostel had been burnt but parts of the structure were still standing. It was actually the women of Phola Park who pushed that hostel down. I was there. They felt like there were still people coming down from Madala Hostel and Khutuza Hostel [further up Khumalo Street] and hiding in the buildings and shooting at Phola Park. Literally one morning they went out, loads and loads of women and just pushing down what was left of the walls and then they took the blocks away and used them to build their own places. It was very much a sort of women's power going on because they were sick and tired of when they went out to the loo or something like that they were getting shot at by people coming down and hiding in what was left of the hostel.[47]

Political neutrality provided no protection from violence and residents were forced to choose sides. As she enjoyed a Black Label beer during an interview, an elderly pensioner from Thokoza's Phenduka section recounted how hostel dwellers had boarded a taxi she was riding and demanded to know everyone's political allegiance. Passengers who could not convince the militants of their loyalty to the IFP were beaten and forced off the taxi. She had no interest in politics and decried, 'I was not in favour of ANC. I was not in favour of IFP. I was only in favour of Black Label.'[48] For township residents any suspected connection to IFP supporters became extremely dangerous. A peace monitoring report discussed the precarious position of township homeowners who rented to migrant Zulus:

Many landlords ... became victims of a violent process of polarization where any association with 'the enemy' was grounds for attack ... they were subject to attack because they had rented their shacks to 'Zulus' or 'IFP' members. Bongani Ndlovu said that the 'comrades held a meeting to plan the elimination of homeowners who were 'being useful to the IFP'.[49]

IFP attacks constituted the foremost danger for many residents, but the militarisation of the townships and the suspicion of strangers could also make movement between sections precarious:

Say you come from work and meet a group of people ... they would do a sign that you didn't know and that would put you in danger, because it served as an indication that you did not belong to the area and that meant that you were an enemy, you see. Sometimes, you would be killed not for doing anything wrong but just because you didn't know the sign.[50]

Township residents also had to deal with predatory SDUs and the backlash against suspected *izimpimpi*. In the 1980s, police informants,

[47] Interview, Sally Sealey, London, July 2006.
[48] Interview, G6, female resident, Thokoza, 12 June 2004.
[49] IBIIR/Peace Action, *Before we were good friends*, p. 22.
[50] Interview, J4, male resident, Thokoza, 11 July 2004.

along with so-called sell-outs to the struggle such as local politicians working for apartheid authorities, were targeted by anti-apartheid militants. Hundreds were killed, including necklacing executions. In the transition period, summary executions were extended to persons suspected of supporting the IFP. In many cases the alleged *izimpimpi* were punished in public spectacles that allowed embattled communities to vent their rage against accessible targets:

> The *impimpi* would carry all information discussed to help and protect the communities to the Zulus and the police. When we found out our information was given to our enemies, then there was a group of people who will hunt those suspected to be *impimpi*. When an *impimpi* was caught it was made sure that the community knows about it and there will be a gathering, and everyone will be beating and kicking that *impimpi* and then he will be set alight using paraffin or petrol, and sometimes they will necklace *impimpi*. I saw one man who was killed that way after one member of the community claimed to have seen him with Inkatha people at his house. People were very angry and disappointed to hear that. Later that evening, which was on Sunday, a group of angry residents went to the *impimpi's* house and dragged him out to the street and beat him until he was unconscious. They burnt down his house including his car and then they poured petrol on his whole body and set him alight ... People were so angry about *impimpi* and they wanted to show anyone who was attempting to be an *impimpi* that his life, including his family, will be in danger as they won't tolerate sell-outs.[51]

Respondents acknowledged that informers were a destructive force and deserved to be punished, but many were dismayed that the campaigns to rid the townships of *izimpimpi* led to widespread abuses:

> There was a problem with trust amongst us township people. People used the violence to justify their bad intentions about others. There was this thing of the necklace, now others would use that to solve their grudges between them and their neighbour. They would then say, so and so is a spy. And without any verifying of that accusation, people would attack that person. And many innocent people died, and their houses were destroyed.[52]

Once accused it was impossible to prove that one was not an informer. In addition to malicious accusations motivated by jealousy or personal grudges, allegations were sometimes based on the thinnest of suspicions. 'One teacher was killed in our school because it was said he was IFP because he said we should come to school during the time when it was very tense. He was then said to be an IFP member because he did not show fear towards the Zulus.'[53] *Izimpimpi* were the prime target of these campaigns, but other undesirables were sometimes singled

[51] Interview, D2, female resident, Thokoza, 3 June 2006.
[52] Interview, T4, male resident, Thokoza, 15 December 2005.
[53] Interview, Z88, male resident, Katlehong, 2006.

out for punishment. In a war situation, those seen to be undermining community cohesion – such as criminals and suspected witches – were also vulnerable to retribution. Some attributed this to the out-of-control nature of young militants:

> I think the problem was that the youth were given so much power and they used it badly ... Some people were real *impimpis* and some were just killed because the youth were used to killing. There was an old granny down the other side of Extension 2, she was killed and for what? They said she was a witch. So many bad things happened because of the violence.[54]

Township residents' reflections on the youth-dominated SDUs ranged widely and often accommodated both appreciation and resentment: 'Without the SDU the Zulus were going to kill us all. But there were problems because some SDU members became uncontrollable and they wanted to rule everybody's lives.'[55] There was also a sense that adults had surrendered community control:

> People's children were prepared to sacrifice their lives for us. But you understand that some of them became so wild that we were scared of them. We were just told that they are going to do something, but we really had no say when it comes to what was to be done. Our children made this their war.[56]

There is no shortage of accounts detailing SDU abuses. Many respondents were sceptical that the money collected by SDUs was spent exclusively on guns and ammunition: 'The violence corrupted our children ... They would say that they were fighting Inkatha, whereas some of them were just silly children out of control. Those kids would make us donate money for protection and some of the money was not accounted for and you were scared to even ask.'[57] Some SDU members preyed on township girls and women, including female pupils:

> The SDUs were sent to watch schools but they ended up raping school girls. If they wanted you as a girl you could not reject them because even if you tried they would take you and sleep with you by force and everyone was scared of SDUs ... They were not all like that but some of them did that.[58]

The SDUs' access to arms made resistance to forced sex very difficult. 'They would terrorise people because they had guns. For instance, if they want a particular woman, even if she had a boyfriend, they would

[54] Interview, T5, male resident, Thokoza, 20 March 2006.
[55] Interview, Z78, male resident, Katlehong, 9 June 2007.
[56] Interview, T6, male resident, Thokoza, 27 April 2006.
[57] Interview, T9, male SDU member, Thokoza, 27 May 2006.
[58] Interview, Z56, female resident, Katlehong, 2006.

make sure that they get the girl and there would be nothing that you could do as a man.'[59] A former SDU member confirmed the routine nature of sexual violence:

> You know during those days, you can find young girls ... actually that was a rape because no one was allowed to have sex with a young age ... sixteen years. That we know ... we are taking advantage to say this is a situation. So, if I want a girlfriend I might choose anyone, and say 'I want that one'. I say 'come here, if you don't like I slap you', she is crying and then I take [her] over to my place and do that, she'll sleep over.[60]

Rape could also be used as a form of punishment. Sibongile Sambo and her sister, Fransisca, were abducted from their Thokoza home on the orders of SDU Commander Ben Mashinini. It was claimed that the two women were IFP informers because men from the nearby Buyafuthi Hostel frequented their shebeen (informal tavern). Both women were stripped, robbed of their jewellery and repeatedly raped before being shot. Unlike her sister, Sibongile survived. 'They raped us. ... and afterwards shot at us. My sister was shot in the back of the head and I was shot in the shoulder, leg and private parts.'[61]

Fighting between rival SDUs and the disruption of schooling featured prominently in residents' concerns. A Thokoza resident explained that, when the SDUs were first formed, communities rallied behind them – people sheltered them, women cooked for them and community members shielded them from the police. But then, 'I don't know what went wrong, they started killing each other. They were under commanders and each section had its commander. One section started attacking other sections and the commanders were blamed for those things because I think they became corrupt and they were into criminal activities.'[62] Inevitably, residents were drawn into these conflicts. Two SDU members from Thokoza Extension 2 were captured stripping a car in another section. The home SDU was called and executed them on the spot as criminals. This killing then precipitated a battle between the two SDUs and a problem for local ANC officials. An ANC representative in Extension 2 argued that the ANC flag should not be raised at the deceased SDU members' funerals because they had been killed in the commission of a criminal act. His stand incurred the wrath of Extension 2 SDU members, who threatened to kill him, and he had to go into hiding before the matter was resolved.[63] Teachers

---

[59] Interview, Z58, male resident, Katlehong, 2006.
[60] Barolsky, *Transitioning out of Violence*, p. 82.
[61] 'Thokoza Violence Victim Tells of Rape and Murder by SDU Members', 1 December, 1998, http://www.justice.gov.za/trc/media%5C1998%5C9812/s981201b.htm. The SDUs involved received amnesty for the abduction and shootings but not for the rapes.
[62] Interview, T5, male resident, Thokoza, 20 March 2006.
[63] Interview, male ANC official, Thokoza, 19 May 2005.

reported being caught between police who harassed their students and SDU members who sometimes brought their guns to school and intimidated teachers and pupils:

> The police would come during school times and demand that we hand some students over to them. They claimed that those students were dangerous. But most of the time we refused and hid the students because we knew what would happen to them if we handed them to the police. Our work as teachers was made difficult. We had to deal with the police on one side, and on the other hand, there were bad elements in the youth at schools. Education in the township was badly affected by the violence. There was a time when it was so bad we were afraid to come and teach. ... As a teacher at a high school I have seen the worst. I have seen students dragging a person they were saying was Inkatha through the township. The youth were coming here to collect fellow youth to go and kill this guy. The mob was a bunch of wild youth and there was nothing we could do as teachers, because if we called the police we knew we were starting another problem. So, we told them that they can do whatever they wanted to do as long as they left the school premises, but the situation got out of control. They broke down the school fence. In a minute, the same students who were in classes had pangas and guns and you could see that there was nothing we could do. The guy was killed right here inside the school yard.[64]

Parents felt powerless to prevent the militarisation of their children. With their communities under attack and with no other force to depend on for protection, it was left to local youth to serve as soldiers. 'Letting your child go to fight was very difficult for many women because they knew what they were risking but there was nothing they could do, it was war and children had to go out.'[65] Acknowledging the inevitability of this development in no way reduced the level of parental anguish:

> As I have said, I have four sons. I thought I was going to lose one of them and none of them sits on top of the other, I love them equally. Every time when I would hear the gun shoot I will hear it right inside my stomach. Remember boys had to be out at night patrolling so anything could happen to them and many young people died during that time and I still thank God that I did not lose a child. In this street, we lost two boys. They were both killed by IFP but on different occasions. Death was normal at that time, but it was difficult to expect it in your house.[66]

In the initial stages of the violence, when young males were often compelled to join defensive structures, parents who objected risked retribution:

---

[64] Interview, T5, male resident, Thokoza, 20 March 2006.
[65] Interview, Z66, female resident, Katlehong, 25 May 2007.
[66] Interview, Z69, female resident, Katlehong, 26 May 2007.

Every boy had to participate in the patrols. Some of the youth were armed and others not and they had to face armed Zulus and the police. So, you understand why some parents were very protective of their children. And if you showed concern over such things you were sometimes seen as a sell-out. And that made the whole experience even harder.[67]

In addition to the assortment of dangers to which people were exposed, many also experienced material losses. Residents located close to the hostels were often driven from their homes and abandoned valuables when they fled to safety. A Katlehong homeowner described her family's forced exodus:

In 1992 the Inkatha people came and chased us away and they occupied our houses and the police did not help us ... You know, when you have your house you work for it, every little cent you get you invest it in your house because you don't think you will lose it. I lost my house for two years. I came back here with my family in 1994. They had taken everything, when we came back here it was empty and filthy.[68]

And, although township residents aligned with the ANC were not subjected to the same isolation as hostel dwellers, Phola Park residents experienced restrictions when the camp was cordoned off by state security forces:

From about the 13th of December 1990 until December 1991 Phola Park was surrounded by razor wire. For all of January and February 1991 there was a [twenty-four] hour presence of SADF, and then SAP, guarding three entrances to Phola Park ... The security forces believed that this wire actually protected the community from attack ... and certainly that it prevented attackers from moving out of Phola Park. But for the [twenty thousand] people who are not going to move out of Phola Park to attack anyone, the struggle for survival became an exercise of living in a concentration camp. Women and children had to be searched to move out into the veldt to relieve themselves. People feared being trapped inside Phola Park, unable to flee in case of an Inkatha attack, which they believed the SAP would allow or assist. The razor wire became a block to removing trash from Phola Park, in fact it became a wall of litter, rags and refuse. The living conditions and health conditions inside Phola Park became dramatically worse.[69]

Conclusion

With Katlehong and Thokoza functioning as war zones, thousands were killed and injured, and all residents were exposed to violence. Many

---

[67] Interview, T9, male SDU member, Thokoza, 27 May 2006.
[68] Interview, Z76, female resident, Katlehong, 8 June 2007.
[69] IBIIR, 'Report from Davin Bremner to Goldstone Commission'.

respondents look back on the conflict years as a period of madness that completely distorted township life. Neighbours turned on neighbours, innocents were slaughtered; hate and suspicion ruled the day. Fear was pervasive as people were targeted based on suspected political affiliation, ethnicity, gender, place of residence and the inability to protect themselves. All armed parties, including state security forces, victimised non-combatants and there was no effective law enforcement. Township, hostel, and informal settlement residents, irrespective of political allegiances, experienced displacement, material destruction, job losses, disruption of education and restrictions on their freedom of movement. No section of the Katlehong or Thokoza population had a premium on suffering.

Conclusion

South Africa's first elections with universal adult suffrage, held on 27 April 1994, marked the end of apartheid. The ANC won more than 60 per cent of the popular vote and formed a Government of National Unity. At the regional level of government, the ANC topped the poll in seven of the nine provinces; the IFP won its home province of KZN and the NP held on to the Western Cape. The elections demonstrated the IFP's political marginalisation on the Rand, as it was trounced at the polls just as its followers were isolated in the hostels and exhausted by the violence. Consequently, the IFP concentrated its political efforts in KZN. For its part, the ANC moved to demilitarise Rand townships, urging SDUs to stand down and comply with disarmament initiatives. Numerous SDUs, fearing a resurgence of hostilities, refused to surrender their weapons, and some SDU rivalries persisted, but the scale of violence immediately and substantially diminished once political sponsors disavowed fighting.

Many combatants had a difficult time transitioning to peace. Notwithstanding the trauma they endured, SDU members achieved a status that evaded most township youth. They were feared, they had power, and in the midst of a war, communities had little choice but to tolerate SDU excesses and accept SDU authority. Once the violence was over, the new ANC government had no use for local militias and any continuing violence was branded as criminal. The communities that had once sheltered and fed SDUs no longer did so. Instead, ex-SDU members were sometimes stigmatised as killers and ostracised by their home communities. There was little in the way of counselling or reintegration programs available to these combatants.[1] A handful were absorbed into the local police as reservists, but the majority of these were dismissed or resigned within a short period of time.[2] Many struggled with post-traumatic

---

[1] Two ex-SDUs interviewed for this study became involved with rehabilitation programs that concentrated on wilderness and outdoor activities sponsored through the National Peace Accord.

[2] Former SDU members report that the police were hostile to this initiative and marginalised SDU reservists at every turn. Moreover, many SDU reservists did not have the required educational qualifications or driver's licences to qualify as regular members of the police. This led to resignations by qualified candidates who left in solidarity with their less fortunate comrades. As one Thokoza SDU member

stress disorder (PTSD) and substance abuse issues along with joblessness and social isolation. SDU members considered themselves to be soldiers of the ANC and pointed out that they had done much more fighting than MK veterans who were eligible for pensions, reintegration packages and enlistment into the post-apartheid military. Some SDU groups lobbied for recognition as statutory combatants, a status that would entitle them to benefits but, despite a short-lived demilitarisation programme in Ekurhuleni, these goals were never realised. Instead, some ex-SDUs turned to crime and these former combatants have been implicated in car-jacking operations, cash-in-transit heists and contract killings.[3] Not one of the two dozen former SDUs interviewed for this study had full-time employment when we met.[4]

Inkatha militants have fared no better. Whereas the TRC was available to SDUs and many told their stories at amnesty hearings, perhaps with some therapeutic effect, this possibility was denied to SPUs and other Inkatha fighters because the IFP instructed its followers to boycott the TRC. A few SPUs attended Ekurhuleni demilitarisation meetings in the mid-2000s and some also took part in Peace Accord outdoor/wilderness rehabilitation programmes, but no formal recognition or benefits were made available to them. Many former SPUs are rumoured to be involved in crime syndicates operating out of the hostels.[5] For IFP followers the only positive outcome from the fighting is that six hostels remain standing and still provide an urban base for migrant Zulus in Katlehong and Thokoza. However, except for Katlehong's Buyafuthi Hostel, which was renovated and upgraded, the hostels in these townships were without electricity or running water twenty years after the conflict ended. A study of urban renewal in Kathorus noted the neglect of the hostels: 'The limited funding for hostel upgrading is particularly unjust in the sense that hostel residents are amongst the poorest and most marginalised of Kathorus residents, and yet they received the least support from the SIPP [Special Integrated Presidential Project for urban planning].'[6] The former Inkatha fortress on

(contd) stated, 'We said if they can't become members we must leave as well because I can't be a traitor to my fellow members. If I must choose between my fellow members and the police, I must stand with my fellow members who don't have those particulars.' Interview, G2, male SDU member, Thokoza, 16 July 2008.

[3] For more on the plight of ex-SDUs and other ex-combatants, see Gear, 'Wishing Us Away'; Barolsky, *Transitioning out of Violence;* and Monique Marks, 'Alternative Policing Structures? A look at youth defense structures in Gauteng in 1995', Research report written for the Centre for the Study of Violence and Reconciliation (Centre for the Study of Violence and Reconciliation, Johannesburg, July 1995), https://www.csvr.org.za/publications/1570-alternative-policing-structures-a-look-at-youth-defense-structures-in-gauteng-in-1995.

[4] Group SDU Interview, Thokoza, 13 July 2008.

[5] Several hostel interviewees made this connection.

[6] Tanya Zack, *Critical Pragmatism in Planning: The Case of the Kathorus Special Integrated Presidential Project in South Africa* (Ph.D. Dissertation, University of the Witwatersrand 2006), pp. 241–2.

Conclusion

Plate 7 Ruined, yet still inhabited building in Mshayazafe Hostel, 2008 (© Theresa Ulicki)

Khumalo Street still houses Zulu migrants who came to the city seeking relief from the grinding poverty of their rural homes. Constructed in the mid twentieth century, many of the buildings are derelict and structures that were partially demolished during the fighting have not been rebuilt. Long stretches of squat cinder block buildings, punctuated with broken windows, form squares around rubbish-filled courtyards. During one visit, an elderly resident exclaimed, 'I'm sure you didn't expect people to be living in a place like this. I'm sure you think that such a place is just for animals.'

The ANC government followed through with some development initiatives in Thokoza, including the construction of hundreds of Reconstruction and Development Programme houses on the site of Phola Park. Hostel residents have no doubt that such projects have bypassed their complexes in favour of ANC-supporting areas. They point to the erection of a concrete barrier around the Khumalo Street hostels as proof of the government's continuing hostility towards the ANC's former enemies. The IFP lacks any meaningful political influence on the Rand, and hostel dwellers have been left to fend for themselves since the end of the violence.

ISD veterans were assigned the thankless task of policing war-torn townships. It was a losing proposition from the start because the prior history of policing in the townships placed them at odds with many residents who regarded them as apartheid enforcers. Even more importantly, the government never prioritised township secu-

Plate 8 Grounds of Madala Hostel, 2008 (© Theresa Ulicki)

rity. All the men interviewed for this study have left the police. Several mentioned that some of their former comrades suffer PTSD, and some men who stated they are battling with PTSD refused interviews. However, ISD veterans do not have to cope with the trials of rebuilding their lives in a war zone and their material circumstances are considerably better than those of the non-state combatants interviewed. Their primary grievance is their portrayal as racist killers who were responsible for much of the township bloodshed. Not only do they insist that this reputation is undeserved, but that it is a profound injustice to police who put their lives at risk in a war in which they otherwise had no stake. They did their duty as best they could in enormously challenging conditions that their fellow South Africans never understood or appreciated:

> A lot of people in South Africa in their homes sitting at six o'clock at night watching their SABC [South African Broadcasting Corporation] news did not understand this. They had no clue what was happening out there … There was a war raging and they had no idea. It was a handful of 120 or 150 people protecting the East Rand.[7]

They particularly resent that, instead of SDUs who necklaced people or Inkatha militants who committed wholesale slaughter, the ISD is often seen as bearing the greatest responsibility for township violence in the transition period.

[7] Interview, ISD2, Unit 6, 2015.

After being the mainstays of Rand violence, Katlehong and Thokoza faded back into obscurity after 1994. Unlike better-known Soweto, with its struggle sites, museums and sightseeing tours, these townships have little to offer visitors. The lone marker of the violence is located on a barren stretch of Khumalo Street. Poorly signed, unattended by employees or volunteers and well set back from the road sits a memorial to Thokoza's dead, a stone edifice etched with the names of some seven hundred victims of the violence.[8] This bleak, forgotten monument is an all too appropriate testament to a brutal civil conflict that often appears as a secondary story in accounts of South Africa's transition to democracy.

Legacies of violence

Even as the ANC election victory effectively ended politicised violence on the Rand, the discursive contest persisted. Here too, the ANC emerged victorious, as the dominant popular and academic narratives locate transition violence firmly within the 'struggle history' framework. This book maintains that the massive militarisation triggered by the ANC–IFP conflict unleashed an explosion of violence and an assortment of armed groups with disparate agendas that is not adequately captured by the oppressor–resister binary. Whereas the price paid by Thokoza and Katlehong residents is relatively easy to assess, the national legacy of transition violence is trickier to pin down. Many Rand townships had well-established histories of violence – state, criminal, vigilante and political – before 1990. However, the unique conditions of the transition period produced an unprecedented level of communal conflict. The ANC and the IFP armed and assisted local militias, and fighters aligned with both sides committed atrocities, often against non-combatants. Along with the IFP conflict, ANC supporters also fought with PAC and AZAPO activists. Some ANC structures were riven by internal conflicts and militants from all parties, but primarily the ANC, clashed with security forces. These same militants sometimes victimised locals and engaged in criminal pursuits for material gain. Amid township fighting, criminal figures who forged political connections rose to prominence.

[8] The Thokoza monument does not include victims from Katlehong. Moreover, great difficulties were experienced in identifying victims, so these names represent a partial roll-call of the dead, which is generally estimated to be in the several thousands. For an account of the process that led to the Thokoza monument see, Lazarus Kgalema, 'Symbols of Hope: Monuments as symbols of remembrance and peace in the process of reconciliation' Research report written for the Centre for the Study of Violence and Reconciliation (October, 1999). http://www.csvr.org.za/publications/1676-symbols-of-hope-monuments-as-symbols-of-remembrance-and-peace-in-the-process-of-reconciliation, accessed 11 April 2017.

Conclusion

The standard narrative positions state security forces as implacably hostile to their historical ANC enemy and presents covert 'third force' units as a primary driver of politicised violence. Although apartheid security forces were ideologically ill-equipped disinterestedly to police township conflicts involving ANC-supporting combatants, transition-era policing was not as one sided as is often depicted. Specialised police and military units supplied significant quantities of weapons, along with training, to IFP fighters, but some black police – especially those residing in conflict areas – provided SDUs with firearms, ammunition and intelligence, and some SADF units actively assisted SDUs against IFP militants. Many security force personnel did not favour either party. There is no credible evidence that covert units had the capacity to direct Rand violence and, despite receiving weapons from state sources, IFP militants pursued their own campaigns that were not subject to 'third force' manipulation. Moreover, as negotiations proceeded and the ANC gained influence, the state was compelled to act against officials and units associated with covert activities. The ability of such forces to fuel the violence waned considerably in the last half of the transition period. More than 'third force' operations, the NP government's approach to township violence guaranteed its continuation. The primary task of the security forces remained the protection of the white population, and the government's efforts at violence reduction in even the worst-afflicted townships were haphazard and half-hearted. State security forces were unable to contain communal conflicts and thousands of bodies were collected by the police with no attempt at criminal investigation. In this anarchic environment, various forms of violence thrived. So, whereas the transformation to democracy granted political rights to black South Africans, it did nothing to address the deep-seated practices of violence that had become rooted in South African society. Instead, it provided the stage for some of the worst expressions of political and communal violence in South African history.

In terms of situating the persistence and resurgence of post-apartheid violence, it is critical to acknowledge that transition conflicts constituted a distinct rupture from the preceding decades of politicised violence. Political conflict prior to 1990 was defined in insurrectionary terms – state repression begot resistance, which provoked further state violence. Many of apartheid's watershed events are closely tied to struggle history. The Sharpeville massacre led the NP to ban the ANC and the PAC, which in turn sparked the formation of MK and Poqo (succeeded by APLA, the Azanian People's Liberation Army) and the beginning of an armed struggle against the apartheid state. The 1976 student uprisings signalled the importance of youth-led resistance, which continued during the 1980s urban insurrections. These resistance campaigns prevailed in the face of brutal state repression, including mass intimidation and arrests, the use of the military to suppress protests, the torture of political activists, targeted assassinations by government death squads and the hanging of convicted dissidents. To be sure, various aspects of criminal, vigilante and communal violence existed alongside and often overlapped with politicised conflict, and nationalist rivalries sometimes flared up, but resistance to and defence of white rule constituted the defining paradigm for political violence until the start of the transition years. Because ANC supporters considered Inkatha militants to be NP pawns, the 1980s UDF–Inkatha rivalry was also viewed as insurrectionary.

The unbanning of nationalist movements in 1990 and the undertaking to negotiate a new political settlement transformed the nature of politicised violence. The ANC returned from exile, suspended its armed struggle and committed to talks with the government. Despite ongoing clashes between some activists and the security forces, ANC violence was no longer directed at overthrowing the state. Negotiations leading to majority rule offered a more promising route to ending apartheid and assuming state power. The prospect of a national election with a non-racial franchise made the struggle for black votes paramount. ANC conflict with the IFP, which had been raging in many parts of KZN since the mid 1980s, intensified and spread to Reef townships. Old animosities between state security forces and ANC supporters did not disappear, but the focus of the violence shifted from insurrectionary to competitive as ANC and IFP supporters engaged in a deadly contest for political influence. At the same time, as the ANC grew rapidly and seemed poised to become the next government, struggles proliferated within and between militarised ANC structures.[9]

Party leadership promoted, armed and provided oversight to local militias that often had competing interests. Groups such as the rival SDU and ANCYL in Katlehong's Moleleki Extension 2 fought to establish local dominance, while others battled over positions within ANC civics or ANC affiliates such as NUMSA. Much of the internecine fighting in the Vaal seems to have followed this course. Prior to the ANC's return from exile, the benefits of support for liberation movement structures were limited and the risks were great. In the transition period, the ANC's status as an emerging political giant greatly expanded the potential rewards associated with party positions. Many activists judged that these opportunities were worth fighting for and the ensuing clashes occurred in a highly charged, militarised atmosphere in which violence was normalised. Trying to manage its own

---

[9] ANC and MK groups in exile had a long history of factionalism and infighting, and their return to South Africa contributed to some of the violent rivalries that erupted in various townships. See Stephen Ellis, *External Mission: The ANC in Exile, 1960–1990* (Oxford University Press, Oxford, 2013).

exponential growth while simultaneously fighting a war with the IFP and conducting contentious political negotiations, the ANC lacked the capacity and often the resolve to effectively mediate such disputes. Instead, it was forced to tolerate the excesses of armed groups to keep them within the fold. Post-apartheid South Africa has been wrestling with this inheritance ever since.

Anthony Collins argues that, while South Africans abhor the impacts of violent crime, 'they are remarkably enthusiastic about many other forms of violence'.[10] This propensity for violence extends into the political sphere. All political parties and many different structures carried their histories and practices of violence into the democratic era and, since 1994, South Africans have been ruled by an ANC government that was deeply implicated in transition conflict. The point here is not to demonise the ANC. Whatever its faults they cannot compare to those of the NP, which founded apartheid and ruled by terror. The NP, IFP and ANC all functioned as belligerents in transition-era hostilities. The focus here is on the ANC because, as the current government, it has yet to demonstrate a decisive break with its violent past.[11] The achievement of ending apartheid through a negotiated election, rather than a full-blown civil war, Nelson Mandela's international stature as a Gandhian figure of reconciliation and humanity, and the fixation with NP and IFP violence, has deflected attention from the ANC's history of violence. The ANC turned to an armed struggle in 1961, endorsed violence against functionaries of the apartheid regime in the 1980s uprisings, avoided outright condemnation of necklacing murders in this same period and brutalised suspected informers and dissidents in some of its military camps.[12] Despite the formal suspension of its armed struggle in 1990, it waged war against the IFP to better secure its political interests in the negotiation period and has consistently disavowed any responsibility for these conflicts. Violence was an essential part of ANC campaigns on the ground in areas of the Rand and KZN, and the party also experienced considerable levels of internecine conflict.

Many of these tendencies have been evident since the ANC attained office. For the first decade, the ANC faced little meaningful opposition or violent protest, but as the state came under increasing pressure in the early 2000s, the ANC's reliance on violence has revealed troubling continuities. The government has often encouraged police to take a hard line with protestors during the epidemic of 'service delivery

[10] A. Collins, 'Violence is not a Crime: The impact of "acceptable" violence on South Africa society', *SA Crime Quarterly* 43 (March 2013), p. 30.

[11] For a discussion of ANC militants who graduated to local governance following the ANC's 1994 election victory, see Ellis, *External Mission* and, Sarah Mathis, 'War Leaders to Freedom Fighters: Violence in Umbumbulu in the Waning Days of Apartheid in South Africa', *African Affairs* 112, 448 (2013), pp. 421–39.

[12] See Ellis, *External Mission* for a comprehensive discussion of violence in exile.

protests'.[13] Police brutality, a hallmark of the apartheid regime, has continued in the democratic era with the Marikana massacre of striking mine workers, and the subsequent cover-up, serving as the most callous example of state oppression. As opposition groups have gathered strength, the ANC has repeatedly demonstrated its intolerance for political challengers. This has included less formal groups, like the shack dwellers movement Abahlali baseMjondolo, as well as its principal political rivals the Democratic Alliance and the Economic Freedom Fighters.[14] If the ANC's grip on power continues to diminish, it is hard to imagine that intimidation and violence will not intensify, especially in the lead-up to elections. Perhaps because of the ANC's dominance, the worst violence to date has occurred within the party. Top government officials engaged in factional disputes have subverted state resources, but the deadliest struggles have occurred at the local level where assassinations have become increasingly common.[15] The enticements of local office are especially alluring in rural municipalities where, in the absence of other remunerative opportunities, such positions offer significant material reward and require nothing in the way of formal qualifications. Assassinations can prevent rivals from running for office or remove incumbents and are also employed to silence whistle-blowers or others who threaten those already in power.

Mark Shaw's observation, 'Hits are used in the South African context to regulate intersecting political, economic and criminal interests', accurately describes much transition violence.[16] Testifying at the Moerane Commission of Inquiry into KZN political killings in 2017, three leading ANC officials 'all played down suggestions that violence had spiralled out of control under their watch, arguing that they had inherited a violent society conditioned to use force to settle political

[13] See, for example, P. Alexander, 'Rebellion of the poor: South Africa's service delivery protests – a preliminary analysis', *Review of African Political Economy* 37, 123 (2010), pp. 25–40; M. Paret, 'Violence and democracy in South Africa's community protests', *Review of African Political Economy* 42, 143 (2015), pp. 107–23; K. von Holdt, M. Langa, S. Molapo, N. Mogapi, K. Ngubeni, J. Dlamini and A. Kirsten (2011) *The Smoke That Calls: Insurgent Citizenship, Collective Violence and the Struggle for a Place in the New South Africa: Eight Case Studies of Community Protests and Xenophobic Violence* (Centre for the Study of Violence and Reconciliation and Society, Work and Development Institute, University of the Witwatersrand, Johannesburg, 2011), http://www.csvr.org.za/docs/thesmokethatcalls.pdf

[14] A report by the Community Agency for Social Enquiry concludes that 'intimidation and the manipulation of the electoral process remain systemic features of political life in South Africa', and identifies the ANC as the 'primary source of intimidation' involving economic threats, physical threats and outright violence. D. Bruce, '"Just singing and dancing"? Intimidation and the manipulation of voters and the electoral process in the build-up to the 2014 elections', Community Agency for Social Enquiry (CASE), April 2014, p. 4.

[15] D. Bruce, 'A Provincial Concern? Political Killings in South Africa' *SA Crime Quarterly* 45 (September 2013), pp. 13–24; Mark Shaw, *Hitmen for Hire: Exposing South Africa's Underworld* (Jonathan Ball Publishers, Johannesburg and Cape Town, 2017).

[16] Shaw, *Hitmen for Hire*, p. 179.

disputes'.[17] ANC KZN Chairperson Sihle Zikalala attributed the killings to competition for local positions: 'Incumbents will want to hang on to public office by hook or by crook because they have no career outside public office. Others will work hard to remove the incumbents so that they also get the positions and get closer to state resources.'[18] These developments are reminiscent of internecine ANC violence during the transition period. Recall, for example, the attempted assassination of Vaal activist Bavumile Vilikazi, reputedly because MK soldiers accused Vilikazi of 'blocking positions for them'. And, just as it was rare for anyone to be held accountable for the transition-era killings, very few post-apartheid assassinations have led to convictions. Many ANC officials and supporters continue to view violence as an acceptable and effective tool for advancing party and individual interests, and the evidence suggests that the ruling party has yet to abandon the violent practices that crystallised in the transition period.[19] Recognising the nature and depth of these conflicts provides a broader perspective for understanding the violence that continues to afflict South Africa – much of it still emanating from the state.

This book has recounted the intense and brutal violence that wracked the black townships of the Witwatersrand between 1990 and 1994. It has examined the excesses of the time, the fissures that they opened, and the scars and memories that are its legacy. It is a history that wove a particularly bloody thread into the contemporary fabric of a society still beset by violence.

---

[17] Paddy Harper, 'ANC KZN: We didn't turn a blind eye to violence and corruption', *Mail & Guardian*, 20 October 2017, https://mg.co.za/article/2017-10-20-anc-kzn-we-didnt-turn-a-blind-eye-to-violence-and-corruption.

[18] Paddy Harper, 'Sihle Zikalala: Apartheid legacy at the root of KZN killings', *Mail & Guardian*, 19 October 2017, https://mg.co.za/article/2017-10-19-sihle-zikalala-apartheid-legacy-at-the-root-of-anc-killings.

[19] Karl van Holdt, 'South Africa: The Transition to Violent Democracy', *Review of African Political Economy* 40, 138 (2013), pp. 589–604.

Bibliography

Government Collections (printed)

Truth and Reconciliation Commission of South Africa Final Report (Truth and Reconciliation Commission, Cape Town, 1999)

Government Collections (online)

Truth and Reconciliation Commission
http://www.justice.gov.za/trc/report
http://sabctrc.saha.org.za

TRC Amnesty Hearings
Nicholas Zwile Chamane, AM0188/96, 7 September 1999, Johannesburg, http://www.justice.gov.za/trc/amntrans/1999/99090609_jhb_990907jh.htm, accessed 9 February 2008.
Mzobona Leonard Hadebe, 2 February 1999, Nelspruit, http://www.doj.gov.za/trc/amntrans/1999/99020105_nel_990202ne.htm, accessed 14 July 2014.
Mr Hlongwane, AM54696, 21 April 1998, Durban, http://sabctrc.saha.org.za/hearing.php?id=54696, accessed 22 November 2012.
Samuel Mafolane Hlophe, AM5878/97, 23 November 1999, http://www.doj.gov.za/trc/amntrans/1999/99112325_jhb_991123jb.htm, accessed 6 January 2009.
Zandisile Patrick Kondile, Langeberg Factory incident, 12 October 1998, http://www.justice.gov.za/trc/amntrans/1998/98101215_jhb_joha1.htm, accessed 19 December 2010.
Victor Wanda Muchacho Mabaso, 2 February 1999, Johannesburg, http://www.justice.gov.za/trc/amntrans%5C1999/99020118_jhb_990202jh.htm, accessed 6 May 2011.
Jeremia Mbongeni Mabuza, AM7633/97, 8 December 1998, Palm Ridge, http://www.justice.gov.za/trc/amntrans%5C1998/9811231210_pr_981208th.htm, accessed 30 January 2015.
Chichela Esau Machitje, AM7634/97, 24 November 1998, Vosloorus, http://www.doj.gov.za/trc/amntrans/1998/9811241202_jhb_981124.

vos.htm, accessed 6 March 2008.

Sipho Japtha Maduna, AM5475/97, 16 February 1999, Johannesburg, http://sabctrc.saha.org.za/hearing.php?id=53191&t=AM5475%2F97&tab=hearings, accessed 9 November 2008.

Stephen Donald Makhura, AM0014/96, 16 November 1998, Welkom, http://sabctrc.saha.org.za/documents/amntrans/welkom/52973.htm, accessed 22 June 2010.

Thomazile Eric Mhlauli, AM7344/97, 3 December 1998, Palm Ridge, http://www.justice.gov.za/trc/amntrans%5C1998/9811231210_pr_981203th.htm, accessed 13 April 2009.

Mohale Oscar Motlokwa, AM3135/96, 22 March 2000, Pretoria, http://sabctrc.saha.org.za/hearing.php?id=54097, accessed 4 September 2009.

Motlana Mphoreng, AM2740/96, 8 June 1998, Johannesburg, http://sabctrc.saha.org.za/hearing.php?id=52691, accessed 19 February 2010.

Mosa Danton Msimango, AM7370/97, 23 November 1998, Pretoria, http://sabctrc.saha.org.za/hearing.php?id=52995&t, accessed 22 January 2009.

Victor Mthandeni Mthembu, AM1707/96, 13 July 1998, Sebokeng, http://sabctrc.saha.org.za/hearing.php?id=52721&t, accessed 20 September 2014.

Thulani Mzokhona Myeza, AM54702, 26 March 1998, Durban, http://sabctrc.saha.org.za/hearing.php?id=54702, accessed 5 May 2009.

Simphiwe Ndlovu, AM7074/97, 25 November 1998, Palm Ridge, http://www.justice.gov.za/trc/amntrans/1998/9811231210_pr_981125th.htm, accessed 19 January 2009.

Bhekindile Davis Ndwangu, AM7055/97, 7 December 1998, Palm Ridge, http://www.justice.gov.za/trc/amntrans/1998/9811231210_pr_981207th.htm, accessed 1 March 2012.

Sipho Steven Ngubane, AM7295/97, 3 December,1998, Palm Ridge, http://www.justice.gov.za/trc/amntrans%5C1998/9811231210_pr_981203th.htm, accessed 14 July 2009.

Jabulani Aaron Ngwenya, AM7300/97, 1 December 1998, Palm Ridge, http://sabctrc.saha.org.za/documents/amntrans/palm_ridge/53024.htm, accessed 27 April 2014.

Bongani Nkosi, AM7268/97, 9 February 1999, Johannesburg, http://sabctrc.saha.org.za/documents/amntrans/johannesburg/53186.htm, accessed 2 April 2014.

Johannes Dingane Nkosi, AM7960/97, 7 December 1998, Palm Ridge, http://www.justice.gov.za/trc/amntrans/1998/9811231210_pr_981207th.htm, accessed 2 June 2011.

Sidney Vincent Nkosi, 2 February 1999, Johannesburg, http://sabctrc.saha.org.za/hearing.php?id=53171&t, accessed 30 May 2014.

Colin Lerato Nteo, AM7278/97, 4 December 1998, Palm Ridge, http://

sabctrc.saha.org.za/documents/amntrans/palm_ridge/53039.htm, accessed 19 October 2016.
Michael Phama, Day 1, AM3155/96, 21 June 1999, Johannesburg, http://sabctrc.saha.org.za/documents/amntrans/johannesburg/53500.htm, accessed 11 August 2008.
—— Day 2, AM3155/96, 22 June 1999, Johannesburg, http://sabctrc.saha.org.za/documents/amntrans/johannesburg/53501.htm, accessed 11 August 2008.
Thulani Terrence Tsotsetse (Mlaba), AM4400/96, Ngema Tavern Shooting, 9 December 1999, Palm Ridge, http://www.doj.gov.za/trc/amntrans/1999/99120910_jhb_991209.htm, accessed 21 April 2011.
Themba Stephen Zimu, AM1806/96, Ngema Tavern Killing, 6 September 1999, Johannesburg, http://sabctrc.saha.org.za/documents/amntrans/palm_ridge/53670.htm, accessed 21 April 2011.
TRC Amnesty Committee Hearings, AM7634/97, 24 November, 199, Vosloorus, http://sabctrc.saha.org.za/hearing.php?id=53075, accessed 25 September 2016.
TRC Amnesty Hearings, 7 October, 1999, Durban, http://sabctrc.saha.org.za/hearing.php?id=53741, accessed 16 April 2009.
—— AM7726/97, 3 October, 2000, Johannesburg, http://sabctrc.saha.org.za/hearing.php?id=54509, accessed 7 June 2010.
TRC Amnesty Hearing, Sally Sealey submission, 23 November, 1998, Palm Ridge, http://www.justice.gov.za/trc/amntrans/1998/9811231210_pr_981123th.htm, accessed 18 September 2009.

TRC Amnesty Decisions
TRC Amnesty Decision, Eugene Alexander de Kock, AM0066/96, AC/2001/225, http://www.doj.gov.za/trc/decisions/2001/ac21225.htm, accessed 29 September 2014.
TRC Amnesty Committee, Sipho Japhta Maduna, AM5475/9702, 18 February 1999, Central Methodist Church, Johannesburg, http://www.doj.gov.za/trc/decisions/1999/ac990348.htmAC/99/0348, accessed 8 April 2008.
—— Phakamani Alex Ndinisani, AM5906/97, 13 March 2001, Cape Town, www.doj.gov.za/trc/decisions/2001/ac21090, accessed 19 January 2009.
—— SDU Amnesty Decisions, Aubrey Stimbeko Radebe, AC/99/0186, 11 February 1999, http://sabctrc.saha.org.za/hearing.php?id=58864&t, accessed 6 May 2012.
TRC Amnesty Decisions, Thembu Zima, Thulani Tsotetsi, Mzwake Khumalo, Mbekhiseni Khumalo, 2000B, AC/2000/0198, http://www.doj.gov.za/trc/decisions/am00b.htm, accessed 14 June 2009.
TRC Amnesty Committee, SDU Amnesty Decisions, AC/99/0243, 1999, Cape Town, http://www.doj.gov.za/trc/decisions/1999/ac990243.htm, accessed 24 April 2008.

TRC Amnesty Committee, AC/2001/118, Cape Town, 2001, http://www. doj.gov.za/trc/decisions/2001/ac21118.htm, accessed 9 January 2010.

Other Hearings
TRC Special Hearings, Children's Hearing, George Ndlozi, 12 June 1997, http://sabctrc.saha.org.za/hearing.php?id=56292&t, accessed 26 October 2016.

Other Collections (online)

University of the Witwatersrand Historical Papers
'Boipatong Inquiry, General Description of the Incident', TRC Investigative Report Submitted by Jan-Ake Kjellberg, (n.d.), http://www. historicalpapers.wits.ac.za/inventories/inv_pdfo/AK2672/AK2672-C2-3-006-jpeg.pdf, accessed 12 February 2017.
Memoranda on the Ongoing Violence and the Failure by the Security Forces to Prevent the Violence, Protect Residents and Bring the Perpetrators of the Violence to Justice, Submitted on Behalf of the ANC (PWV), ANC (Vaal) and Vaal Council of Churches (n.d.), Submission to the Goldstone Commission, http://www.historicalpapers.wits. ac.za/inventories/inv_pdfo/AK2672/AK2672-B14-2-001-jpeg.pdf, accessed 9 February 2017.
Goldstone Commission Interim Report to the Commission of Inquiry Regarding the Prevention of Public Violence and Intimidation from the Committee established to inquire into the involvement of 32 Battalion at Phola Park, 3 June, 1992, http://www.historicalpapers. wits.ac.za/inventories/inv_pdfo/AK2702/AK2702-A12-001-jpeg.pdf, accessed 12 April 20014.

O'Malley Archives
The Heart of Hope: South Africa's Transition from Apartheid to Democracy, O'Malley Interviews 1985–2005, www.nelsonmandela.org/omalley
'Further Submissions and Responses by the ANC to Questions raised by the Commission for Truth and Reconciliation', 12 May 1997, Manifesto: Nature of the South African Conflict, https://www.nelsonmandela.org/omalley/cis/omalley/OMalleyWeb/03lv02167/04lv02264/05lv02303/06lv02304/07lv02315.htm, accessed 9 September 2016.
'Interview with Gertrude and Abraham Mzizi', 4 August 1993, https://omalley.nelsonmandela.org/omalley/index.php/site/q/03lv00017/04lv00344/05lv00730/06lv00758.htm, accessed 14 September 2016.
'Interview with Thokoza Hostel Residents', 18 December 1990, https://omalley.nelsonmandela.org/omalley/index.php/site/q/03lv00

017/04lv00344/05lv00389/06lv00507.htm, accessed 14 September 2016.

Centre for the Study of Violence and Reconciliation (Johannesburg)

Barolsky, V. *Transitioning out of Violence: Snapshots from Kathorus* (2005), http://www.csvr.org.za/wits/papers/papvtp11.pdf, accessed 7 May 2009.

Kgalema, L. 'Symbols of Hope: Monuments as symbols of remembrance and peace in the process of reconciliation'. Research report written for the Centre for the Study of Violence and Reconciliation (October 1999) http://www.csvr.org.za/publications/1676-symbols-of-hope-monuments-as-symbols-of-remembrance-and-peace-in-the-process-of-reconciliation, accessed 11 April 2017.

Marks, M. 'Alternative Policing Structures? A look at youth defense structures in Gauteng in 1995', Research report written for the Centre for the Study of Violence and Reconciliation (July 1995), https://www.csvr.org.za/publications/1570-alternative-policing-structures-a-look-at-youth-defense-structures-in-gauteng-in-1995, accessed 4 August 2012.

Rauch, J. and Storey, D. 'The Policing of Public Gatherings and Demonstrations in South Africa, 1960–1994' (1998), http://www.csvr.org.za/wits/papers/papjrds.htm, accessed 29 August 2008.

von Holdt et al., *The Smoke That Calls: Insurgent Citizenship, Collective Violence and the Struggle for a Place in the New South Africa: Eight Case Studies of Community Protests and Xenophobic Violence* (Centre for the Study of Violence and Reconciliation and Society, Work and Development Institute, University of the Witwatersrand, Johannesburg, 2011), http://www.csvr.org.za/docs/thesmokethatcalls.pdf, accessed 9 March 2012.

Other Collections (printed)

University of the Witwatersrand Historical Papers, Missing Voices Project, SDU Interviews by
Sally Sealey, A3079
Interview no. 1, Victor Mngomezulu, SDU Commander, Phenduka section, Thokoza, June 2004
Interview no. 6, Sidney Vincent Nkosi, SDU Thokoza Gardens, Thokoza, 9 June 2004
Interview no. 10, Sephiwe Leslie Mokoena, SDU Phooko section Katlehong, 12 June 2004
Interview no. 11, George Melusi Ndlozi, SDU Mokoena section, Katlehong, 14 June 2004
Interview no. 12, Aubrey 'Mgidi' Radebe, SDU Thokoza, 14 June 2004

Interview no. 17, Mandla Alfred Sibeko, SDU Ncala section, Katlehong, 15 June 2004
Interview no. 18, Inspector Charles Dlamini, SAP Thokoza, 11 June 2004
Interview no. 19, Mlungisi Duke Tshabalala, SDU Thokoza, 10 June 2004
Interview no. 20, Moses 'Bla' Mduduzi Khubeka, SDU Commander, Phenduka section Thokoza, 8 June 2004
Interview no. 21, Jeremiah Mbongeni Mabuza 'Boikie', SDU Katlehong, 10 June 2004
Interview no. 27, Nkosinathi Jimmy Makhondo, SDU Ext. 2, Thokoza, 18 June 2004
Interview no. 29, Bongani Caswell Nkosi, Chief Commander, Thokoza SDUs, 27 July 2004
Interview no. 30, Dalixolo 'Meneer' Mqubi, SDU Commander, Ext. 2, Thokoza, 21 June 2004

University of the Witwatersrand Historical Papers, Independent Board of Inquiry into Informal Repression (IBIIR) Collection
Monthly Reports of the IBIIR
August 1990
November 1990
December 1990/January 1991
April 1992
March 1993
May 1993
June/July 1993
October/November 1993
December 1993/January 1994
February/March 1994
Election Special, April 1994
Other Reports
IBIIR, 'Statement of Prince Mhlambi and Pola Park Committee with regard to various aspects of evidence and contextual aspects of the violence in the East Rand and its impact on Pola Park', 22 November, 1991, AG2543, C18
IBIIR, Memorandum: 'Crisis in Sharpeville', [undated, but written after September 1993], AG2543 3.1-3.42
IBIIR, Memorandum: 'Update on Sharpeville', 16 January, 1994, AG2543 C21
IBIIR Kwa-Thema, *Commission of Inquiry into Incidents of Violence in Kwa-Thema presented to the Honourable Premier of the Province of Gauteng*, January 1997, by Advocate Clive van der Spuy, AG 2543, C-12
IBIIR, 'Confidential Report on Sebokeng Vigil Shootings', 18 January, 1991, AG2543, C20
IBIIR, Kheswa file, AG2543, C20

IBIIR, Memorandum on the Activities of Mbhekisini Khumalo, 24 February, 1993, AG 2543 3.1-3.42
IBIIR TRC, Section 29 Hearing, 'In Camera', 'Khumalo Gang', AG2543, A13
IBIIR, 'Briefing documents on the murders of Constance, Margaret and Sabata Sotsu on July 3', 1991, AG2543, C20
IBIIR Thokoza, 'Briefing on the Violence in Thokoza since May 22, 1993', AG2543 C26
IBIIR, 'Memoranda on Reef Violence', 16 August 1993, AG2544 3.3-3.7
IBIIR, Memoranda, ISU, SADF and the NPKF, Undated [but almost certainly April 1994], AG2543 3.1-3.42
IBIIR Thokoza Files, C26
IBIIR, 'Report from Davin Bremner to Goldstone Commission', 25 March 1992, C26
IBIIR/Peace Action, *Before we were good friends: An account and analysis of displacement in the East Rand Townships of Thokoza and Katlehong*, April 1994

University of the Witwatersrand Historical Papers, Miscellaneous
Local Disputes Resolution Committee, 1992–93, Annexure D, ANC Peace Desk, 'Report to the 4th Regional Conference', 29–31 October, 1993, AK2832 A-C9
Local Disputes Resolution Committee, 1992–93, Report: 'Vaal Commission of Inquiry', AK2832 A-C9

Centre for the Study of Violence and Reconciliation (Johannesburg)
Gear, S., 'Wishing Us Away: Challenges Facing Ex-Combatants in the "New" South Africa', Violence and Transition series, vol. 8 (2002)
Rakgoadi, P., 'The Role of the Self-Defence Units (SDUs) in a Changing Political Context' (Johannesburg, January 1995)

Periodicals

Business Day
Christian Science Monitor
Citizen
City Press
Independent
Los Angeles Times
New York Times
New York Times Magazine
Saturday Star
South
Sowetan

Star
Sunday Star
Sunday Times
Weekly Mail

Theses and Grey Literature

Barolsky, V., 'The Moleleki Execution: A Radical Problem of Understanding' (PhD dissertation, University of the Witwatersrand, 2010)

Bruce, D., '"Just singing and dancing"? Intimidation and the manipulation of voters and the electoral process in the build-up to the 2014 elections', Community Agency for Social Enquiry (CASE), April 2014

Human Sciences Research Council and the Institute for Defence Policy, *The National Peacekeeping Force, Violence on the East Rand and Public Perceptions of the NPKF in Katorus*, Pretoria, June 1994

Marx, C. and M. Rubin, *Divisible Spaces: Land Biographies in Diepkloof, Thokoza and Doornfontein, Gauteng* Report prepared for Urban LandMark, May 2008, http://www.urbanlandmark.org.za/downloads/Land_Biographies_Full_Report_LowRes.pdf

Xeketwane, B.M.K., 'The Relation Between Hostels and the Political Violence on the Reef from July 1990 to December 1993: A Case Study of Merafe and Meadowlands Hostel in Soweto' (M.A. dissertation, University of the Witwatersrand, 1995)

Zack, T. *Critical Pragmatism in Planning: The Case of the Kathorus Special Integrated Presidential Project in South Africa* (Ph.D. Dissertation, University of the Witwatersrand, 2006)

Commissions

Goldstone Commission
Report of the Committee of Inquiry into the Phenomenon and Causes of Violence in the Tokoza Area, Under the Chairmanship of Mr M.N.S Sithole. Presented to the State President by R.J. Goldstone, Chairman of the Commission of Inquiry Regarding the Prevention of Public Violence and Intimidation, 17 November 1992.

Miscellaneous Online Sources

African National Congress, '5.3 People's Committees and Self Defence Units' in *African National Congress: Statement to the Truth and Reconciliation Commission*, August 1996, http://www.anc.org.

za/content/anc-statement-truth-and-reconciliation-commission, accessed 22 September 2016.

'The Nobel Peace Prize 1993', *Nobelprize.org* (Nobel Media AB 2014), https://www.nobelprize.org/nobel_prizes/peace/laureates/1993/, accessed 4 October 2016.

Judy Seidman and NomaRussia Bonasa, '*Tsogang Basadi:* Finding women's voice from South Africa's political conflict', http://www.judyseidman.com/tsogang%20basadi%20paper.html, accessed 11 June 2017.

'Thokoza Violence Victim Tells of Rape and Murder by SDU Members', 1 December, 1998, http://www.justice.gov.za/trc/media%5C1998%5C9812/s981201b.htm, accessed 19 September 2017.

Interviews

Township interviews
G6, female, Thokoza, 12 June 2004
J1, male, Thokoza, 19 June 2004
J2, female, Thokoza, 11 July 2004
J3, female, Thokoza, 12 July 2004
J4, male, Thokoza, 11 July 2004
T1, male, Thokoza, 5 July 2005
T2, male, Thokoza, 29 July 2005
T3, male, Thokoza, 12 January 2006
T4, male, Thokoza, 15 December 2005
T5, male, Thokoza, 20 March 2006
T6, male, Thokoza, 27 April 2006
T7, female, Thokoza, 23 April 2006
T8, male, Thokoza, 22 May 2006
T10, female, Thokoza, 3 June 2006
T12, male, Thokoza, 3 June 2006
T13, male, Thokoza, 5 June 2006
T15, male, Thokoza, 7 June 2006
T16, female, Thokoza, 7 June 2006
D1, female, Thokoza, 2 June 2006
D2, female, Thokoza, 3 June 2006
D3, male, Thokoza, 7 June 2006
Z56, female, Katlehong, 2006
Z58, male, Katlehong, 2006
Z59, female, Katlehong, 2006
Z60, male, Katlehong, 2006
Z61, female, Katlehong, 2006
Z62, male, Katlehong, 2006
Z63, male, Katlehong, 2006

Bibliography

Z64, male, Katlehong, 2006
Z65, male, Katlehong, 2006
Z66, female, Katlehong, 25 May 2007
Z67, female, Katlehong, 25 May 2007
Z68, female, Katlehong, 26 May 2007
Z69, female, Katlehong, 26 May 2007
Z70, male, Katlehong, 26 May 2007
Z71, female, Thokoza, 1 June 2007
Z72, male, Thokoza, 1 June 2007
Z73, male, Katlehong, 1 June 2007
Z74, female, Thokoza, 2 June 2007
Z75, male, Thokoza, 2 June 2007
Z76, female, Katlehong, 8 June 2007
Z77, female, Katlehong, 8 June 2007
Z78, male, Katlehong, 9 June 2007
Z79, female, Katlehong, 9 June 2007
Z80, female, Katlehong, 9 June 2007
Z81, male, Katlehong, August 2006
Z83, female, Katlehong, 2006
Z84, female, Katlehong, 2006
Z85, male police officer, Katlehong, 2006
Z86, male, Katlehong, 2006
Z87, female, Katlehong, 2006
Z88, male, Katlehong, 2006
Z89, female, Katlehong, 2007

Hostel interviews
JH1, male, Mshayazafe Hostel, 10 July 2004
JH2, male, Buyafuthi Hostel, 18 July 2004
Z1, male, Buyafuthi Hostel, 29 May 2006
Z2, male, Buyafuthi Hostel, 10 June 2006
Z3, male, Buyafuthi Hostel, 10 June 2006
Z4, male, Mshayazafe Hostel, 14 June 2006
Z5, male, Mshayazafe Hostel, 14 June 2006
Z6, male, Mshayazafe Hostel, 19 June 2006
Z7, male, Buyafuthi Hostel, 24 June 2006
Z8, male, Buyafuthi Hostel, 24 June 2006
Z9, male, Buyafuthi Hostel, 4 July 2006
Z10, male, Buyafuthi Hostel, 4 July 2006
Z11, male, Buyafuthi Hostel, 4 July 2006
Z13, male, Madala Hostel, 10 July 2006
Z12, female, Mshayazafe Hostel, 19 June 2006
Z14, male, Madala Hostel, 10 July 2006
Z15, female, Buyafuthi Hostel, 10 July 2006
Z16, female, Buyafuthi Hostel, 12 July 2006

Z17, female, Kwesine Hostel, 12 July 2006
Z18, female, Kwesine Hostel, 18 July 2006
Z19, male, Buyafuthi Hostel, 18, July 2006
Z20, male, Madala Hostel, 18 July 2006
Z21, male, Madala Hostel, 19 July 2006
Z22, male, Kwesine Hostel, 19 July 2006
Z23, male, Kwesine Hostel, 19 July 2006
Z24, male, Buyafuthi Hostel, 8 August 2006
Z25, male, Madala Hostel, 8 August 2006
Z26, male, Kwesine Hostel, 18 October 2006
Z27, male, Kwesine Hostel, 18 October 2006
Z28, male, Mazibuko Hostel, 18 October 2006
Z29, female, Kwesine Hostel, 19 October 2006
Z30, female, Kwesine Hostel, 19 October 2006
Z31, male, Kwesine Hostel, 20 October 2006
Z32, male, Kwesine Hostel, 20 October 2006
Z33, male, Mazibuko Hostel, 20 October 2006
Z35, male, Mazibuko Hostel, 23 October 2006
Z36, female, Mazibuko Hostel, 23 October 2006
Z37, male, Mazibuko Hostel, 24 October 2006
Z38, male, Mazibuko Hostel, 24 October 2006
Z39, female, Mazibuko Hostel, 25 October 2006
Z40, male, Mazibuko Hostel, 25 October 2006
Z41, male, Mazibuko Hostel, 2006
Z42, female, Mazibuko Hostel, 2006
Z43, female, Mazibuko Hostel, 2006
Z44, female, Mazibuko Hostel, 2006
Z45, male, Mazibuko Hostel, July 2006
Z46, male, Mazibuko Hostel, 2006
Z47, male, Mazibuko Hostel, 2006
Z48, female, Mazibuko Hostel, 2006
Z49, female, Kwesine Hostel, 2006
Z50, male, Mazibuko Hostel, August 2006
Z51, male, Mazibuko Hostel, 2006
Z52, male, Mazibuko Hostel, 2006
Z53, male, Mazibuko Hostel, 2006
Z54, male, Kwesine Hostel, 2006

SDU interviews
J51, male, Thokoza, 20 June 2004
G1, male, Thokoza, 11 June 2004
G2, male, Thokoza, 16 July 2008
G3, male, Thokoza, 16 July 2008
Group interview, Thokoza,13 July 2008
T9, male, Thokoza, 27 May 2006

Z57, male, Katlehong, 2006
Z82, male, Katlehong, 2006
Z90, male, Katlehong, 2006
Z91, male, Katlehong, 2006
Z92, male, Katlehong, 2006
Z93, male, Katlehong, 2006
Z94, male, Katlehong, 2006
Z95, male, Katlehong, 2006
Z96, male, Thokoza, 21 June 2008
Z97, male, Thokoza, 21 June 2008
Z98, male, Thokoza, 21 June 2008
Z99, female, Thokoza, 24 June 2008
Z100, male, Thokoza, 24 June 2008
Z101, female, Thokoza, 24 June 2008
Z102, male, Thokoza, 23 November 2008
Z103, male, Thokoza, 23 November 2008
Z104, male, Thokoza, 23 November 2008

ISD interviews
Hein Kilian, Unit 6 Commanding Officer, 2017
ISD1, Unit 6, 2015
ISD2, Unit 6, 2015
ISD3, Unit 19, 2017
ISD5, Unit 6, 2017
ISD6, Unit 6, 2017
ISD7, Unit 6, 2017

Other interviews
Female IFP official, Johannesburg, 21 June 2004
Male ANC official, Thokoza, 1 July 2004
Male ANC official, Thokoza, 19 May 2005
David Storey, Johannesburg, 26 May 2006
Robert McBride, Johannesburg, 21 June 2006
Greg Marinovich, Johannesburg, 4 July 2006
Sally Sealey, London, July 2006
Duma Nkosi, Ekurhuleni, 27 June 2008

Books and articles

Adam, H. and Kogila Moodley, 'Political Violence, "Tribalism", and Inkatha', *Journal of Modern African Studies* 30, 3 (1992): pp. 485–510

Alexander, P., 'Rebellion of the poor: South Africa's service delivery protests – a preliminary analysis', *Review of African Political Economy* 37, 123 (2010), pp. 25–40

Bibliography

Andreas, P., 'The Clandestine Political Economy of War and Peace in Bosnia', *International Studies Quarterly* 28 (2004), pp. 29–51

Anglin, D., 'The Life and Death of South Africa's National Peacekeeping Force', *Journal of Modern African Studies* 33, 1 (1995), pp. 21–52

Bank, L., 'The Making of the Qwaqwa "Mafia": Patronage and Protection in the Migrant Taxi Business', *African Studies* 49, 1 (1990), pp. 71–93

Bøås, M. 'Marginalized Youth' in Bøås and Kevin Dunn (eds) *African Guerrillas: Raging Against the Machine* (Lynne Reinner Publishers, Boulder, 2007), pp. 39–54

Bonner P. and Noor Nieftagodien, *Alexandra: A History* (Wits University Press, Johannesburg, 2008)

—— *Kathorus: A History* (Maskew Miller Longman, Cape Town, 2001)

—— 'The Truth and Reconciliation Commission and the Pursuit of "Social Truth": The Case of Kathorus' in Deborah Posel and Graeme Simpson (eds), *Commissioning the Past: Understanding South Africa's Truth and Reconciliation Commission* (Wits University Press, Johannesburg, 2002), pp. 173–203

Bonner P. and Noor Nieftagodien with Sello Mathabatha, *Ekurhuleni: The Making of an Urban Region* (Wits University Press, Johannesburg, 2012)

Bonner P. and Vusi Ndima, 'The Roots of Violence and Martial Zuluness on the East Rand' in Benedict Carton, John Laband and Jabulani Sithole (eds), *Zulu Identities: Being Zulu past and present* (Columbia University Press, New York, 2009), pp. 363–82

Branch, D., *Defeating Mau Mau, Creating Kenya: Counterinsurgency, Civil War and Decolonisation* (Cambridge University Press, New York, 2009)

Bremner, L., 'Development and Resistance: The Lessons for the Planners of Phola Park', *Urban Forum* 5, 1 (1994), pp. 23–44

—— 'The Thokoza Peace Process' in L. Douwes-Dekker, A. Majola, P. Visser and D. Bremner (eds), *Community Conflict: The challenge facing South Africa* (Juta & Co. Limited, Cape Town, 1995)

Bremner, D., 'South African Experiences with Identity and Community Conflicts', *Journal of Peace Research*, 38, 3 (2001), pp. 393–405

Bridger, E. 'Soweto's Female Comrades: Gender, Youth and Violence in South Africas's Township Uprisings, 1984-1990', *Journal of Southern African Studies* 44, 4 (2018).

Brown, J., *South Africa's Insurgent Citizens* (Jacana Media, Johannesburg, 2016)

Bruce, D., 'A Provincial Concern? Political Killings in South Africa', *SA Crime Quarterly* 45 (September 2013), pp. 13–24.

Chipkin, I., *Do South Africans Exist? Nationalism, Democracy and the Identity of 'the People'* (Wits University Press, Johannesburg, 2007)

—— 'Nationalism as Such: Violence during South Africa's Political

Transition', *Public Culture* 16, 2 (2004), pp. 315–335

Collins, A., 'Violence is not a Crime: The impact of "acceptable" violence on South Africa society', *SA Crime Quarterly* 43 (March 2013), pp. 27–37

de Haas, M., 'Violence in Natal and Zululand: The 1990s' in *The Road to Democracy in South Africa,* vol. 6, part 2, South African Democracy Education Trust (Unisa Press, Pretoria, 2013), pp. 876–957

de Kock, E., *A Long Night's Damage: Working for the Apartheid State* (Contra Press, Johannesburg, 1992)

de Waal, A., *Demilitarizing the Mind: African Agendas for Peace and Security* (Africa World Press, Philadelphia, 2003)

Denis, P., Radikobo Ntsimane and Thomas Cannel, *Indians versus Russians: An oral history of political violence in Nxamalala (1987–1993)* (Cluster Publications, Pietermaritzburg, 2010)

Douwes-Dekker, L., A. Majola, P. Visser and D. Bremner (eds), *Community Conflict: The challenge facing South Africa* (Juta & Co. Limited, Cape Town, 1995)

Du Toit, C.P, 'Peacekeeping in East Rand Townships' in Mark Shaw and Jackie Cilliers (eds), *South Africa and Peacekeeping in Africa*, vol. 1 (Institute for Security Studies, Pretoria, 1995), pp. 71–86, http://www.issafrica.org/pubs/Books/BlurbPk1.html

Dugard, J., 'From Low Intensity War to Mafia War: Taxi Violence in South Africa (1987–2000)', Centre for the Study of Violence and Reconciliation, *Violence and Transition Series*, vol. 4 (May 2001), pp. 1–46

Ellis, S. *External Mission: The ANC in Exile, 1960–1990* (Oxford University Press, Oxford, 2013)

—— 'The Historical Significance of South Africa's Third Force', *Journal of Southern African Studies* 24, 2 (1998), pp. 261–99

—— *The Mask of Anarchy: The Destruction of Liberia and the Religious Dimensions of an African Civil War* (New York University Press, New York, 1999)

Everatt, D., 'Analysing political violence on the Reef, 1990–1994' in R. Greenstein (ed.), *The Role of Political Violence in South Africa's Democratisation* (Community Agency for Social Enquiry, Johannesburg, 2003), pp. 95–142

Foster, D., Paul Haupt and Maresa de Beer, *The Theatre of Violence: Narratives of Protagonists in the South African Conflict* (HSRC Press, Cape Town, 2005)

Gerhart, G. and Clive Glaser, *From Protest to Challenge: A Documentary History of African Politics in South Africa, 1882–1990, Volume 6: Challenge and Victory, 1980–1990* (Indiana University Press, Bloomington, 2010)

Gibbs, T., 'Inkatha's young militants: reconsidering political violence in South Africa', *Africa* 87, 2 (2017), pp. 362–86.

Giliomee, H., *The Last Afrikaner Leaders: A Supreme Test of Power* (Tafelberg Publishers Limited, Cape Town, 2012)

Guelke, A., 'Interpretations of political violence during South Africa's transition', *Politikon* 27, 2 (2000), pp. 239–54.

Harris, P., *Birth: The Conspiracy to Stop the '94 Election* (Struik Publishers, Cape Town, 2010)

Hickel, J., *Democracy as Death: The Moral Order of Anti-Liberal Politics in South Africa* (University of California Press, Oakland, 2015)

Howarth, N., *War in Peace: The truth about the South African Police's East Rand Riot Unit, 1986–1994* (Galago Books, Johannesburg, 2012)

Jeffrey, A., *People's War: New light on the struggle for South Africa* (Jonathan Ball Publishers, Johannesburg, 2009)

Kalyvas, S., *The Logic of Violence in Civil War* (Cambridge University Press, New York, 2006)

Kaufman, S., *Nationalist Passions* (Cornell University Press, Ithaca, 2015)

Keller, B., 'Island of Fear: Inside a Soweto Hostel', *New York Times Magazine* (20 September 1992), http://www.nytimes.com/1992/09/20/magazine/island-of-fear-inside-a-soweto-hostel.html

Khosa, M., 'Routes, Ranks and Rebels: Feuding in the Taxi Revolution', *Journal of Southern African Studies* 18, 1, (1992), pp. 232–51

Kynoch, G., 'Crime, Conflict and Politics in Transition Era South Africa', *African Affairs* 104, 416 (2005), pp. 493–514

—— 'Reassessing Transition Violence: Voices from South Africa's Township Wars, 1990–94', *African Affairs* 112, 447 (2013), pp. 283–303

Lekgoathi, S.P. and Sifiso Mxolisi Ndlovu, 'Political Violence in the PWV region, 1990–94' in *The Road to Democracy in South Africa*, vol. 6, part 2, South African Democracy Education Trust (Unisa Press, Pretoria, 2013), pp. 958–1019

Maake, N., 'Multi-Cultural Relations in a Post-Apartheid South Africa', *African Affairs* 91, (1992), pp. 583–604

Marinovich, G. and Joao Silva, *The Bang Bang Club: Snapshots from a hidden war* (Arrow Books, London, 2001)

Mathis, S., 'From War Leaders to Freedom Fighters: Violence in Umbumbulu in the Waning Days of Apartheid in South Africa', *African Affairs* 112, 448 (2013), pp. 421–39.

Minnaar, A., 'Hostels and Violent Conflict on the Reef' in Minnaar (ed.), *Communities in Isolation: Perspectives on Hostels in South Africa* (Human Sciences Research Council, Pretoria, 1993), pp. 10–47

Mueller, J., 'The Banality of Ethnic War', *International Security* 25, 1 (2000), pp. 42–70

Nortje, P., *32 Battalion: The Inside Story of South Africa's Elite Fighting Unit* (Zebra Press, Cape Town, 2003)

Paret, M., 'Violence and democracy in South Africa's community protests', *Review of African Political Economy* 42, 143 (2015), pp. 107–23.

Reed, D., *Beloved Country: South Africa's Silent Wars* (BBC Books, London, 1994)

Seekings, J., 'Hostel Hostilities: Township Wars on the Reef', *Indicator SA* 8, 3 (1991), pp. 11–15.

—— *The UDF: A History of the United Democratic Front in South Africa 1983–1991* (David Philip Publishers, Cape Town, 2000)

Segal, L., 'The Human Face of Violence: Hostel Dwellers Speak' *Journal of Southern African Studies* 18, 1 (1992), pp. 190–231

Shaw, M. *Hitmen for Hire: Exposing South Africa's Underworld* (Jonathan Ball Publishers, Johannesburg and Cape Town, 2017)

Simpson, J., 'Boipatong: The Politics of a Massacre and the South African Transition', *Journal of Southern African Studies* 38, 3 (2012), pp. 623–47

Sitas, A., 'The New Tribalism: Hostels and Violence', *Journal of Southern African Studies* 22, 2 (1996), pp. 235–48

Szeftel, M., 'Manoeuvres of war in South Africa', *Review of African Political Economy* 19, 51 (1991), pp. 63–76

Taylor, R. and M. Shaw, 'The Dying Days of Apartheid' in D. Howarth and A. Norval (eds), *South Africa in Transition: New Theoretical Perspectives* (MacMillan Press Ltd., London, 1998), pp. 13–30

Thotse, M.L. and J.E.H. Grobler, 'Standpoints on "Black-on-Black" vs "Third Force" Violence during South Africa's Transitional Negotiations', *Historia* 48, 2 (2003), pp. 143–60

van Holdt, K., 'South Africa: The Transition to Violent Democracy', *Review of African Political Economy* 40, 138 (2013), pp. 589–604.

Waddington, P.A.J., 'Policing South Africa: The View from Boipatong', *Policing and Society* 4, (1994), pp. 83–95

Waldmeir, P., *Anatomy of a Miracle: The End of Apartheid and the Birth of the New South Africa* (W.W. Norton & Co., New York, 1997)

Wilson, R., *The Politics of Truth and Reconciliation in South Africa: Legitimizing the Post-Apartheid State* (Cambridge University Press, Cambridge, 2001)

Index

32 Battalion 88, 96, 113–15

Adam, Heribert 31
ANC (African National Congress)
  and conflict with AZAPO/PAC
    13, 19–20, 36, 73–5, 197
  and conflict with IFP
    biased narrative about 1,
      7–11
    history of 3–5, 142, 197, 199
    and hostel violence 4, 11–12,
      20–23, 25–6, 31–3, 123–9,
      133–7, 138–42 see also hostels
    in KZN 4, 7, 17, 26, 30–31, 32,
      55, 107, 199
    and political campaigning
      17, 23–6, 30–32, 34, 199
    and squatter settlement
      violence 125–9, 132–3
    taxi wars 28–30, 123, 137–8
    and 'third force' 5–8, 14, 85,
      107–9, 198
    and train violence 54, 140–41
    workplace violence 52–4,
      58–9, 60
  and foreign media 7–10
  Freedom Charter 19
  as government 10, 193, 200–2
  and internecine violence
    62–72, 197, 199–202
  and liberation struggle 3, 5, 18,
    25, 198–9, 200
  and negotiations with state/
    NP 25, 26, 30, 41, 87–9, 117, 198,
    199–200
  and National Peace Accord
    40–41, 61, 88, 129–30
  Peace Desk 41, 62, 83 see also
    McBride, Robert
  and SDUs 9, 13, 36, 37, 39–52,
    64, 68–70, 82–4, 146
  Umkhonto weSizwe (MK)
    as armed wing 13, 18, 25, 198
    and criminality 81–4
    and intra-ANC violence 62,
      66
    and SDUs 25, 39, 43–5, 51,
      64, 67–70
    and SPUs 60
  and unions 21–22
  Women's League 13
  Youth League (ANCYL) 3, 13,
    38, 62, 68–72, 74, 78–9, 147
  and Zulus 24, 25, 31, 183
  see also hostels; SDUs;
    townships
Andreas, Peter 13
apartheid
  end of 1, 2, 3, 193–200
  discrediting of 7
  and oppressor–resister
    narrative 1, 197
  and post-apartheid violence
    198–200, 198–202
  struggle against 3, 18–19, 73,
    102, 198–9
  and unions 21–2
  and white privilege 5, 119
  see also NP, state security
    forces
AZAPO (Azanian People's
  Organisation) 13, 19–20, 36, 73–5,
  197

Barolsky, Vanessa 71, 72
Basotho 73
Bekker, Hennie 111
Bekkersdal 73
Beyco (Bekkersdal Youth Congress)
  73
Bisho massacre 87 n.3
Boipatong massacre 9–10, 32, 56, 87,
  157
Bonner, Philip 10, 27, 31, 176

Branch, Daniel 11
Bremner, Davin 129
Buthelezi, Mangosuthu 3–4, 7, 24, 31
　see also IFP

Cebekulu, Mr 29
Chamane, Zwile 58
Charterists 19–20, 73
Chipkin, Ivor 22
Collins, Anthony 200
Community Agency for Social
　Enquiry (CASE) 8
COSAS (Congress of South African
　Students) 28, 29, 34, 62, 69, 74
COSATU (Congress of South African
　Trade Unions) 21, 22, 31, 53, 77
criminal violence
　and political conflict 12–13,
　　75–84, 199
　and SDUs 45, 48–9, 64, 69,
　　81–4, 188–9, 193, 197
　and state security forces 77–8,
　　80–81
　in townships 17–18
　see also gangs
Crossroads (squatter settlement) 124,
　125, 127, 132–3

de Klerk, F.W. 1, 3, 4, 11, 26, 31, 87, 88
de Kock, Eugene 59, 107–9
Desai, Barney 74–5
de Waal, Alex 12

East Rand see Ekurhuleni
Ekurhuleni 6, 27, 194
Ellis, Stephen 5–6, 87, 113
ethnic violence 4, 24, 28–9, 32–4, 38,
　124–7, 176–7, 179, 182–3
　see also Xhosas; Zulus
Everatt, David 6

FAWU (Food and Allied Workers
　Union) 52–3, 60
FOSATU (Federation of South
　African Trade Unions) 21

gangs
　Germans 69
　Russians 73
　Mugabe 78
　Kheswa 76–8
　Khumalo 79–81, 128
　Toaster 83–4

Gear, Sasha 82, 143
Gerhart, Gail 20
Germiston and District Taxi
　Association (G & D) 27–30, 34
Giliomee, Herman 7
Goldstone Commission 9, 48, 63, 88,
　107, 114–15, 118, 128–9, 132

Hadebe, Mzobona 58–59, 60
Hani, Chris 43, 51, 64, 127
Hickel, Jason 22
Holomisa, Bantu 65
hostels
　and arms dealing 52
　Bayafuthi Hostel, 60, 101, 111,
　　124, 133, 139, 194
　Daveyton Hostel 52
　after demilitarisation 194–5
　history and demographics of
　　20–21, 124 see also indunas
　hostel–township conflicts 4,
　　11–12, 20–23, 25–6, 31–3, 37, 56,
　　123–9, 133–7, 138–42, 176–91
　and IFP 22, 23, 24, 25–6, 33,
　　36, 55–61, 84, 131, 133–4,
　　138–42
　Khalanyoni Hostels 32–3, 35,
　　38, 63, 125–6, 158, 177
　Khutuza Hostel 124
　KwaMadala Hostel 9–10, 31,
　　76–7
　kwaMasiza Hostel 65, 67–8
　Kwesine Hostel 28, 124, 125,
　　133, 139, 179
　Lindela Hostel 10, 124, 125–6,
　　158, 177
　Madala 95, 124, 125, 159
　Mazibuko Hostel 44, 59, 124,
　　139, 158, 177–8
　Meadowlands Hostel 60
　Mshayazafe Hostel 58, 116, 124,
　　132, 141–2
　Ratanda Hostel 58, 60
　residents of 11–12, 20–21, 23,
　　55–7, 101, 178–81
　and SDUs 138–42, 180
　Sebokeng Hostel 31–2, 65–7
　and security forces 65, 142
　see also Katlehong; Thokoza;
　　Xhosas; Zulus
Howarth, Nick 90, 131, 162
Human Rights Commission (HRC)
　8, 9

IBIIR *see* Independent Board of Inquiry into Informal Repression
IDT (Interdependent Development Trust) 63
IFP (Inkatha Freedom Party) 1
   and association with state 4–8, 9–11, 14, 17, 26, 31, 59–60, 75, 107–9, 198 *see also under* state security forces
   and Bekkersdal conflict 74
   and boycott of TRC 10, 57
   Buthelezi, Mangosuthu 3–4, 7, 24, 31
   and conflict with ANC
      biased narrative about 1, 7–11
      history of 3–5, 142, 197, 199
      and hostel violence 4, 11–12, 20–23, 25–6, 31–3, 123–9, 133–7, 138–42 *see also* hostels
      in KZN 4, 7, 17, 26, 30–31, 32, 55, 107, 199
      and political campaigning 17, 23–6, 30–32, 34, 199
      and squatter settlement violence 125–9, 132–3
      taxi wars 28–30, 123, 137–8
      and 'third force' 5–8, 14, 85, 87–8, 107–9, 198
      and train violence 54, 140–41
      workplace violence 52–4, 58–9, 60
   and foreign media/monitoring groups 7–9
   formation of 3–5, 31
   and hostels 22, 23, 24, 25–6, 33, 36, 55–61, 84, 131, 133–4, 138–42
   Inkatha Youth Brigade 59
   and internecine conflict 72–3
   and Kheswa, Victor Khetisi 'Vaal Monster' 75–8
   and Khumalo, Mbhekiseni 'the Archbishop' 75–6, 78–81
   and National Peace Accord 40, 61, 129–30, 194
   and National Peacekeeping Force 115–16
   and SPUs (Self Protection Units) 26, 55, 57–61, 135, 145, 153, 156–61, 194–5 *see also* indunas; Zulus

and taxi wars 28–30, 123, 137–8
Transvaal leaders 31, 59, 107
and unions 22–3
and Zonkizizwe (squatter settlement) 126
and Zulus 3–4, 5, 10, 17, 24, 25–6, 31–33, 57, 124, 144–5, 176, 184–6
impis 56
impimpi/izimpimpi 18, 37, 49, 53, 64, 150, 186–7
Independent Board of Inquiry into Informal Repression (IBIIR)
   and ANC 8–9
   on black police 91, 92
   on ISD 98
   on Phola Park 114, 126, 133
   on security force partiality 107
   on SDUs 68, 69–70, 82, 83
   on taxi violence 137
   and Thokoza LPC 130
indunas 2 n.3, 26, 56, 58–9, 61, 104, 178, 183
Inkatha *see* IFP
Inkatha Freedom Party *see* IFP
ISCOR (Iron and Steel Corporation) 66–7
ISD (Internal Stability Division)
   association with IFP 80, 86, 97–8, 99–101, 102–6, 170
   biased portrayal of 167–70, 196
   creation and deployment of 95–7, 106–7, 161
   after demilitarisation 195–6
   distrust of 71, 96–7, 98–9, 162
   and excessive force 98–100, 101, 165–6, 171
   experiences of, personal 163–7
   and SADF 101, 111–12, 114
   and SAP 91–2, 161
   and SDUs 86, 98, 99–100, 103, 105, 164, 170–71
   and state negotiations 63, 88–9
   and trauma 171–2, 196
   veterans' accounts of 101–7, 161–72
   see also state security forces
ISU *see* ISD

Kalyvas, Stathis 12, 61
Kasrils, Ronnie 50, 51

Index

Katlehong
  and ANC support 42
  after demilitarisation 197
  and hostel–township conflicts
    4, 11–12, 20–23, 25–6, 31–3, 37,
    56, 123–9, 133–7, 138–42, 176–91
  ISD in 123, 161–72
  and political territory 135–8
  population and demographics
    of 124–5
  SDUs in 37, 41, 44, 57, 70–72,
    131, 133–42, 143–56
  and taxi wars 27–30, 34–5, 123,
    137–8, 139, 184
  see also ethnic violence;
    hostels; Khalanyoni; Moleleki;
    squatter settlements; Thokoza;
    townships; Xhosas; Zulus
Katlehong Taxi Association (KATO)
  27–30
Khalanyoni (Hostels) 32–3, 35, 38, 63,
  125–6, 158, 177
Kheswa, Victor Khetisi 'the Vaal
  Monster' 65, 75–8
Khoza, Themba 59, 107–8, 111, 176
Khumalo, Joshua 'Chipper' 69
Khumalo, Mbhekiseni 'the
  Archbishop' 75–6, 78–81
Kiyana, Malusi 'Blanko' 71
Kondile, Zandisile 52–4
KwaZulu 3, 4 see also KZN
KZN (KwaZulu-Natal province)
  and ANC–IFP conflict 4, 7, 17,
    26, 30–31, 32, 55, 107, 199
  and elections 193
  fighters from 60, 124
  Moerane Commission of
    Inquiry 201
  and Zulu migrants 20, 23, 27, 55,
    125, 177

Langa, Pius 66
Lawyers for Human Rights (LHR)
  8
Legal Reference Centre (LRC) 8
Lekgoathi, Sekibakiba 6

Maake, Nhlanhla 30
Mabuza, Mbongeni 116, 135, 140
Machitje, Chichela 43
Mahlatsi, Masoli 77
Makhondo, Nkosinathi 144
Makhura, Stephen 51

Mandela, Nelson
  intervention in Sebokeng 66
  and Nobel Peace Prize 1
  and release from prison 2, 3, 17,
    33, 96–7, 102–3, 162
  political significance of 6, 24,
    87, 200
Mandela, Winnie Madikizela 51
Manete, Oupa 69
Marikana massacre 201
Marinovich, Greg 116
Mashinini, Ben 189
Mbaso, Wanda 144
Mbele, Piet 137
McBride, Robert
  on ANC 42–3, 48, 83, 130
  on ISD 101
  on Peace Accord 131
  and SDUs 41, 43, 46–7, 48, 83,
    140, 151
  and weapons smuggling 50–51
MDM (mass democratic movement)
  21–3, 28
Mhlambi, Prince 63–5
migrant workers 20–23
MK see Umkhonto weSizwe
Mngomezulu, Victor 51, 81–2, 133–4,
  136, 150
Modise, Joe 45
Moleleki 70–72, 147, 199
monitoring/press groups 6, 7–10
Motlokwa, Mohale 54
Mozambicans 29, 43, 51, 52, 60,
  64
Mthembu, Victor 157
Mueller, John 36
Mzizi, Gertrude 48, 130

Naidoo, Jay 30–31
Nangalemebe, Christopher 76
Natal 4, 29, 55, 144, 185 see also KZN
National Party see NP
National Peace Accord see NPA
National Peacekeeping Force see
  NPKF
Ndamase, Jeffrey 66–8
Ndebele 72–3
Ndinisani, Phakamani 72–3
Ndlovu, Humphrey 108
Ndlovu, Simphiwe 138
Ndlovu, Victor 108
Ndlozi, George 29
Ndondolo, Njebe 71–2

Index

necklacing 18, 74, 181–2, 185, 187, 200
Nemorani, Sydney 43
Ngema Tavern 79
Ngubane, Sipho 81
Ngwenya, Jabulani 135
Nkondo, Jimmy 148–9
Nkosi, Bongani 43, 150, 152, 186
Nkosi, Duma 9, 43, 48, 49, 174, 182–3
Nkosi, Johannes 29
Nkosi, Sidney 136, 149, 150, 152
NP (National Party)
   anti-ANC actions/sentiment 4, 5, 26, 34, 86–8 *see also* state security forces
   and association with IFP 4–8, 9–11, 14, 17, 26, 31, 59–60, 75, 107–9, 198 *see also* state security forces
   and Buthelezi, Mangosuthu 4, 7, 24, 31
   as governing party 1, 21, 26
   and foreign media 7–9
   and National Peace Accord 40
   and negotiations with ANC 25, 26, 30, 41, 87–9, 117, 198, 199–200
   and racist rule 2, 3, 6–7, 17–18
   unbanning of opposition parties 1, 3–4, 13, 199
   and white security 5, 34–5, 86, 90, 119, 163, 198
   see also state security forces
NPA (National Peace Accord) 8, 40–41, 50, 61, 88–9, 129–31, 132, 294
NPKF (National Peacekeeping Force) 88, 115–17, 141
Nteo, Lerato 150
Ntuli, Sam 80, 128–9
NUMSA (National Union of Metalworkers of South Africa) 21, 54, 65–7, 199

PAC (Pan Africanist Congress) 1, 13, 19, 28, 36, 40, 67, 197
PASO (Pan Africanist Student Organisation) 74
Peace Action 9
Peens, Detective Sergeant 'Pedro' 77–8
Phama, Michael 128, 133, 151
Phenduka section (Thokoza) 92, 133–6, 139, 151–2, 155 *see also* Thokoza
Phola Park (squatter settlement)
   and 32 Battalion 114–15
   development of 63–5, 195
   and negotiations with police 63, 88–9
   SDUs in 37–8, 48–9, 63–5, 128
   and state security forces 191
   as weapons and training base 51–52
   war with Khalanyoni 32–3, 35, 38, 63, 125–6
   war with other hostels 126–9, 132–3
   see also Thokoza
Planact 63

racist rule 2, 3, 6–7, 17–18 *see also* apartheid; NP
Ramaphosa, Cyril 66
Ramushwana, Brigadier Gabriel 115
Rand, the *see* Witwatersrand
Rani, Siza 69
Rauch, Janine 95
Reed, Daniel 49, 51, 64, 94, 99, 126, 128, 135, 139, 179
Reef, the *see* Witwatersrand
riot units *see* ISD

SACP (South African Communist Party) 2, 43
SADF (South African Defence Force)
   and 32 Battalion 113–15
   and association with ANC 86, 110–13
   and black soldiers 86, 109, 111, 115
   history of 109
   and IFP 26, 60, 107
   and ISD 96, 97, 101, 111–12, 114
   supressing political violence, general 8, 18, 90, 92
   and NPKF 116–17
Sambo, Sibongile 189
SAP (South African Police) 8, 19, 31, 53–4, 59, 90–2, 107, 109
   see also ISD; state security forces
SDUs (Self Defence Units)
   activities of, general 145–7

223

and ANC 9, 13, 36, 37, 39–52, 64, 68–70, 82–4, 146
and black police or soldiers 86, 91, 93
and conflict with ANC affiliates 68–72, 199
control and discipline of 9, 36, 45–50, 64, 68–70, 82–4, 146
and criminal violence 45, 48–9, 64, 69, 81–4, 188–9, 193, 197
and demilitarisation 193–4
and hostels 138–42, 180
and intra-SDU violence 45–6, 49, 61, 62–3, 65, 67–70, 189–90
and ISD 86, 98, 99–100, 103, 105, 164, 170–71
in Katlehong 37, 41, 44, 57, 70–72, 131, 133–42, 143–56
and MK 25, 39, 43–5, 51, 64, 67–70
and NPKF 116
origin and composition of 6, 13, 25, 37–9, 126–7, 144–6, 153–6
in Phola Park 37–8, 48–9, 63–5, 128
political oversight of 39–45
and state security forces 39, 51, 63–4, 112, 131–2, 146, 149
in Thokoza 37, 40, 41, 43–4, 52, 57, 131–2, 133–42, 143–56
and trauma 148–53, 193–4
weapon supplies to 50–52
and women 38, 145, 153–5
and Xhosas 38–9, 52, 70
youth in 38–9, 47, 69, 145, 155–6, 188–9, 189–90
see also Katlehong; Phola Park; Thokoza
Sealy, Sally 9, 46, 155
Sebokeng 4, 30–32, 35, 49–50, 52, 65–70, 76, 77
Seekings, Jeremy 19
Segal, Lauren 11–12, 60–61, 94
Sexwale, Tokyo 45, 64, 102
Sharpeville 62, 68, 69, 198
Shaw, Mark 201
Sibiya, Jeffrey 101, 110–11
Siepe, Michael Lucky 43
Silva, Joao 116, 160
Simpson, James 9
Sitas, Ari 21, 56
'Skosana' 49–50
Sotsu, Ernest 52, 65–8, 77

South African Broadcasting Corporation 8
South African Communist Party *see* SACP
South African Defence Force *see* SADF
South African Police *see* SAP
Soweto 20, 32, 62, 197
SPUs (Self Protection Units) 26, 55, 57–61, 135, 145, 153, 156–61, 194–5
see also indunas; Zulus
squatter settlements
  Crossroads 124, 125, 127, 132–3
  Holomisa Park 127, 128–9, 132
  Mandela Park 65, 127, 133
  Phola Park *see* Phola Park
  Zonkizizwe 72, 124, 125–6, 127, 132
state security forces
  anti-ANC sentiment of 4, 14, 26, 59, 69, 75, 85, 86–8, 102–5, 107, 117, 161–2, 163, 198
  association with IFP 4–8, 14, 17, 26, 31, 59–60, 75, 80, 85–6, 97–8, 99–101, 102–6, 107–9, 117, 170, 198
  black police and soldiers
    and ISD 91–2, 96
    and SADF 86, 109, 111, 198
    and SDUs 86, 91, 93
    as sell-outs 86, 90–91
    and support for liberation struggle 93, 94, 198
    as township police 19, 89–95
    Xhosa police officers 35, 94–5
    Zulu police officers 35, 94–5
  and criminal involvement 77–8, 80–81
  ISD (Internal Stability Division)
    association with IFP 80, 86, 97–8, 99–101, 102–6, 170
    biased portrayal of 167–70, 196
    creation and deployment of 95–7, 106–7, 161
    after demilitarisation 195–6
    distrust of 71, 96–7, 98–9, 162
    and excessive force 98–100, 101, 165–6, 171
    experiences of, personal 163–7
    and SADF 101, 111–12, 114
    and SAP 91–2, 161

Index

and SDUs 86, 98, 99–100, 103, 105, 164, 170–71
and state negotiations 63, 88–9
and trauma 171–2, 196
veterans' accounts of 101–7, 161–72
negotiations with 63, 88–9
repression of anti-apartheid activists 7, 18, 59, 75
SAP (South African Police) 8, 19, 31, 53–4, 59, 90–92, 107, 109
see also ISD
SADF (South African Defence Force)
and 32 Battalion 113–15
and association with ANC 86, 110–13
and black soldiers 86, 109, 111, 115
history of 109
and IFP 26, 60, 107
and ISD 96, 97, 101, 111–12, 114
and NPKF 116–17
supressing political violence, general 8, 18, 90, 92
'third force' 5–8, 14, 85, 87–8, 107–9, 198
Thokoza Police Station 92
transition violence involvement, general 1–2, 9–10, 13, 17, 18–19, 26, 34–5, 77, 117–18, 198
unpredictability of 118–19
Vlakplaas 59, 86, 88, 107–9, 117, 168
and white security 5, 34–35, 86, 90, 119, 163, 198
see also NP
Storey, David 88, 95, 112, 129–31

Taylor, Rupert 6
taxi wars 27–30, 34–5, 123, 137–8, 139, 184
TEC (Transitional Executive Council) 88, 115
'third force' 5–8, 14, 85, 87–8, 107–9, 198
Thokoza
after demilitarisation 197
and hostel–township conflicts 4, 11–12, 20–23, 25–6, 31–3, 37, 56, 123–9, 133–7, 138–42, 176–91
ISD in 123, 161–72
and NPKF 115–17
Phenduka section 92, 133–6, 139, 151–2, 155
and political territory 135–8
population and demographics of 124–5
SDUs in 37, 40, 41, 43–4, 52, 57, 131–2, 133–42, 143–56
and taxi wars 27–30, 34–5, 123, 137–8, 139, 184
Thokoza Hostel Dwellers Association 128
Thokoza Local Peace Committee (LPC) 129–30, 183
Thokoza Police Station 92
Thokoza Stadium massacre 128–9, 151
Thokoza Taxi Association (TTA) 137
see also ethnic violence; hostels; Katlehong; Khalanyoni; Moleleki; Phola Park; squatter settlements; townships; Xhosas; Zulus
Thotse, M.L. 8
Thotsese, Thulani 134
Thulo, Seko 43
toyi-toyi 49, 54
townships
Alexandra 91–2
Bekkersdal 73
Daveyton 52, 62, 106, 165
histories 17–20
hostel–township conflicts 4, 11–12, 20–23, 25–6, 31–3, 37, 56, 123–9, 133–7, 138–42, 176–91
in Johannesburg, general 19–20
Katlehong *see* Katlehong
Moleleki 70–72
in Port Elizabeth, general 19–20
Sebokeng 4
Tembisa 83–4
Thokoza *see* Thokoza
Vosloorus 41, 43–4, 52, 101
see also hostels; ISD; SDUs; Xhosas; Zulus
train violence 54, 140–41
Transvaal *see under* IFP
Truth and Reconciliation Commission (TRC)

225

Index

Amnesty Committee 79, 80, 107–8
ANC submission to 39–40
applications for amnesty 29, 58, 72, 134
and children's experiences 148–9
establishment of 10
IFP boycott of 10, 57, 194
investigations 77–8
testimonies to 43, 45, 49, 50, 51, 52, 59, 60, 75, 80

UDF (United Democratic Front) 4, 18, 19–20, 21, 60, 199
Umkhonto weSizwe (MK)
as ANC's armed wing 13, 18, 25
and criminality 81–4
and demilitarisation 194
and intra-ANC violence 62, 66
and SDUs 25, 39, 43–5, 51, 64, 67–70
and SPUs 60
unionism 21–3
UWUSA (United Workers' Union of South Africa) 22–3, 60

Vaal (region) 31–2, 65–70, 74–5, 199, 202 *see also* Kheswa, Victor Khetisi 'the Vaal Monster'
Van der Merwe, Commissioner Johan 86–7
Vikikazi, Bavumile 202
Vlakplaas 59, 86, 88, 107–9, 117, 168

Witwatersrand
description of 1
political campaigning and violence in 4, 17, 23–6, 34, 123, 200
reports about 8–9
and threats to democracy 6
see also ethnic violence; Ekurhuleni; hostels; Katlehong; Phola Park; SDUs; squatter settlements; taxi wars; townships; Thokoza
women
ANC Women's League 13
and IFP 160–61
in SDUs 38, 145, 153–5
and sexual violence 45, 75, 114–15, 154–5, 178–9, 185, 188–9
tearing down hostel remains 185–6
workplace violence 52–4, 58–9, 60

Xhosas
and ANC 4, 24, 38, 65
and hostels 20, 31–2, 65, 179
and SDUs 38–9, 52, 70
in Phola Park 32–3, 64, 94, 125–6
as police officers 35, 94–5
see also ethnic violence; hostels; taxi wars; townships; Zulus

youth
activist, general 18, 28, 31
in ANC Youth League (ANCYL) 3, 13, 38, 62, 68–72, 74, 78–9, 147
in COSAS (Congress of South African Students) 28, 29, 34, 62, 69, 74
and the 'Germans' (gang) 69
Inkatha Youth Brigade 59
and parents 190–91
in SDUs 38–9, 47, 69, 145, 155–6, 188, 189–90
in SPUs 57–8, 60–1, 145
and taxi wars 27–30

Zikalala, Sihle 202
Zonkizizwe (squatter settlement) 72, 124, 125–6, 127, 132
Zulus
and ANC 24, 25, 183
and arms dealing 52
in hostels 125–6, 133, 144, 157–60, 176–82, 194–5
and IFP 3–4, 5, 10, 17, 24, 25–6, 31–3, 57, 124, 144–5, 176, 184–6
as *impis* 56
as migrants/migrant workers 17, 20–23, 31, 55, 125, 152–3, 157–60, 176–82, 194–5
as police officers 35, 94–5
in townships 144–5, 182–91
see also ethnic violence; hostels; KZN; taxi wars; townships; Xhosas
Zwane, Bulelwa 71